THE ENCYCLOPEDIA OF

World Wildlife

THE ENCYCLOPEDIA OF

World Wildlife

Mike and Peggy Briggs

This is a Parragon book
First published in 2005

Parragon
Queen Street House
4 Queen Street
Bath, BA1 1HE

For details of the photograph copyrights see page 314
Produced by Atlantic Publishing

A catalogue record for this book is available from the British Library.

This book is dedicated to
our father and father-in-law Bill Briggs and
our sister and sister-in-law Gwen Adams.

ISBN 1-40545-680-9

Printed in China

Contents

Introduction

In writing this book it became very clear to us, as it will to the reader, that the natural world, diverse though it is with its 10–20 million species, is under threat as never before. Many of the familiar creatures featured here may be extinct by the middle of this century; some might be gone in just a year or two. Very few large mammals have an absolutely secure foothold on the planet, many of the birds we take for granted are disappearing (the Japanese crested ibis, the national symbol, became extinct in its home country during the writing of this book), fish are being over-harvested and only reptiles and insects appear to be relatively safe from the effects of the greatest destroyer of all – mankind.

The statistics are alarming. Recent research has shown that 83 per cent of the Earth's total land surface is directly influenced by human activity. The oceans, over-fished and easily polluted, have not escaped either. Wide open spaces are fast disappearing (one fifth of the US land mass is within 500m of a paved road) and forests are being destroyed at an alarming rate (over 6,000 square metres of Amazon rainforest is lost every second). Then there are unforeseen disasters like the TB and FIV epidemic which has reduced the number of African lions to just 20,000 – less than ten per cent of the population 20 years ago.

Humans have direct influences on nature (for example, a million vertebrates are killed each day on US roads) and indirect ones, such as the introduction of foreign species that compete with and often eliminate native species. Some scientists estimate that 40–100 species become extinct each day. And all the time *Homo sapiens* is increasing by 200,000 daily.

But it is not all bad news. One creature whose numbers are growing fast is the conservation worker. People have never been so well informed about the need to maintain biodiversity and to keep the planet healthy. And then there are the occasional pleasant surprises: in 2003 the long-lost, long-legged Fijian warbler was rediscovered after having been presumed extinct for 109 years. Its haunting song, which led to it being called the spirit bird, was once again heard in the remote forest and its numbers appear to be increasing. Perhaps we will be able to include it in a future edition of this book.

Although we have tried to take in all the most familiar species here, a few people might be disappointed not to find their favourites, in which case we hope the absence will be compensated for by the inclusion of some less well-known but nevertheless fascinating creatures and by the chance to learn something new about the world's wildlife.

THE ENCYCLOPEDIA OF World Wildlife

Mammals

WEASEL (*Mustela nivalis*)

SIZE:	20–22cm excluding tail
DISTRIBUTION:	Holarctic: northern North America (Alaska to northeastern USA), western Europe to eastern Siberia, Asia including Japan, northern Africa. Absent from Ireland
IDENTIFICATION:	Small, slender body, reddish-brown fur with white underside. Short tail without a black tip

The weasel is one of the world's smallest carnivores and takes advantage of its size and streamlined shape to follow its prey down burrows. It pursues mice, rabbits, and voles, and has a reputation for being a relentless hunter, partly because it needs to eat one third of its body weight each day to survive.

The weasel is very similar to the stoat in appearance but smaller and without the black tip to the tail. Both weasels and stoats living in northern lands turn white during winter.

Young weasels, which are cared for by their mother for 9–12 weeks, can kill prey when they are only 8 weeks old.

MINK (*Mustela vison*)

SIZE:	Length, body, 40cm (tail 20cm)
DISTRIBUTION:	North America and British Isles
IDENTIFICATION:	Dark-brown, almost black, thick glossy fur. Pointed snout, small eyes and ears, white spot under the chin

In the days when it was the norm for every wealthy woman to own a mink coat, this native of North America was hunted relentlessly for its luxurious pelt. Such was its popularity that mink ranching was established to cope with demand and by the mid-1960s there were 7,200 ranches competing to produce superior pelts.

Mink farming prospered in Britain for a while but fashions change and escapees from mink farms have had a more lasting impact than fur coats. With no natural predators, these ferocious little creatures thrived and multiplied with devastating results for British wildlife and domestic poultry. With its webbed feet, the mink is a strong swimmer, catching fish and waterfowl without too much trouble. On land, ground-nesting birds are seriously threatened as their nests are so easily accessible and millions of pounds are being spent on trying to eradicate this pest from Scottish islands.

ERMINE (*Mustela erminea*)

SIZE:	Length 15–30cm including tail of 4–12cm
DISTRIBUTION:	North America and Eurasia
IDENTIFICATION:	Long body, short legs, long neck with triangular head. Reddish-brown fur with white underside in summer, white in winter

The demands the ermine makes on its body mean at least one daily meal is essential. It prefers small mammals but will eat birds, fish, eggs or insects if necessary, leftovers being cached for future consumption. The female is roughly half the size of the male, allowing her to hunt underground, tracking down lemmings in their burrows. Above ground, the ermine is a bold hunter, winding its body and feet around its victim to hold it fast before killing with a bite to the back of the neck.

Fur or feathers from the kill are used to line the ermine's underground nest, ready for the litter of four to nine offspring. By the time they are two months old, the young are able to join their mother on the daily food hunt.

PINE MARTEN (*Martes martes*)

SIZE:	Length 44–55cm excluding tail of up to 26cm
DISTRIBUTION:	North America, Europe, Asia and southern Asian islands
IDENTIFICATION:	Reddish-brown fur, yellowish-white throat, long body and long fluffy tail. Large rounded ears with paler edges

In well-wooded areas or deep forest with plenty of cover, the pine marten marks out its territory of 10–25 square km. It climbs with great agility but hunts by night on the ground. In northern Europe, the red squirrel is the main mammal in its diet but voles are easier to find. The pine marten frequently nests among the roots of Scots pine, which is probably the source of its common name. Formerly killed for its fur, the pine marten is now fully protected in Great Britain.

The North American marten is renowned for being the only creature to get the better of a porcupine. Undeterred by the lashing of a spiny tail, the marten circles and confuses the porcupine until it can attack its vulnerable head.

POLECAT (*Mustela putorius*)

SIZE:	Length 30–45cm, weight 0.7–1.7kg
DISTRIBUTION:	Europe, although limited to Wales in Great Britain. Introduced to New Zealand
IDENTIFICATION:	Long slender body covered with brown fur and buff underfur, short legs and short furry tail. Round face with dark mask around the eyes and white markings

The common name of the polecat comes from the French *poule chat* meaning 'chicken cat', reflecting its reputation for raiding chicken coops. It is a fierce hunter. Once a polecat bites its victim it is almost impossible to dislodge due to the 'key-lock' formation of the jaw – strong enough to bear the animal's weight if it is lifted by whatever it is gripping.

A polecat ranges over approximately 21 square km and marks its territory with a strong-smelling secretion. This strong odour is also released when it is threatened. The polecat lives a solitary life – only when the female is in season do the sexes mix. The young leave their mother at about three months.

Otter

Throughout most of Asia, north Africa and Europe, as far north as the Arctic circle, rivers, lakes, swamps and coastal areas are home to the **Eurasian river otter** (*Lutra lutra*). This magnificent animal was hunted almost to extinction, partly for its luxurious fur and partly because it was considered a pest and competition for fishermen. At one time the Swiss government even paid a bounty for each one killed. It is now listed as vulnerable and protected by law in some countries.

Henry Williamson's novel *Tarka the Otter* endeared this shy creature to many people and it tops the list of wild animals most people would like to see. Loss of habitat and road accidents continue to reduce numbers so there are very few left in Britain – the west coast and Scottish islands being the best places to see them.

Otters are renowned for being playful. They can spend hours tobogganing down mud banks on their chests into the water only to climb out and slide down again. They also play in the water, the mother encouraging her cubs to perfect their swimming and hunting techniques. If the young are reluctant to enter the water, she pushes them in and lures them deeper with the promise of fish. A family of otters can often be heard before they are seen, as they communicate with whistles and squeaks.

In Alaska, Canada and the northern United States *Lontra canadensis*, the **North American river otter**, suffered a similar fate from over-hunting. More than 33,000 pelts were sold in 1983/4 hunting season (for $18.71 each), but it is now protected internationally and trade is controlled.

This otter is a similar size to the Eurasian otters, growing up to 90cm long with a 45cm tail, and has the same dark brown dense fur with paler undersides. Its den or holt is built into the river bank, often with an underwater entrance. Here the litter of 1–5 cubs is born and, although the mother chases the male away soon after giving birth, he is later allowed back to help care for them.

With its webbed feet and agility in the water, the otter is an excellent fisherman. Otters have been tamed and trained to hunt fish for their handlers.

North American river otter

SEA OTTER (*Enhydra lutris*)

SIZE:	Length, body, 1–1.4m (tail up to 33cm)
DISTRIBUTION:	North Pacific Ocean and Bering Sea
IDENTIFICATION:	Dark-brown luxurious fur, paler head. Short legs and powerful, webbed hind feet

The rare and beautiful sea otter is one of the few mammals to use tools. Floating on its back, it breaks open its favourite mussels and sea urchins by clasping a rock to its chest and smashing the shells onto it.

It seldom comes ashore. Even the pup is born at sea although it cannot swim until taught by its mother. Until then its fur is constantly groomed to keep it buoyant enough to float while the mother dives for food. To escape predators she clasps the pup to her and dives for as long as its breath holds out. The sea otter was once hunted almost to extinction for its pelt, said to be the most valuable in the world – warmer than sable, more durable than mink. It has been protected since 1911 but more than 5,000 died in the 1998 *Exxon Valdez* oil spill in the Gulf of Alaska.

BADGER (*Meles meles*)

SIZE:	Length up to 90cm, weight 10–14kg
DISTRIBUTION:	Europe, Japan and south China
IDENTIFICATION:	Dark-grey, stocky body with distinctive black-and-white-striped face

An unobtrusive, nocturnal animal, the badger is most often seen as roadkill. In Great Britain alone it is estimated that 50,000 badgers die on the roads every year.

Badgers have been hunted, baited and persecuted over much of Europe for hundreds of years, not least because they are believed to spread bovine TB in cattle.

Mating takes place at any time of the year as the badger uses delayed implantation of the fertilized eggs to ensure the young are born in late winter or early spring. A litter of one to six blind and helpless young are born in separate nesting chambers within the badger's complex burrow, known as a sett. The badger is a social animal living in family groups with up to a dozen members and can sometimes be seen romping playfully with the rest of the clan.

Western Spotted Skunk

(*Spilogale putorius gracilis*)

Size:	Length, body, 17–29cm (plus tail 13cm). Weight 368–565g
Distribution:	Western North America
Identification:	Black and white with lateral stripes along body, white spots on forehead, in front of ears, on each side of rump and at base of tail. Underside of tail white to halfway, tip white

When a western spotted skunk starts doing handstands it is time to get out of its way. It is about to dowse you with butyl mercaptan – an extremely smelly sulphurous liquid. Other warning postures include tail raising, stamping, hissing, floor scratching and charging and lead to the final pay-off, which it delivers with a swaying movement designed to cover as large an area as possible. Even skunks dislike skunk smell and will not spray anywhere near their dens. Any creature drenched by a skunk forever associates its warning black-and-white markings with a nasty experience.

Skunks eat eggs, young rabbits, fruit, berries, mice, voles, roots, grasshoppers and even scorpions.

Ratel or Honey Badger

(*Mellivora capensis*)

Size:	Height 23–28cm. Weight 8–14.5kg
Distribution:	Asia and Africa
Identification:	Stocky animal with well developed neck and shoulders. Coarse white fur covers the back, head and neck, whereas the face and lower body are black

The sweet tooth of this fierce creature and its fondness for honey have led to its common name of honey badger. It works in co-operation with a honeyguide bird to find a bees' nest. The honeyguide first alerts the ratel by calling and swooping until the animal follows the bird to the booty. Most of the bees flee from the ratel's foul-smelling secretions, leaving their honey for the invader who, in turn, leaves grubs and honeycomb for its guide.

Described as having the courage of a lion, the ratel has a formidable reputation as a hunter, undaunted by the size of its prey. It has been known to attack buffalo and wildebeest and even cattle and horses. Strangely enough, in captivity the ratel shows another side to its character, becoming tame, playful and easy to train.

WOLVERINE (*Gulo gulo*)

SIZE:	Weight, males 10–18kg, females 5.8–12kg
DISTRIBUTION:	North America, Scandinavia, eastern Europe, Siberia and Asia
IDENTIFICATION:	Glossy, dark-brown coat with yellowish-buff stripes from shoulder to rump, sometimes with pale collar or socks. Long bushy tail

With its overall appearance of a small bear, its habit of marking with musk or urine, and the pale striping of its body, it is not surprising that this fiendish creature is also known as the skunk bear, although it is actually a member of the weasel family. The wolverine has a fearsome reputation as a vandal and a murderer although stories of it killing moose are probably exaggerated. Carrion makes up the larger part of the wolverine's diet. Its ferocity is respected in the animal world and even grizzly bears have been observed to give up their kill when faced with a wolverine's bared teeth. It is also renowned for raiding bait from traps, burying food for future consumption and vandalizing cabins in its search for anything edible, earning its species name *Gulo*, meaning glutton.

Wolverine fur is valued for trimming coat hoods as it is the only fur that can be breathed on in the cold without frosting up.

RACCOON (*Procyon lotor*)

SIZE:	Length 60–102cm including tail of up to 25cm
DISTRIBUTION:	Southern Canada to northern South America. Fur farm escapees in parts of Russia and Europe
IDENTIFICATION:	Characteristic black mask across the eyes and between four and ten black rings around the bushy tail. Stocky body with thick fur, varying in colour

The Latin name *lotor* means 'the washer', as the raccoon has been seen apparently washing its food before eating. This is instinctive mimicry, a need to replicate catching aquatic prey. The raccoon is omnivorous, with a penchant for fruit and nuts. In agricultural areas corn is a favourite meal but the raccoon is a pest to farmers, damaging more than it can eat.

During the day, or in bad weather, the raccoon sleeps in its den, which might be a hollow tree or a crevice between rocks, emerging at dusk to forage for food. It is not unknown for the raccoon to take over a crow or magpie nest 3.9–4.8m above ground.

Giant Panda

(*Ailuropoda melanoleuca*)

Size:	Weight 80–125kg. Length 1.5–1.8m. Height at shoulder 65–70cm
Distribution:	Central China
Identification:	Stocky body, rounded head and short tail. Legs, eyes, ears and shoulders black, rest of body white. Thick, dense fur. Eats bamboo shoots

A panda skin is worth $180,000 on the black market in Japan but Chinese poachers tempted to trade in this endangered species face the death penalty if they are caught. Several poachers have been executed and China has shown its further commitment to protecting this much-loved bear by stopping commercial logging within its range and introducing a national conservation programme. Numbers are stable but the population is small and the habitat under threat – ironically, partially from tourism development centred on the panda itself. Attempts at captive breeding have been extremely unsuccessful. An ancient Chinese tale explains that the panda got its markings when a young girl, a friend of the bears, died. They wept at the funeral and rubbed their arms over their eyes, smudging them with black. Then they hugged each other for comfort and blackened their ears, shoulders and rumps as well.

Asian black bear

Black Bear (*Ursus americanus*)
Asian Black Bear (*Ursus thibetanus*)

A **black bear** hauls a huge sockeye salmon from the waters of Clayoquot Sound on Vancouver Island, British Columbia, and rumbles off into the forest to eat it. It gets a meal and helps preserve this unique forest habitat by fertilizing it with fish scraps. It is estimated that black bears drag more than 60 million kg of salmon 'fertilizer' into the woods each year, providing up to 20 per cent of the annual nitrogen requirements of waterside plants.

The black bear once roamed throughout North America. European colonizers saw this intelligent animal as a pest and hunted it ruthlessly right up to modern times. Numbers fell to about 175,000 before it began to make a comeback. The male black bear weighs up to 409kg and is up to 2m long; females are about two-thirds as large. Colouring varies from blonde through brownish cinnamon to pure black, usually with a pale muzzle and sometimes a white chest spot. Across most of its range the black bear eats grasses, greenery, nuts and berries as well as insects and some carrion. They also visit bird tables.

The **Asian black bear** hunts and eats mostly at night and has less interaction with humans. It is killed by farmers but mostly for body parts which are used in folk medicine. Numbers are falling and it is considered endangered. It is smaller than its American cousin with males reaching 115kg and females 90kg in weight. It too is a good a swimmer, climber and runner. The Asian black bear is found mostly in the upland wet forests of Pakistan, Afghanistan, India, China, Russia, Korea, Taiwan and Japan. It eats insects, honey, fruit, nuts, berries, green shoots and grasses but will take small animals. During hibernation from late November until early April its heart rate drops to 8–12 beats per minute and its body temperature to just 3–7 °C (37–44 °F).

Black bear

Brown Bear (Grizzly Bear)

(Ursus arctos)

Size:	Length up to 3m, weight up to 612kg
Distribution:	Alaska, western Canada and small numbers in western Europe, Siberia, Palestine and the Himalayas
Identification:	Stocky body with shaggy coat, usually dark brown, sometimes lighter. Long nose has a light-golden muzzle

Tales of grizzly bear encounters surely equal in tallness fishermen's stories of the ones that got away. Its legendary ferocity has resulted in the grizzly being valued as a big game trophy. Unfortunately, it does not always get away and has been hunted almost to extinction. The shaggy coat has longer hairs on the back and shoulders, sometimes frosted with white – a grizzled look that led to the bear's common name.

Surviving in the harsh tundra is no easy feat and the brown bear will eat almost anything to store up fat for the winter. Tubers, fish and carrion are staples and, in late summer, a treat of berries, fruit and nuts.

A cave or den is chosen as a winter retreat where the bear makes a bed of dry vegetation before going into a state of dormancy, but as its body temperature does not drop this is not a true state of hibernation. In this warm refuge the young are born blind and hairless. They remain with their mother for three to four years.

The **Kodiak bear** (*Ursus arctos middendorffi*) is a sub-species of the brown bear, and named after its exclusive habitat, Kodiak Island.

Polar Bear (*Ursus maritimus*)

Size:	Length, male up to 3.4m; female up to 2.8m. Height up to 1.5m at shoulders. Weight, male up to 545kg, female up to 364kg
Distribution:	Throughout Arctic surrounding North Pole. Prefers to stay on pack ice. Reported as far south as the southern tips of Greenland and Iceland
Identification:	Distinctive large stocky body covered in white fur (sometimes yellowish or even brown or grey, depending on season and light). Relatively smaller head than other bears, elongated neck, black nose

The ringed seal has drawn the short straw in life. It is the main prey of the polar bear, one of nature's most efficient and determined hunters. A seal pup might feel safe tucked up in its lair deep in the snow, but a hungry female polar bear can smell it from more than 2km away. Near starvation after a four-month birthing spell in her winter den, she needs blubber to produce milk to feed her cubs. She pads delicately across the sea ice to within a few metres of the lair, her huge, furred feet making no sound. Having chosen her target she leaps into the air, crashes down with her front legs and

smashes through the snow. If the seal has not swum to safety through its escape hole she scoops it out with sharp claws. A fully-grown polar bear needs the equivalent of one adult seal every six days, so the hunt is relentless and a bear might travel 50km or more between meals.

Polar bears have two other hunting strategies. Still-hunting involves finding a seal's breathing hole in the ice and waiting for it to surface to make the kill. Bears will also stalk their quarry in the open (they can smell seal blubber from 35km), either crouching and creeping up on the surface or swimming through channels in the ice. Polar bears are superb swimmers and have been seen in the open sea miles from land, paddling at up to 7kph. On land they can run at 40kph.

When humans moved into the Arctic regions 4,000 years ago they learned their hunting techniques from the bears, techniques that are still used by the Inuit or Eskimo people. Polar bears, called *nanuk* by the Inuit, were the most highly prized of all quarry and played a large part in their cultural and spiritual life. Killing a bear was a major event incorporating much ceremony. Sometimes, of course, it was the bear that killed the person: the predator–prey relationship works both ways.

MEERKAT (*Suricata suricatta*)

SIZE:	Length, body, 25–35cm (tail 17.5–25cm). Weight 600–900g
DISTRIBUTION:	Angola, Namibia, South Africa, southern Botswana
IDENTIFICATION:	Grey and tan with brownish banding on back and sides. Head and throat greyish-white. Eyes ringed with black, rounded black ears and long, black-tipped tail

Cooperation is the keynote to meerkat survival. All members benefit if a group is large and healthy, providing more sentinels and greater power to resist encroachments by neighbouring groups. A mother must forage each day to keep up her milk supply and her mate guards her, so other group members take turns in providing nursery care. All groups post sentries to look out for eagles, cobras or other predators. On sighting a threat the guard, with its distinctive upright stance, calls an alarm and every meerkat within earshot dives underground. To reassure the group that it is still on watch the guard keeps up a low, steady peeping. The meerkat eats beetles, insect larvae, scorpions and small reptiles.

WATER MONGOOSE ▲

(*Atilax paludinosus*)

SIZE:	Length, body, 46–62cm (tail 32–53cm)
DISTRIBUTION:	Africa, south of the Sahara Desert
IDENTIFICATION:	Chestnut-brown to black glossy coat, paler head and underside

The water mongoose can be found in a variety of habitats but swamps, marshes and reed beds – in fact anywhere with plenty of mud – suit it best. Sometimes known as the marsh mongoose, this dextrous mammal uses its soft, sensitive forefeet to sift through mud, feeling for food. It spends a lot of time in the water but not always swimming. It finds more to eat by wading along beside the bank poking its feet into holes and crevices searching for frogs and crabs. The hard shells of crabs and mussels pose no problem: the mongoose stands and throws them at a rock to break them open.

The water mongoose is a solitary creature and highly territorial. The boundaries are scent-marked and the mongoose performs a handstand in order to reach higher to deposit secretions from its anal glands.

NORTHERN WATER VOLE

(*Arvicola terrestris*)

SIZE:	Length, body, 18–22cm (tail 12cm)
DISTRIBUTION:	Northern Europe, Russia, North America
IDENTIFICATION:	Dark-brown or black fur, blunt nose and long, thin, lightly-furred tail

In Kenneth Graham's novel *The Wind in the Willows* the famous Ratty was actually a water vole, a fact that has long endeared this creature to the British despite its being considered a pest in the rest of Europe. The introduction of mink in Britain has been blamed for declining numbers of water voles but in Holland they are so abundant they can seriously damage the flower industry by eating tulip bulbs in winter.

Usually living at the water's edge, this vole burrows into banks, making entrances both above and below the water line. Balls of dried grass or plants are made into nests within the burrows or occasionally under driftwood on the bank. The water vole is a strong swimmer, paddling along with just its head above water. If pursued, it will stir up mud to cloud the water and act as a 'smokescreen'.

SMALL SPOTTED GENET

(*Genetta genetta*)

SIZE:	Length 50–60cm plus tail 41–52cm. Weight 1–2.9kg
DISTRIBUTION:	France, Spain, Portugal and northern Africa
IDENTIFICATION:	Slim body with yellowish-grey fur marked with dark spots. Long, banded tail

The small spotted genet is a long, slender cat-like animal with incredibly soft fur and a tail almost as long as its body. However, this shy, nocturnal creature is seldom seen even in areas where it is common. An excellent climber, the genet also has semi-retractable claws that allow it to pin down its prey. It leads a solitary life, hunting by stealth, and is considered beneficial in controlling vermin. Like a cat it will kill its victim with a quick bite to the back of the neck. The genet also makes cat-like hisses and meows, particularly when mating.

There are eleven species of genet with regional colour variations including one that is all black.

SPOTTED HYAENA (*Crocuta crocuta*) ▲

SIZE:	Height at shoulder 110–120cm. Weight 48–55kg
DISTRIBUTION:	Africa, south of the Sahara, and Ethiopia
IDENTIFICATION:	Well developed neck and shoulders, smaller hindquarters. Various shades of brown with dark spots, facial mask

In the African savannah most carnivores either scavenge leftovers from a larger hunter's kill or seek smaller prey that they can tackle themselves. But the spotted hyaena frequently intimidates leopards and cheetahs into giving up their catch and wages constant war with the lion, the two creatures snarling and threatening each other over territorial boundaries.

Hyaena clans are dominated by the larger, more aggressive females, which are so masculinized that it's difficult to tell the genders apart until the female has had pups. The females fight over food, they fight the males and they fight each other. Occasionally, the males will 'bait' a female in retaliation, but it takes a gang of four or five to do so. The spotted hyaena's massive jaws and acidic stomach means it can consume bones, horns and teeth as well as meat.

STRIPED HYAENA (*Hyaena hyaena*)

SIZE:	Height 65–80cm. Weight 25–45kg
DISTRIBUTION:	Northern and eastern Africa, Middle East, India and Asia to southern Siberia
IDENTIFICATION:	Grey or straw-coloured with black muzzle and black stripes on head, torso and legs. Long hair and large, pointed ears

The striped hyaena is a creature of the dark. Unlike its cousins on the grasslands farther south, which hunt in packs during the day, the striped hyaena scavenges at night. Its diet is mostly carrion, insects and human refuse but it has retained the hyaena's ability to crunch through bone and will devour an entire carcass, regurgitating the horns, hooves and anything else its powerful digestive system cannot crush and dissolve. Some African villages leave their rubbish outside at night for the striped hyaena to 'collect'. It rarely attacks livestock or people and is not aggressive.

GREY WOLF (*Canis lupus*)

SIZE:	Height 60–90cm. Length 70–150cm. Weight 25–80kg
DISTRIBUTION:	Originally throughout northern hemisphere, now scattered in North America and Europe. Several Asian populations
IDENTIFICATION:	Large dog with thick fur. Colour mixture of greys, black, brown and cinnamon with pale belly and muzzle

We are all familiar with tales of ravaging wolves but attacks are now virtually unheard of despite the fact that there are about 2,600 grey wolves in the lower 48 states of America, 8,000 in Alaska and 50,000 in Canada. Wolves have learned to be wary of well-armed, two-legged humans and most attacks are provoked by illness (such as rabies), hunger or a perceived threat to young or prey.

The grey wolf was once the world's most widely dispersed carnivore, but its numbers have been reduced by steady human persecution and destruction of its habitat. Wolves live as packs, family groups of 8–12, all related and headed by a principal breeding pair.

They will hunt beavers and rabbits on their own but operate as a pack to bring down moose, elk, bison, musk ox and reindeer, animals that are many times their own body weight. A wolf living near human habitation will rummage through rubbish bins for titbits.

ARCTIC WOLF *(Canis lupis arctos)* ▶

SIZE:	Shoulder height 60–75cm. Weight, male up to 80kg
DISTRIBUTION:	Throughout Arctic region
IDENTIFICATION:	Colour varies from white through grey and red to almost black

The Arctic wolf spends autumn and winter roaming singly or in small packs in its constant quest for food. In these months of darkness it can survive sub-freezing temperatures and weeks without eating. Alone, the wolf will seize Arctic hare and lemmings. In the hunt for larger prey the pack work together, following migrating herds of caribou, and separate the young or weaker animals unable to outrun them. A caribou or musk ox will feed the pack for several days.

A small pack of Arctic wolves is quite often a family group comprising the alpha male and alpha female, and their offspring. The cubs are born blind and helpless, relying on their mother's milk for the first four weeks and then the pack co-operates in feeding, regurgitating meat from the kill.

MANED WOLF *(Chrysocyon brachyurus)*

SIZE:	Length, body, 120–130cm (tail 28–45cm)
DISTRIBUTION:	South America
IDENTIFICATION:	Golden or rust-coloured coat, erectile mane and long legs

The maned wolf has exceptionally long, slender legs. It inhabits open regions with tall vegetation cover so the extra height helps it to see over the long grass. These wolves pair for life although they seem to live fairly independently within their territory of 25–30 square km. They lead such secretive lives that not a great deal is known about their behaviour. Attempts to breed and study them in captivity have had little success as captive females often abandon or even eat their newborn pups.

Mainly nocturnal, the maned wolf has a varied diet, eating rabbits, mice and birds, ants, grubs, berries and fruit. According to South American folklore, children can avoid dental problems by wearing a maned wolf's tooth on a chain around their neck and snakebite victims can avoid death by eating two small pieces of its heart.

Coyote (Prairie Wolf)

(Canis latrans)

Size:	Height 45–53cm. Length, body, 70–97cm (tail 30–38cm). Weight 10–22kg
Distribution:	Central and North America
Identification:	Variable colouration from light-grey with black flecks and pale underparts, to almost completely dark (in mountains) or yellowish (desert). Thick fur among northern varieties

The coyote is a great survivor and one of the most successful predators on Earth. Despite being shot, trapped and poisoned its numbers are on the increase and its range expanding. It has a distinctive yapping howl, which floats for several kms on a still night. Where wolves are eliminated, the coyote becomes top predator, eating everything from snakes and insects to small mammals, domestic fowl and pets, fruit, carrion and domestic rubbish. It usually hunts alone. However, intriguingly, individual coyotes have been observed teaming up with a badger to hunt burrowing rodents: the coyote scents the quarry, the badger digs it out and they share the spoils.

Dingo *(Canis lupus familiaris dingo)*

Size:	Height 50cm. Length 117–124cm. Weight 10–20kg
Distribution:	Throughout Australia and in scattered groups in Southeast Asia
Identification:	Usually ginger or rusty-yellow-coloured but occasionally pure black. Sharply defined head with erect, triangular ears. Short-haired but with fairly bushy tail.

The dingo is probably descended from the Asian wolf, introduced to Australia by seafarers and traders around 2,000 BC. Because of inbreeding with domestic dogs there are few 'pure' dingoes left. The dingo eats small mammals, lizards, birds, carrion and kangaroo. It hunts alone but a pack will form to tackle larger prey. Infamously, dingoes have been implicated in the taking and killing of babies and small children in some public areas.

ARCTIC FOX *(Alopex lagopus)*

SIZE:	Body length 50–65cm, plus tail 30–38cm. Weight 2.5–8kg
DISTRIBUTION:	Arctic regions of Europe, Asia and North America
IDENTIFICATION:	Thick fur, pure white in winter, grey-brown to bluish-black in summer. Stocky, compact body, small ears and long bushy tail

All foxes are renowned for their cunning and the Arctic fox is no exception. In this harsh environment with scarce prey, it will follow the polar bear's footprints in the snow in the hope of scavenging from a seal carcass. If unsuccessful it will use its keen senses of sight and smell to hunt for smaller mammals, eggs or berries. Occasionally it will sniff out a newly born seal pup and dig down to its lair.

The thick fur of the Arctic fox traps air and provides excellent insulation, allowing it to doze unharmed in the snow for an hour or so at temperatures as low as –50 °C (–58 °F). Even the undersides of its paws are covered with fur and when severe winds blow relentlessly across this barren landscape, the Arctic fox uses its furry paws to dig a den several feet deep in the snow.

◄ Fennec Fox *(Fennecus zerda)*

Size:	Height 19–21cm. Length, body, 24–41cm (tail 18–31cm). Weight 1–1.5kg
Distribution:	Morocco, Algeria, Tunisia, Libya, Egypt, northern Sudan
Identification:	Tiny dog with large ears and golden or fawn coat with white 'edging' and dark flecks. Long black whiskers

Despite its disproportionately huge ears, there is nothing monstrous about the fennec. It feeds on small mammals, lizards, birds, eggs, insects and plants and only becomes troublesome when another fennec tries to steal its hard-won meal. Furious scraps break out with screaming, hip slamming and pushing. The fennec's enormous ears help pick up the sound of insects crawling over the sand but they are also thought to help disperse body heat. This nocturnal fox shelters in a burrow that may be linked to others in a complex tunnel system occupied by many individuals. It is not endangered although it is trapped for fur and sold as a pet.

Swift Fox *(Vulpes velox)*

Size:	Height at shoulder 18–35cm. Length, body, 37–53cm. Weight 1.8–3kg
Distribution:	Southwestern United States. Reintroduced to Canada
Identification:	Dark-grey in summer, ochre-tan in winter. Throat, chest, underside and inside ears creamy white. Large ears, broad face. Long bushy tail with dark tip

The swift fox was once widespread in Canada and the United States. By the 1930s it had been cleared from the north and much of the south, the victim of poisoning aimed to kill wolves, coyotes and ground squirrels. It was declared extinct in Canada in 1978 but has been reintroduced through captive breeding and release. It can run at up to 50kph, allowing it to chase down small mammals, birds and reptiles and outrun predators such as red-tailed hawk. It also eats fish, insects, berries and grasses, hunting by night and spending most of the day in its burrow.

Red Fox

(*Vulpes vulpes*)

Size:	Length up to 150cm including tail of up to 60cm
Distribution:	Europe, Asia, North America and introduced to Australia
Identification:	Reddish-brown coat with paler chest and underside. Distinctive bushy tail usually tipped with white. Pointed ears and paws sometimes darker-brown to black

Throughout history the red fox has been the subject of folklore and fables, its name synonymous with cunning and wiliness. The fox is usually the culprit when farmers lose their chickens and, if not, it gets the blame anyway. As a nocturnal hunter, it is not often seen in the countryside but urban foxes are on the increase and becoming bolder, scavenging in gardens and exploring rubbish bins. Despite being hunted for its fur as well as by farmers, numbers continue to increase and it is now the most widespread and abundant wild carnivore in the world.

During the mating season in early spring, the vixen can sometimes be heard calling to her mate with a high-pitched yelp and the dog fox answering with a shrill bark sounding across the valley. A hollowed-out tree stump makes an ideal den or 'earth' where the vixen and her cubs spend the daylight hours before emerging at dusk to creep silently about the countryside.

Eurasian Lynx

(*Lynx lynx*)

Size:	Length up to 100cm, weight up to 38.5kg
Distribution:	Europe and northern Asia
Identification:	Light grey to reddish-brown fur with spots or short stripes. Distinctive 'brush ears' and sideburns

The rear view of the lynx is not impressive, its short stubby tail seems incongruous on such a large cat. This is compensated for by its magnificent face with tufted ears and sideburns that are more than just a fashion accessory. As it cannot use its tail to communicate in the same way as other cats, the lynx moves its ears and sideburns to the same effect, each movement having a certain meaning. The lynx hunts in forested areas, hiding in the undergrowth to stalk its prey, which can be ground-dwelling birds or small mammals, from mice to roe deer.

The **Iberian lynx** is an endangered species. A Spanish survey in 1999 indicated only 400–600 remaining in the wild. The numbers of **Canadian lynx** fluctuate in direct proportion to those of its main food source, the snowshoe hare, which is named for its large, flat hind paws.

BOBCAT (*Lynx rufus*)

SIZE:	Height 45–58cm. Length, body 65–105cm (tail 11–19cm). Weight 4–15kg
DISTRIBUTION:	Throughout North America; greater densities in southeast
IDENTIFICATION:	Short tail, tufted ears and hairy ruffs on sides of head. Various shades of buff and brown with dark stripes and spots

The bobcat is renowned for its ferocity but it rarely attacks humans. There are probably about a million bobcats in the United States with greater population densities in some areas than in others where it has been driven out as a pest. It will eat small domestic animals and poultry but is more likely to hunt rodents, rabbits, large birds, reptiles and small deer. It stalks its prey and pounces on the unwary victim, snapping the neck with its jaws. Once extensively hunted for its pelt, it is now listed as a species of special concern and although some states allow regulated hunting it is protected in others. It lives a solitary life and males and females come together only to mate in the early spring.

CARACAL (*Lynx caracal*)

SIZE:	Length, body, 60–105cm (tail 20–35cm)
DISTRIBUTION:	Africa, Arabian peninsular and southwest Asia
IDENTIFICATION:	Long-legged cat with short, reddish-brown coat, white undersides. Black tufted ears

The caracal's name comes from the Turkish *karakal*, meaning 'black ears' so it is not surprising that these are its most distinguishing feature. The black tufts can be two inches long. The eyespots – white spots on the back of each ear – are clearly visible when the caracal displays its ears in anger.

Rock hyrax make up the largest part of the caracal's diet but it is an aggressive hunter and has been known to attack bigger prey such as gazelles. It is extremely agile and climbs well, sometimes taking its prey up into a tree to eat in a leopard-like manner. If the meal is too large to consume in one sitting, the caracal might return to it later. In India and Iran this feline has been tamed and, like the cheetah, trained to hunt for man.

EUROPEAN WILD CAT (*Felis silvestris*)

SIZE:	Length 44–70cm excluding tail. Weight 2.9–7.9kg
DISTRIBUTION:	Europe, excluding Scandinavia
IDENTIFICATION:	Dark-grey or reddish-brown with soft tabby markings, broad head with distinctive 'M' on the forehead. Blunt-ended tail marked with black rings. Golden-amber eyes, black paw pads

Scattered populations of wild cat are found in remote forest areas of Spain, Portugal and Eastern Europe, but its range and numbers are declining rapidly. Hybridization is its greatest threat, as many live close enough to civilization to mate with feral or even domestic cats. The Scottish wild cat is an endangered species as it has been widely hunted. However, in a court case in 1990 a Scottish gamekeeper was acquitted of killing three wild cats because an expert witness could not identify the remains as pure specimens.

In Turkey and around the Caucasus mountains, the subspecies *F.s. caucasica* can sometimes be completely black although experts cannot agree whether these are pure or hybrids. The Scottish black-coated 'Kellas cat', as it is known, has been established as a pure melanistic wild cat.

Sand Cat ▲

(*Felis margarita*)

Size:	Height 24–30cm. Length, body, 40–57cm (tail 27–35cm). Weight 1.5–3.4kg
Distribution:	From Algeria to Pakistan
Identification:	Very small with large, wide head, short legs and big ears. Soft fur coloured from light-grey to sandy with dark bands around legs

Sound does not travel well in the soft sand of the desert, especially when made by a gerbil asleep in its burrow beneath the surface. That is one reason why the nocturnal sand cat has such keen hearing. Once it has located its prey it digs furiously to reach its meal. The dense black, wiry hair on the soles of its feet insulates it against intense heat and cold and aids burrowing. It also eats jerboas, birds, rabbits, insects and lizards and is renowned among Saharan nomads for being a snake hunter, particularly of vipers. It never drinks water, getting all the moisture it needs from its food. Sand cats have been sold as pets, shot for sport and killed for their pelts.

Pallas's Cat (Manul, Steppe Cat)

(*Otocolobus manul*)

Size:	Length, body, 50–65cm (tail 21–31cm). Weight 3–4.5kg
Distribution:	From Caspian Sea to Kazakhstan
Identification:	Short, broad head, small round ears, large eyes. Long greyish or russet-red coat, spotted with black. Long dark fur on underside

Pallas's cat is a feline oddity: it has round rather than vertical pupils, it is a very poor runner, and it yelps like a dog. It lives at altitudes above 4,000m where its extremely thick fur protects it against the cold. Fur hunters have eliminated the cat from large areas of its original range. It is now protected (although some hunting still goes on) and does a good job of keeping down pika and rodents, which are pests and carriers of disease. It also eats larks, sandgrouse and ptarmigan. It is now further threatened by the drive to eliminate its main prey, pika, from large areas of Russia and China.

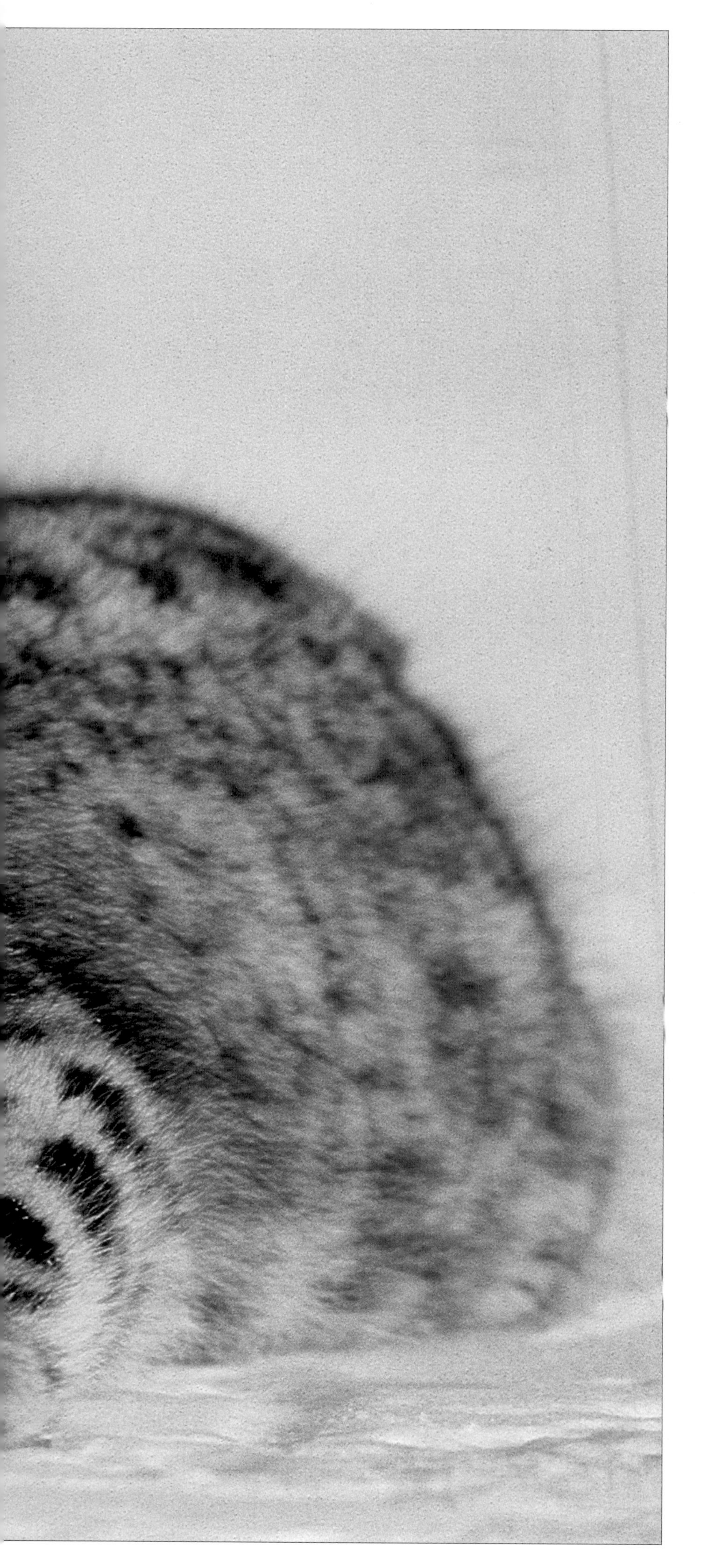

Snow Leopard (*Uncia uncia*)

There are few sights in nature as breathtaking as a snow leopard moving across the mountain. This muscular, agile cat, with its huge paws and long hind legs, can leap 15m horizontally and 6m vertically as it traverses the broken landscape. The average annual diet for one snow leopard has been calculated as five blue sheep (or *bharal*), nine Tibetan woolly hares, 25 marmots, five domestic goats, one domestic sheep and 15 birds.

Most active at dawn and dusk, the snow leopard grows to a height of 50–70cm, is up to 130cm long in the body and can weigh 75kg. Its thick fur is light or smoky grey, tinged with yellow, shading to pure white on its belly and with 'rosettes' of dark spots scattered all over. Its thick tail is nearly a metre long and it has dense, woolly underfur.

Although endangered and protected and with total numbers down to 4,500–7,500, the snow leopard is still hunted, not only for its pelt but also for bones and body parts used in traditional Chinese medicine. This, together with depletion of its natural prey, habitat degradation and fragmentation and reprisal attacks by herdsmen for loss of livestock, means the snow leopard faces an uncertain future.

Its geographical range mirrors that of two of its largest prey species, the blue sheep and the ibex: the mountains of China, Bhutan, Nepal, India, Pakistan, Afghanistan, Tajikistan, Uzbekistan, Kyrgyzstan, Kazakhstan, Russia, and Mongolia.

OCELOT *(Leopardus pardalis)*

Size:	Length, body, 55–100cm (tail 30–45cm). Weight 8.8–11.5kg
Distribution:	Central America, northern South America
Identification:	Short, tawny to reddish-brown coat marked with black spots and rosettes. Lighter beneath. Single white spot on back of each ear. Two black lines either side of face. Black-banded tail

This small, slender cat was once hunted for its beautiful coat but is now internationally protected. It remains a great attraction in zoos. It is solitary and hunts at night over a range of about 18 square km, taking mostly small mammals (deer, rabbits and other rodents), reptiles and amphibians, including iguanas and lizards, frogs, turtles and crabs. It can swim well and will catch fish. The ocelot will also climb trees to hunt for birds and sleep in the lower branches.

Although they are territorial cats, a male's territory will frequently overlap a female's. Kittens are born throughout the year and raised in a den by their mother. Unusually for a big cat, she is provided with food by the male while suckling her young.

Clouded Leopard (*Neofelis nebulosa*)

Size:	Length, body, 75–110cm (tail up to 90cm)
Distribution:	Southeastern Asia
Identification:	Yellowish-brown fur with distinctive cloud pattern. Flattened skull and extremely long tail

Rimaudahan, meaning 'tree tiger', is the Malay name for the clouded leopard. It is an accomplished climber – its long tail helping it to balance – and spends a great deal of time up in the trees. Lying still on an overhanging branch in dappled sunlight, the clouded leopard is difficult to spot and is in an excellent position to ambush its prey. A single bite with its long canines is usually enough to despatch its victim swiftly and these teeth, which can be up to 45mm long, have earned it the name 'modern-day sabre-tooth'.

A shy, solitary creature, the clouded leopard stays well away from civilization, seeking peace and seclusion deep in the tropical forests. It does not always manage to escape man and has been heavily hunted not just for its fur but also for its teeth and bones, which have reputed medicinal qualities.

Cougar (Mountain Lion, Puma, Panther)

(*Puma concolor*)

Size:	Height 61–76cm. Length, body, 110–243cm (tail 53–82cm). Weight 30–103kg
Distribution:	Western North America and throughout South America. Possibly introduced elsewhere
Identification:	Short, coarse hair from yellow-brown to grey-brown with creamy belly and muzzle. Long black-tipped tail

The cougar is the usual subject of those regular reports of mysterious big cats seen in gardens and farmland, terrifying people and killing livestock. Victims of a cougar attack would be unlikely to live to tell the tale, however, as this cat is a supreme and stealthy hunter, which can deliver instant death with a bite through the neck. An 18-year-old jogger was killed in an attack in 1991 in Idaho Springs, Colorado and many more deaths occur in South America. Once widespread in the United States, the cougar was driven into more inhospitable regions by humans. It eats everything from insects and small birds to domestic cattle and moose.

JAGUAR (*Panthera onca*)

SIZE:	Length, body, 100–180cm (tail 40–70cm). Weight 70–120kg
DISTRIBUTION:	Southwest USA, Central and South America
IDENTIFICATION:	Brownish-yellow fur, similar to a leopard but has dots within the dark rosette markings and is stockier with a larger head

In American folklore, the Maya revered the jaguar as God of the Underworld, believing that it helped the sun to travel under the earth every night so it could rise safely each morning. Many legends are told about the jaguar, partly because it is solitary and elusive and has been studied less than other big cats. Known facts are few. Often living in dense jungle close to water, the jaguar not only hunts its prey on the ground but will take fish or turtles from rivers and seek monkeys in the lower branches of trees.

An estimated 15,000 jaguars remain in their natural habitat and are protected by international agreement. Completely black jaguars are not unusual and, like black leopards, are known as black panthers.

CHEETAH *(Acinonyx jubatus)*

SIZE:	Length, body, 110–150cm (tail 65–90cm)
DISTRIBUTION:	Sub-Saharan Africa and southwest Asia
IDENTIFICATION:	Long, slender legs, long tail and lithe body. Tawny-golden coat with solid spots

This beautiful cat is the fastest land animal in the world. With its greyhound-like body, flexible spine, and long tail, it can sprint at up to 110kph but is built for speed rather than endurance and cannot keep this up for more than 400m. Chases usually only last about 20 seconds. In fact, the cheetah is usually so exhausted after a chase that she needs to recover for about half an hour before she can consume her prey or take it to her cubs. During this time she is vulnerable to scavengers – typically lions, wild dogs, hyaenas, baboons, or vultures – who will steal her catch. The males fare a little better as they form small groups and hunt together.

AFRICAN LION (*Panthera leo*)

SIZE:	Length, body, 1.7–2.5m (tail 60–100cm)
DISTRIBUTION:	Sub-Saharan Africa
IDENTIFICATION:	Powerful, muscular body covered with short, dense fur, usually tawny-brown. Males have long, darkish manes

The 'King of Beasts' has symbolized strength, power and courage in many civilizations through the ages. Its image has been used by companies to denote grandeur (such as the famous roaring lion which introduces MGM films) and to imply dependability (like the little lion logos stamped on British eggs). Countless warriors have had their lionheartedness emphasized on their epitaphs.

The impressive mane of the male lion takes 5–7 years to grow to full length and the fuller and darker it is, the more appeal it has for the female. This macho attire has its disadvantages, though: a large-maned, fully-grown male is too slow and conspicuous to hunt. Fortunately, the pride females co-operate to hunt for him and his offspring, some chasing the prey towards others lying in wait. After the kill the females allow the males to eat their fill before they take their turn, although there is often a great deal of snarling and snapping at mealtimes. A full-grown lion can consume up to 18kg of meat at one sitting and might not eat again for two or three days.

A group or pride of lions has a core of related females and their cubs. The adult males, usually no more than three, will come and go over the years. Male cubs are ejected from the pride when they are about three years old and often form coalitions with one or two other males. When the members of this group are 5–7 years old they seek out a pride to take over. This usually happens when the existing pride leader is old or sick or simply outnumbered by the invaders. The takeover is swift and brutal: not only is the old leader killed but so too are any suckling young of his. The newcomers want to spread their genes and cannot do so if the females are bringing up another lion's cubs. In their turn the new leaders will last about two years before being deposed.

African lions are on the decrease due to disease and persecution by farmers. On average a lion eats one cow or three sheep per year and it is cheaper to shoot or poison the predators than it is to put up effective fencing. The cattle they consume are infecting lions with bovine TB and, worst of all, thousands are dying from an Aids-like condition, their immune systems destroyed by lentivirus, an auto-immune virus also known as FIV (Feline Immunodeficiency Virus). One estimate has put lion numbers at just 23,000, down from 230,000 in the 1980s – and some pessimistic assessments put numbers even lower than that.

TIGER *(Panthera tigris)*

Size:	Length, body, 190–330cm (tail up to 110cm). Weight 180–260kg (male), 130–160kg (female)
Distribution:	India to Siberia and Southeast Asia
Identification:	Large cat with orange body and thick black vertical stripes. Long hind limbs and tail, powerful shoulders and forelimbs

The tiger has always had a fearsome reputation and the notorious 'Man-eater of Champawat' in India was reputed to have killed 436 people. Today it is generally accepted that only old or injured tigers, unable to capture their usual prey, will attack humans.

This powerful cat has no predators other than man. It has suffered drastically from being hunted as a trophy, for its strikingly beautiful skin and for many of its body parts, which are used in traditional Chinese medicine. Three of the original eight sub-species are now extinct and the others threatened. The Siberian or Amur tiger, the largest sub-species, is the most at risk. Only about 400 remain in the wild and, despite the protection afforded by international treaties, the WWF protection group reported three Amur tigers killed by poachers in December 2003.

The tiger's famous stripe patterns are unique: like human fingerprints, no two are the same.

Tigers are solitary rather than pack animals. The usual social group is a female and her young, who stay together until the cubs are ready to establish their own territory, at around 24–30 months.

Tigers hunt alone. One bite from their exceptionally powerful jaws is usually fatal.

Weddell seal

Seals

Sleek and graceful though seals are in the water, they are easy prey as they shuffle along on land and in the freezing expanses of the polar regions they have always provided a perfect source of food, clothing, heat and lighting.

Elephant seals are enormous: 5.7m long and weighing up to 2,200kg. There are two types, **northern** (*Mirounga angoustrirostris*) and **southern** (*M. leonina*). Both were almost wiped out before hunting was stopped in 1964 and the seals protected. These impressive creatures – the males have huge floppy, inflatable noses and battle-scarred neck shields – can stay underwater for two hours, reaching depths of 1,170m.

Wherever you find **ringed seals** (*Phoca hispida*) you will find polar bears. The former are a main dish for the latter. These relatively small seals, up to 1.2m long, are found mostly in Arctic waters but also in the Baltic and some freshwater Finnish lakes. They can dive for up to 20 minutes as they seek out small fish and crustaceans. The pups are born in tunnels in the snow and their dense, pure white fur makes them a target for hunters. Ringed seal numbers are declining.

Unfortunately for the **harp seal** (*Phoca groenlandica*), which takes its name from a dark, harp-shaped marking on its back, its thick fur is quite beautiful with subtly toned creams and greys and it is heavily hunted, particularly in Canada. It grows to about 1.8m long and can dive to over 270m, staying underwater for up to half an hour.

The Pribilof Islands are the breeding grounds for the **Pribilof fur seal** (*Callorhinus ursinus*), and are home to the largest colonies of fur seal in the world. They were at the heart of the fur trade for almost 200 years until it ground to a halt under pressure from animal rights activists and a dwindling market. The value of the pelt lies in its dense underfur, which has approximately 45,000 hairs per square cm.

Weddell seals (*Leptonychotes weddellii*) are stealthy hunters. They drift to within a few centimetres before grabbing the unsuspecting cod that make up most of their diet. Weddells have acute underwater vision and often use the under-ice surface for backlighting prey. They have also been seen puffing small fish out of ice crevices with blasts of air. The Weddell is found in the Antarctic pack ice and breeds on the solid ice and on islands north to South Georgia. Adult males grow to almost 3m and weigh up to 400kg. Weddell seals' inaccessibility shields them from hunting though many used to be killed to feed sled dogs.

In July 2003 a scientist was killed by a **leopard seal** (*Hydrurga leptonyx*) while snorkelling at a research station on the Antarctic peninsula. A fellow scientist warned that these huge-headed, reptilian-looking killers were sizing up people as prey. Leopard seals, which grow to 400kg and can swim at 40kph, will eat anything from krill, which they filter from the water through their teeth, to juvenile elephant seals. The scientist's was the first recorded death but there have been other non-fatal attacks and some research scientists now fit special protective guards to their inflatable boats to prevent punctures caused by leopard seals.

WALRUS (*Odobenus rosmarus*)

SIZE:	Weight, male 1,215kg, female 812kg. Length, male up to 3.6m, female up to 3m
DISTRIBUTION:	**Pacific walruses** (*O. r. rosmarus*) inhabit Bering, Chukchi, and Laptev seas. **Atlantic walruses** (*O. r. divergens*) inhabit coastal areas of northeastern Canada and Greenland
IDENTIFICATION:	Large cinnamon-coloured, spindle-shaped bodies. Two long ivory tusks in both male and female. Long whiskers on either side of snout

Odobenus is ancient Greek for 'tooth walker' and refers to the way walruses pull themselves up on to the ice with their tusks, which are also used to dig clams and mussels out of the seabed.

The 50,000-strong Atlantic population is stable but Pacific walruses, which have been hunted to depletion and allowed to recover several times, have probably reached saturation point. In the early 1980s, they began to appear leaner and increased their consumption of alternative foods such as fish (their preferred diet is mussels and clams). Natural mortality increased, birth rates decreased. There was just not enough food to go round and, added to an increase in subsistence catches by indigenous Arctic peoples, the Pacific walrus is on the verge of yet another decline.

THREE-TOED SLOTH

(Bradypus variegates)

SIZE:	Length, body, 33–71cm (tail up to 9cm)
DISTRIBUTION:	Central and South America
IDENTIFICATION:	Slender body with grey-brown coarse hair, long limbs with permanently curved claws. Three fingers on front limbs

This creature is as sluggish as its names suggests. Not only does it rest or sleep for up to 20 hours a day, but every move it makes is made incredibly slowly. The three-toed sloth is particularly slow on the ground. Its curved feet and weak limbs prevent it from standing so it can only crawl or grasp something to haul itself up. This gentle animal is far more at home in the tops or middle layers of trees where it hangs upside down from all four limbs, moving slowly paw-by-paw along the branches. All activities are carried out in this position including eating, mating and giving birth. A single offspring is born once a year and spends the first five weeks or so of its life clinging to its mother's belly.

Sloths eat tree leaves, shoots and foliage, mainly of the cecropia tree that grows near clearings, river banks and forest edges.

COMMON LONG-NOSED ARMADILLO *(Dasypus novemcinctus)*

SIZE:	Length, body, 24–43cm (tail up to 37cm)
DISTRIBUTION:	Southern USA through Central America south to Argentina
IDENTIFICATION:	Body, tail and head protected by bony plates. Mid-section 7–11 bands connected by soft skin. Pointed head, pig-like snout and short legs

Some armadillos can roll themselves into a complete ball for protection but the common long-nosed, or nine-banded, armadillo prefers to escape to the safety of its burrow where it wedges itself in, arching its back against the burrow walls. A master of escape, this armadillo has been known to outrun dogs despite its short legs and is adept at crossing water. Not just a good swimmer, the armadillo can run along the bottom of shallow waterways, escaping unseen.

Armadillos are unique in that their litter always includes identical quadruplets that develop from a single egg. For this reason, they are valued for medical research into multiple births. Similarly, they are used for research into leprosy as they are the only creature other than man to suffer from this disease.

GIANT PANGOLIN *(Manis gigantean)*

SIZE:	Length, body, 80–90cm (tail up to 65cm)
DISTRIBUTION:	Equatorial from West Africa to Uganda
IDENTIFICATION:	Head, tapering body and wide, tapering tail covered with brown scales, short legs

Looking like a reptile, the pangolin is the only mammal covered in scales. These sharp, horny scales resemble a pine cone and are used for both attack and defence: sometimes just twitching them is enough to deter a would-be predator. One folk legend describes how the pangolin traps ants by lying in its nest and raising its scales to allow the ants to crawl in. The scales are then lowered, crushing the inquisitive insects, and the pangolin eats them later by lifting its scales in water and letting the ants float out. The pangolin's more usual method of feeding is similar to that of the anteaters, breaking open termites' nests with its front paws and using its long, sticky tongue to pick up the insects.

Pangolins are hunted for their meat and the Chinese prize the scales for their supposed medicinal value.

Common Rabbit (Coney)

(Oryctolagus cuniculus)

Size:	Length 41–59cm, weight 1–2kg
Distribution:	Originally Iberian peninsula and northwest Africa but introduced to all continents except Antarctica and many islands
Identification:	Generally buff brown with lighter underparts and short white tail. Compact with long ears and long hind legs.

The rabbit has a deserved reputation for rapid reproduction. A healthy female often has more than one litter of up to eight young within a breeding season. They are born helpless and without sight or fur, but within four to five months are themselves ready to breed. Rabbits live in large groups, burrowing to form complex warrens with living chambers. A strict hierarchy is maintained and adults can be surprisingly aggressive with one another. Active day or night, they crop grass closely and damage crops by scraping away soil. As a prey species they are always alert and signal danger by drumming their feet. The flashing white tail is also an alarm sign.

Now considered a pest in many areas around the world, rabbits played a major role in the extinction of some marsupials following their introduction to Australia in the 1800s. At Easter Australians celebrate with chocolate replicas of the bilby, a long-eared marsupial now threatened by the rabbit's success.

Arctic Hare *(Lepus arcticus)*

Size:	Length 50cm, weight 5.4kg
Distribution:	North America, Newfoundland, Greenland
Identification:	White fur with black ear tips in winter, greyish-brown in summer, small ears and small white tail

On the high Arctic islands in the far north, the Arctic hare remains white all the year round with just its characteristic black ear tips visible in the snow. The ears are shorter than those of other hares to minimize heat loss. The wolf is its main predator, although the young leverets are also taken by snowy owls, ermine and the Arctic fox. Preferring the open tundra where the wind keeps the snow cover light, the Arctic hare forages for grass and shoots, sometimes congregating in groups of 200 or more. This allows some members of the group to keep watch for predators while others feed, digging for willow under the snow.

When startled, the Arctic hare stands on its powerful hind feet and bounds away like a kangaroo, reaching speeds of 50–60kph, before dropping back to all fours. Unlike rabbits the young leverets are born furred and with their eyes open. A litter of four to eight is guarded by the mother for the first three days after which they lie very still, trying not to attract attention, while she is away from the nest.

Eurasian Red Squirrel

(*Sciurus vulgaris*)

Size:	Length 18–24cm excluding tail
Distribution:	Throughout Europe, from British Isles south to Mediterranean, east to southern Urals, Altai and north-east China. Also Sakhalin Island off eastern Russia and Hokkaido, Japan
Identification:	Reddish-brown fur with tufts of hair on the ears. Long bushy tail

Various small mammals store food for the winter in a cache near their nest, but the squirrel is a scatter hoarder, storing its winter food in several different places. Nuts and seeds are buried by digging a small pit with the front paws, dropping in the food and pressing down with the teeth, finally camouflaging the area with leaves or stones. It is useful to have a series of secret supplies if another foraging animal catches you retrieving your breakfast.

Once common in Britain but now rare, the red squirrel is widespread throughout most of Europe. During the mating season several males leap spectacularly through the branches and up and down tree trunks in pursuit of one female.

Grey Squirrel (*Sciurus carolinensis*)

Size:	Length up to 30cm excluding tail of up to 24cm
Distribution:	Great Britain, eastern United States, Canada and Italy
Identification:	Grey fur tinged with orange-red on back. Large, distinctive, curled, bushy tail

The grey squirrel's magnificent bushy tail is used as a blanket in cold weather, as a parachute to slow its descent from a tree and as a shield when fighting. Its abundance in American gardens means squirrels, and their destruction, are a fact of life for the gardener, although nature lovers appreciate the intelligence and antics of this attractive creature, and squirrel watching is said to be second in popularity only to bird watching.

When a predator approaches, the grey squirrel will freeze rather than flee or fight, darting round to the back of a tree trunk and keeping absolutely still until the danger passes. If the hunter prowls around, the squirrel simply flits to the blind side of the tree and freezes again.

Eastern Chipmunk

(*Tamias striatus*)

▶

Size:	Weight 60 g
Distribution:	Southeastern Canada and eastern USA
Identification:	Reddish fur with dark brown to black stripes on the face and extending along the sides and back and white fur on the stomach. Bushy tail, held erect when running.

Visitors to North American forests are frequently rewarded by the sight of this charming creature scurrying around in its search for food. If they are very lucky they will see one having a sand bath, rolling from side to side on the dry ground.

The eastern chipmunk spends much of its time foraging for food in trees, displaying the typical chipmunk habit of collecting dry food in cheek pouches to store underground. Chipmunks do not hibernate in winter but drop into a period of torpor for up to eight days at a time. The body temperature and heart rate drop to conserve energy and the chipmunk occasionally boosts its reserves by raiding its cache of food.

Abert's Squirrel (*Sciurus aberti*)

Size:	Length 46–58cm plus tail of 19.5–25.5cm
Distribution:	Wyoming to New Mexico, Arizona and Utah in the United States. Also in Mexico
Identification:	Grey coat with white underparts, broad tail. Characteristic tufts of hair on the ears

These handsome tree squirrels make their homes in the pine forests of North America, which provide their main food source. The distinctive tufts of fur on the ears led to the other common name of tassel-eared squirrel. The tough, curved claws are invaluable for climbing and leaping between trees and the broad tails are used to aid balance. There are spectacular chases in the breeding season with one female attracting several suitors and leading them a merry dance through the trees until she is ready to choose a partner and mate.

Hoary Marmot (*Marmota caligata*)

Size:	Length 45–57cm plus tail of 17–25cm
Distribution:	Alaska, Idaho and Washington
Identification:	Brown tail and back with creamy white over the shoulders. Hairy ears, the nose and lips are outlined in white

Like its relative the groundhog, the hoary marmot is also called a 'whistlepig' because of its shrill alarm call. Researchers have found that different calls tell the rest of the colony whether the intruder is approaching by air or overland. The hoary marmot lives in colonies when food is plentiful, otherwise it is each marmot for himself. The dominant male is the only one permitted to mate with the females. A younger or smaller subordinate male sometimes challenges the colony male and if he is driven off he will often leave to form his own colony.

The burrows are used as nests and retreats, to escape from golden eagles, bears or wolverines, and hot summer sun. Marmots emerge from the burrows at dusk to feed.

Muskrat (*Ondatra zibethicus*)

Size:	Length, body, 41–63cm (tail 18–31cm). Weight 0.6–1.8kg
Distribution:	Most of Canada and United States except Arctic, far west, southwest and Florida. Introduced to northern Eurasia
Identification:	Robust body. Dense, glossy, dark-brown fur. Flattish, scaly tail. Short legs, big feet

It is the strong-smelling scent emitted by breeding males which gives the muskrat its name. Like the beaver, it makes its home on the water, building a house of sticks, grass, rushes, leaves and mud on a platform with at least one underwater entrance. These conspicuous structures can be 3m in diameter and up to 1.5m high with one or more dry chambers inside. The muskrat is a superb swimmer, able to go forwards or backwards underwater with ease, and capable of staying submerged for up to 20 minutes. It usually eats stems, leaves and roots, but also takes crayfish and amphibians when necessary. It can be a nuisance on farms: raiding cornfields, blocking drains and destroying dykes by building on them. The muskrat was once a mainstay of the fur trade and its fur is still used, as is its meat.

Black-tailed Prairie Dog

(*Cynomys ludovicianus*)

Size:	Length, body, 28–34cm (tail 75–98mm)
Distribution:	Central and North America
Identification:	Golden-brown squirrel-like mammal with short, black-tipped tail and short legs

Early American settlers named these sociable animals 'little dogs' because they wag their tails when excited and yap or bark a warning call. Numbers reached pest proportions in the nineteenth century despite the fact that their meat is said to taste better than wild rabbit.

Black-tailed prairie dogs live in huge colonies, known as towns, covering several hundred hectares. The largest prairie dog town ever found was in western Texas. About 160km wide and 400km long, and covering an area the size of Belgium, the town was home to an estimated 400 million prairie dogs. The burrow system is complex, the first tunnel going straight down for about 4.5m providing a quick escape from predators. Throughout the town there are escape hatches – tunnels built up to within a few inches of the surface – to be used in case of flooding.

Groundhog (Woodchuck)

(*Marmota monax*)

Size:	40–70cm
Distribution:	Eastern United States, southern Canada, east central Alaska
Identification:	Sturdy body with greyish-brown fur mixed with yellow or reddish tint. Bushy slightly flattened tail, small ears

According to American folklore, if the groundhog emerges from hibernation on February 2 and is able to see its own shadow, frosty winter weather will continue for another six weeks. This rodent member of the squirrel family is also known as 'whistle pig' because of its alarm call. The groundhog barks and squeals when fighting and chatters when cornered. Formerly killed for its fur and meat, it is now hunted only for sport.

Farm machinery and buildings are occasionally damaged by the immense burrows that make up the groundhog's den. These extend as far as 2.4m under ground and can be 13.5m long, with several entrances. As winter approaches, the groundhog builds up a good store of fat and hibernates in a side chamber, rolled into a ball with its head tucked between its hind legs.

BEAVER (*Castor canadensis*)

SIZE:	Up to 120cm long
DISTRIBUTION:	North America
IDENTIFICATION:	Dense, water-repelling brown fur, webbed hind feet, broad flat tail which is used as a paddle

The beaver is an architect. Its complex creation of dams and lodges has earned it a reputation as one of nature's greatest engineers. A beaver gnaws its way round the trunk of a tree and can fell a sapling in under 30 minutes. Thus begins the dam, the beaver using its hand-like front paws to fill the gaps with mud, stones and vegetation. The lake formed behind the dam provides a safe retreat from predators, a storehouse for essential winter supplies of timber for food, and an underwater entrance to the family home.

The beaver and its extended family work together at night, posting a sentry that spanks the water with its tail to warn of danger. Closing its ears and nostrils, and lowering its heart rate, the beaver can stay submerged for up to 15 minutes.

Black Rat (*Rattus rattus*)

Size:	Length 16–23cm plus tail of same length
Distribution:	Almost universal although absent from northern Europe
Identification:	Black furry body, paler undersides, long tail and large ears

As a transmitter of diseases, rats have been blamed for more human deaths over the past thousand years than all the wars and revolutions together. They have developed a dependence on human beings, raiding food stores and damaging more than they consume. It is no wonder that rats are among the most deeply hated mammals.

The black rat is sometimes known as the ship rat, house rat, or roof rat, because of its tendency to flee upwards and make its home in roofs or trees. It is exceptionally adept at climbing and can travel across a wire just 1.5mm in diameter. A single dominant male heads a social group of up to 60 rats with two or three of his wives dominating the others. The females can be particularly aggressive, defending their territory fiercely, even standing on their hind legs and striking invaders with their scrabbling front paws.

Brown Rat (*Rattus norvegicus*)

Size:	Length up to 21cm, plus tail of up to 22cm
Distribution:	Almost universal
Identification:	Greyish-brown fur with a greasy appearance. Long scaly tail is shorter than the body

This rat can be found close to human habitation throughout the world. It is considered a serious pest to farmers, spoiling what it does not eat with its urine and droppings. Poisoning and trapping seem to have only a temporary effect as the rat can produce six to eight litters a year. Its reputation is not enhanced by its penchant for living in rubbish dumps and sewers and its tendency to spread diseases. A modern-day Pied Piper of Hamelin would earn a fortune.

Brown rats form large social groups with a large dominant male guarding his harem against other suitors. Females will defend the group aggressively. Rats sleep for up to 13 hours a day becoming more active at night. They must ensure their diet contains liquid, as they cannot survive for long without water.

Harvest Mouse *(Micromys minutus)* ▼

Size:	Length 4–6cm, plus tail of up to 5cm
Distribution:	Europe (excluding most of Scandinavia), east Russia, Korea and south China
Identification:	Reddish or yellowish-brown fur with white undersides, blunt muzzle and small hairy ears. Long, slender tail

Originally it was thought that the harvest mouse was only to be found in cereal crops, but it is now known to adapt to a wide range of habitats wherever tall vegetation is found. This tiny mouse is the only Old World mammal to have a truly prehensile tail. It can grip a stem with each hind foot and its tail, allowing it to use both forepaws to collect food.

After mating the male will help the female build a breeding nest, weaving grasses and securing the tennis-ball size nest high among the tallest stems. The female chases her mate away and does not allow him into the nest. In fact she does not seem to show a great deal of love to any of her kin: she abandons her offspring after 15 or 16 days and builds a new nest for her next litter.

Wood Mouse *(Apodemus sylvaticus)*

Size:	Length 6–11cm, excluding tail of up to 10cm. Weight 7–12g
Distribution:	Europe except northern Scandinavia, central and southwest Asia and northwest Africa
Identification:	Dark-brown fur with greyish-white underside, large ears and a long tail

The wood mouse is regarded as a pest by farmers and gardeners, digging up seeds before they have germinated and damaging seedlings in commercial woods. In the past, gardeners would roll their beans and peas in red lead before planting but this would not be allowed today. A more eco-friendly solution was to bathe the cat and sprinkle the bathwater over the seedbed, deterring the mice with cat scent.

The wood mouse is extremely agile, adept at climbing and jumping, and a good swimmer. It builds a system of tunnels with underground nests and larders. Social groups share these burrows but the females prevent males from entering nesting areas while they are rearing litters.

Edible Dormouse

(*Glis* (*Myoxus*) *glis*)

Size:	Length 9–19cm excluding tail. Weight 50–250g
Distribution:	Europe and Asia
Identification:	Greyish-brown fur with dark stripes on the legs and dark rings around the eyes. Thick, bushy tail

Dormice have been hunted in Slovenia since the middle of the thirteenth century. Their meat was an important supplement to an otherwise meagre diet, and uses were found for the grease and hides. Nowadays trapping continues and although the meat might not be so necessary, it is regarded as a local speciality in goulash or stews. Dormouse-fur hats used to be part of men's traditional dress and a few are still made today.

Mature deciduous woodland makes the ideal home for the edible dormouse. It will eat nuts and fruit, buds and even tree bark. Cosy nests are made in tree holes or below ground in abandoned rabbit warrens and the whole family group hibernates together until spring.

Hamster (*Cricetus cricetus*)

Size:	Length up to 30cm, weight 100–900g
Distribution:	Throughout Eurasia. Mostly in farmland and open areas
Identification:	Chunky body, generally light brown on the back, white on the sides and black beneath, with soft, thick fur. Short, hairless tail. Cheek pouches

In western Europe the common hamster has been driven to the edge of extinction through habitat destruction. It is now protected by the Bern Convention. However, in eastern Europe it is ubiquitous and regularly poisoned or trapped for its skin. The east cannot understand why the west wants to protect a pest. But protected it is, and vigorously.

The common hamster feeds on grains, beans, lentils, roots, insect larvae, and frogs. It lives a solitary life in its burrow, which can be over six feet deep and which has a chamber for storing up to 90kg of food needed for the winter. Although it hibernates, it wakes every five to seven days to feed. Breeding lasts from April to August with two litters of four to twelve young per year.

Grasshopper Mouse

(*Onychomys torridus*) ▼

Size:	Length, body, 9–13cm (tail 3–6cm)
Distribution:	USA and Mexico
Identification:	Grey or pinkish-brown mouse with dense fur and a long tail tipped with white

Instead of squeaking faintly behind the skirting board like its domestic cousin, this small rodent actually howls. It stands up on its hind legs, points its nose in the air and howls like a miniature wolf. This eerie sound is a sign of aggression and is made before launching into battle with another mouse. The other mouse might even be its mate: the grasshopper mouse frequently kills and eats its partner if short of food.

As its name suggests, grasshoppers make up a large part of this mouse's diet. It also eats scorpions and caterpillars and is the only creature to have found a way of eating a darkling beetle. This beetle emits a foul-tasting anal secretion but the mouse wedges the darkling's rear into the soil and eats it head first, leaving the unpalatable part in the ground.

Lemming

(*Lemmus norvegicus*)

Size:	Length 10–12cm
Distribution:	Scandinavia (similar species in eastern Europe, and north America)
Identification:	Yellowish-brown fur with darker spots, round head with small eyes and ears almost hidden in the fur, short tail

Contrary to popular myth, lemmings do not commit mass suicide. Lemming populations fluctuate tremendously and mass dispersal, rather than suicide, takes place when the local food supply runs out.

A courageous and aggressive little rodent, the lemming will stand and face up to an antagonist, hissing in anger rather than trying to escape. It is a prolific breeder, producing at least two broods of about five young each year in nests under clumps of grass or stones. When migrating the lemming reproduces even more frequently, perhaps to compensate for the loss of pack members as they attempt to cross rivers and lakes during their journey.

North American Porcupine

(*Erethizon dorsatum*)

Size:	Length 75–100cm. Weight 3–7kg (occasionally up to 18kg)
Distribution:	North America
Identification:	Dark-brown but varying throughout range. Back covered with thick, sharp, barbed quills amid stiff guard hair and woolly underfur. Short, thick tail

The porcupine loves salt and given the chance will chew up saddles, riding tack, rifle butts, boots, tool handles – anything with a trace of sweat on it. This placid herbivore can adapt to a wide range of environments. When threatened it hides its nose under a rock or log (a blow on the nose can be fatal), raises and rattles its quills. It backs towards its molester, slaps its tail and drives its jagged, hollow spines deep into the attacker's flesh. These snap off and stay embedded. Minute barbs work the quills ever inwards, eventually killing victims as large as mountain lions and bears.

Prehensile-tailed Tree Porcupine (*Coendou prehensilis*)

Size:	Length, body, 30–60cm (tail 33–48.5cm)
Distribution:	South America
Identification:	Black or yellow and black body, the back is covered with short spines. Long, smooth tail, short legs with well-developed claws

The spines of the prehensile-tailed tree porcupine are 40–50mm long, considerably shorter than the crested species from Africa but no less effective if it needs them. They are usually laid smoothly along the porcupine's back and raised if it is threatened. This porcupine cannot shoot out its quills but they are so loosely attached that when the barbs latch on to an assailant, the quill pulls free and usually becomes embedded in the attacker. Often remaining for a few painful days, the quills work their way into the skin and occasionally cause death by puncturing internal organs.

Tree porcupines are nocturnal, resting inconspicuously in a tree crown during the day. This species curls its tail around branches as it climbs, grazing on leaves and shoots. In winter, this rodent can be a pest, eating bark in a ring round the tree trunk and killing the tree.

CHINCHILLA *(Chinchilla lanigera)*

SIZE:	Length 22.5–38cm plus tail of 7.5–15cm
DISTRIBUTION:	Chile
IDENTIFICATION:	Soft, dense fur of varying colours, usually brownish-grey but can be beige or almost black. Broad head with large, black eyes and long ears. Long, furry tail

Most commonly seen as pets, you have to go to the mountains of northern Chile – at altitudes above 5000m – to see chinchilla living in the wild today. Chinchilla live in colonies and make dens in holes among the rocks, and need their thick coats to withstand extremes of temperature. They keep themselves clean with 'dry shampoos' in lava dust. Chinchilla fur is considered one of the most valuable in the world. It is still available but only from commercially farmed animals, as chinchilla are now officially endangered.

Aardvark

(*Orycteropus afer*)

Size:	Length, body, 105–160cm (tail 45–80cm). Weight 40–100kg
Distribution:	Sub-Saharan Africa, except thick forest
Identification:	Pig-like, stocky body, curved back, short neck, long snout and large ears. Long, muscular tail. Bristly light-brown hair on thick pink-to-black skin

The aadvark, a peculiar beast in an order, family and genus all by itself, is a phenomenal digger and a prodigious eater of ants. Although it has a very small brain and poor eyesight, it has an excellent sense of smell that it uses to locate ants and termites. Once it has smashed into an ant nest or termite mound, the aardvark pokes its long nose in and laps up the insects with its 45cm-long, sticky tongue, consuming as many as 50,000 in a night. The insects have little chance of fighting back: the aardvark's tough skin is impenetrable, its nostrils are thick with hairs to keep things out and its rabbit-like ears can be folded closed. Most insects are swallowed whole but one type of ant is chewed using flat cheek teeth which have no enamel covering and which grow and wear down constantly.

DUGONG (*Dugong dugon*) ▶

Size:	Length up to 3m. Weight up to 500kg
Distribution:	Indian and Pacific Oceans
Identification:	Large, seal-shaped body with small flippers and broad, powerful, flattened whale-like tail. Distinctive fleshy upper lip like squashed trunk

The dugong is found in shallow waters from East Africa to the island of Vanuatu in the Pacific. This wide range, coinciding with seagrass distribution, is its best bet for survival at a time when all sirenians, or sea cows, are threatened with extinction. While the river-based manatee is confined to the populous Caribbean, the dugong can escape the worst ravages of mankind in more desolate areas of ocean. Despite this, numbers are thought to have dropped, mainly due to the destruction of seagrass by dredging, trawling, mining and land reclamation. Sewage, fertilizers and pesticide run-off from farms and cities also kill the grass on which this gentle giant relies. Many dugongs die by becoming entangled in fishing nets and many others are killed to provide meat, oil, medicine, aphrodisiacs, lucky charms and leather. Its stronghold is off Northern Australia where its numbers are estimated to be 85,000.

WEST INDIAN MANATEE

(*Trichechus manatus manatus*)

Size:	Length 3.9m. Weight 1,500kg
Distribution:	Southern United States to Caribbean islands and south to northeast Brazil
Identification:	Large seal-like creature with big snout and horizontal, paddle-shaped, beaver-like tail

When the manatee appeared between 5 and 24 million years ago, conditions favoured freshwater plants in South American coastal rivers but these plants contained a lot of silica. This wore down the manatee's teeth so it adapted by continuously replacing its molars, old ones being shed from the front of the jaw as new ones sprang up at the back. The manatee, which prefers living in large, shallow estuaries, now eats mostly seagrass, consuming up to 9 per cent of its body weight each day. Despite being protected this slow, docile and friendly sea cow is still hunted for its meat in some countries and is often killed or injured in collisions with boats. Its numbers are declining and the most significant populations are now in Florida where habitat degradation and human pressure threaten extinction. Conservation programmes have had limited success.

African Elephant

(*Loxodonta africana*)

Size:	Male: Height 4m. Weight 6,000kg. Female: Height 2.7m. Weight 2,767kg
Distribution:	Sub-Saharan Africa (limited to reserves and parks)
Identification:	Largest land mammal. Greyish, wrinkled skin, large ears, long trunk, concave back. Tusks in both sexes

African elephants are great communicators and when they have something to celebrate they let the world know. These intelligent, socially complex creatures have strong family ties and when there is a reunion, a birth or a mating within their group they acknowledge the occasion, spinning around, defecating and urinating in excitement, trumpeting and roaring. Their calls can reach almost 110 decibels and travel 10km with many of the rumbling sounds at such a low pitch they are inaudible to humans. When death occurs, however, they are solemn and touchingly mournful and seem, unlike other animals, to understand what has happened and grieve for their loss. For days after a death a family might stand round the body, touching it gently with their trunks and covering the body with leaves and twigs.

Asian Elephant

(Elephus maximus)

Size:	Height 3m (average male). Weight 5,500kg (average male)
Distribution:	India and Southeast Asia
Identification:	Smaller than African elephant with smoother, darker skin, smaller ears and convex back. Female does not have tusks. Single, finger-like projection on trunk rather than two

Each Asian elephant needs 200–300 square km of forest to sustain it – a tall order in some of the most densely populated areas on Earth. Habitat destruction and ivory poaching have driven this revered creature into ever smaller pockets of land and there are only about 40,000 at most left in the wild. The elephant has long been a symbol of wisdom in India and man's association with it goes back 5,000 years. It is an important part of the country's folklore and, under the control of a *mahout*, or handler, the elephant has played a major role in the transport of goods and people, in heavy forestry and agricultural work and as a hunting platform. It eats and drinks a prodigious amount: 150kg of vegetation and 140 litres of water per day. It strips the bark off a large branch by rotating it in its mouth with its trunk and peeling with its teeth – rather as a person eats corn on the cob.

Burchell's or Plains Zebra

(*Equus burchellii*)

Size:	Height at shoulder 1.4m. Weight 290–340kg
Distribution:	East Africa
Identification:	Distinctive, black-and-white-striped colouring with faint intermediate 'shadow' stripes on hindquarters. Each animal with unique pattern

The purpose of the zebra's stripes is unclear. None of the three species is more closely related to the others than it is to horses or asses; each species is a kind of equid which just happens to be striped like the others.

Burchell's zebra is the only species – the others being Grevy's (*E. grevyi*) and mountain (*E. zebra*) – which is not endangered. Some 200,000 are on a never-ending migration, making a 480km clockwise circuit of the Serengeti and Masai Mara National Parks in East Africa as the seasons dictate the grazing. Plains zebras mix with herds of wildebeest for protection and eat the grasses that wildebeest cannot eat. They have been hunted for hide and meat but are now a mainstay attraction for the tourist industry.

Przewalski's Horse

(*Equus przewalski*)

Size:	Height at shoulder 12–14 hands (122–142cm)
Distribution:	Mongolia
Identification:	Heavily-built. Dun-coloured coat with a black stripe over back, and black markings on legs. Dark mane and tail

Wild horses were believed to have died out in the nineteenth century so it caused a sensation in 1879, when the naturalist Colonel Nikolai Przewalski discovered some herds near the Gobi desert. Named after their Russian discoverer, Przewalski's horse is now the national symbol of Mongolia. At the turn of the century foals were captured for private collectors, so beginning the difficult task of breeding in captivity. The last confirmed sighting in the wild was in 1969. The Foundation for the Preservation and Protection of the Przewalski Horse advises zoos on breeding and the horse has been reintroduced to the wild. The small herds are either a family group – a stallion with three or four mares and their offspring – or a bachelor group of stallions.

BRAZILIAN TAPIR (*Tapirus terrestris*)

SIZE:	Height at shoulder 75–120cm. Weight 150–300kg
DISTRIBUTION:	South America
IDENTIFICATION:	Dark-brown barrel shaped body, stout legs, short tail and large head with long fleshy nose and a bristly mane

It is easy to see that the tapir, with its heavy body and short legs, is related to the rhinoceros and, like its cousin, it enjoys regular mud baths to rid itself of parasites. A creature of habit, the Brazilian tapir will always take the same route to its favourite wallowing hole, creating a well-trodden path easily followed by predators. It is listed as endangered but is still hunted for meat and for its tough hide. The tapir is quite at home in the water, plunging into the river to escape predators and perhaps staying a while to browse on aquatic vegetation.

A shrill call from a tapir expresses fear but the male also uses squealing and clicking to attract his mate. Generally a single young is born, staying with its mother for about two years. The juveniles have striking pale markings on a chestnut brown background, providing excellent camouflage.

RHINOCEROS

The **black rhinoceros** (*Diceros bicornis*), a long-time favourite trophy for big game hunters, saw its numbers fall by 96 per cent at the end of the last century. In 1970 about 65,000 of these lumbering monsters were found in non-forested parts of sub-Saharan Africa. By 1992 there were just 2,300 left in game reserves. Poachers killed most of them for their horns, which are used for dagger handles, or are ground up for use as an aphrodisiac.

The black rhino, which can weigh 1.4 tonnes, has a hooked, prehensile lip for browsing among trees and shrubs.

The **white rhinoceros** (*Ceratotherium simum*) is much larger – up to 3.6 tonnes – and has a flat front lip which, although flexible, is not hooked (the name 'white' comes from the Afrikaans word *weit*, meaning wide and referring to the lip). It feeds on grass rather than leaves. It too is killed for its horn and, although more numerous with a population of 11,600, is also endangered and protected. In an attempt to prevent poaching wardens have sedated rhinos and removed their horns (which are not essential to survival). However, poachers often kill hornless animals to save themselves the bother of tracking them again.

Black rhinocero

White rhinoceros

WILD BOAR (*Sus scrofa*) ▼

SIZE:	Length 105–180cm. Height 105cm. Weight, male 50–200kg, female 36–150kg
DISTRIBUTION:	Local but widespread throughout Europe, Asia and North Africa
IDENTIFICATION:	Strong neck, conical elongated head, small eyes, erect triangular ears. Compact flanks. Brown coat of long, coarse bristles and thick down. Male has sharp tusks. Young striped black, brown and white along their length

The wild boar, hunted to extinction across much of its former range, is now making a comeback because its meat is so highly prized. Escapees from boar farms are establishing themselves in parts of Great Britain and Europe and adding to a wild population that is still extensively hunted as game on mainland Europe. Mostly active at dusk and dawn, wild boar will come surprisingly close to human habitation and can seriously damage crops. The females build a domed nest to shelter their young and give birth at any time of year, including winter. They can have several litters a year.

WHITE-LIPPED PECCARY (*Tayassu pecari*)

SIZE:	Length, body, 75–100cm (tail 15–55mm)
DISTRIBUTION:	Central and South America
IDENTIFICATION:	Dark-brown to black body with paler undersides, large head with a long snout and thick neck

Most animals communicate with each other, some managing to do so silently with the twitch of an ear or tail. But the white-lipped peccary engages in loud tooth clacking and a supporting chorus of bellowing and shrieking. A herd of two or three hundred can be heard from quite a distance making them an easy target for hunters. These pig-like creatures are hunted for food and for their hide, which is simply known as peccary or South American pigskin.

The herds of white-lipped peccaries are constantly moving, searching for food and water. The peccary's long snout is used like a plough churning through the top layer of soil in its search for roots and tubers. This can be a problem in agricultural areas where sweet potatoes are a particular favourite.

WARTHOG *(Phacochoerus aethiopicus)*

SIZE:	Weight: males 68–100kg, females 45–71kg
DISTRIBUTION:	Africa south of the Sahara desert
IDENTIFICATION:	Long legs, shovel-shaped head with tusks in both upper and lower jaws. Grey coat and mane

Warthogs are not glamorous: the bristly, mud-coloured coat, the odd tuft of hair on the tail and the warts on the face of the male add little to his beauty. A family group trotting across the savannah with tails pointing straight up, piglets following mother single file, is comical rather than poetic.

Warthogs often inhabit burrows dug by aardvarks, relying on these subterranean shelters to protect them from temperature extremes as well as predators. When fleeing from hungry carnivores, the piglets charge head first into the burrow but the adults reverse in after them so they can use their tusks for defence should the pursuer try to follow them in.

HIPPOPOTAMUS (*Hippopotamus amphibius*)

SIZE:	Height at shoulder 1.5m. Length 3.8–4.7m. Weight 3–4.5 tonnes
DISTRIBUTION:	Sub-Saharan Africa, mostly Nile valley, East Africa
IDENTIFICATION:	Like huge pig. Slate to muddy-brown with purplish tinges. Protruding eyes and nostrils, small ears. Short, stumpy legs

Hippos are usually placid, occasionally vicious and often very curious. One famously inquisitive and innocently friendly animal was a hippo called Hubert which wandered around the South African Cape and Natal provinces from late 1928 until early 1930, peeping into doorways, trampling gardens, blocking roads and, on one occasion, stopping a train by lying on the tracks. He was eventually shot by an irate farmer whereupon he was discovered to be a female. There is little chance of a similar occurrence now as the hippo population has been drastically reduced everywhere except in the Nile valley in East Africa. The hippo, despite its bulk, is a graceful swimmer, can run faster than a man and is surprisingly agile when clambering up the rocky precipices beside rivers. When angry it is fearsome and, with its huge canine teeth, is capable of chomping through alligators, boats and people.

Dromedary and Bactrian Camels

Contrary to popular belief, a camel does not store water in its hump. It stores fat, which is used as an energy source or can be converted into water by oxidation. It drinks when water is available, gulping down as much as 30 per cent of its body weight in just a few minutes – something that would be fatal to any other mammal. Its system then uses the water very sparingly and a camel can go for as long as 17 days before needing to drink again.

The camel has three main ways of conserving fluid. Firstly, it is very temperature tolerant. Its body can heat up to 41 °C (106 °F) before it begins to sweat and, at night, it can drop to 35 °C (95 °F) without ill effect, allowing it to get rid of excess heat. Secondly, unlike most animals which lose water because they must wash away waste products in their urine, the camel re-routes waste products from its liver and synthesizes them as proteins in its stomach. Thirdly, the camel is capable of preventing its blood system losing water at the same rate as the rest of the body. Blood plasma loss is the main cause of damage in other species during dehydration. Incidentally, the camel's red blood cells are elliptical and contain a nucleus – an anomaly among mammals.

There are about 14 million camels in the world of which 90 per cent are the one-humped **dromedary** (*Camelus dromedarius*), which was first domesticated 4,000 years ago. It no longer exists in the wild in Africa but there are thousands of wild dromedaries in the deserts of Australia, descendants of domesticated animals abandoned early in the last century. The two-humped **bactrian** (*Camelus bactrianus*) of the Asian deserts was also domesticated about 3,500 years ago. It was heavily hunted for meat and hide. Now just 500–1,000 remain in small areas of northwest China and Mongolia. These are smaller than domestic bactrians.

Both species are herbivores, surviving on dry vegetation, thorns and salty plants that other animals avoid. Camels, although generally placid, have large combat teeth with not only canines but also first pre-molars formed into fighting weapons.

Dromedary cam

Bactrian camel

◄ LLAMA (*Lama glama*)

SIZE:	Height at shoulder 100–125cm. Length 153–200cm. Weight 130–155kg
DISTRIBUTION:	Peru, Bolivia, Chile, Northern Argentina. Introduced worldwide
IDENTIFICATION:	Long, dense, fine wool. Long limbs, slender feet. Colouring varies from all white to brown, yellow, bluish and black

Llamas have been used as beasts of burden in South America for at least 5,000 years but, as road building increased in the Andes, the llama population in the mountain areas declined. Now these graceful herbivores have become very fashionable pack animals in the more affluent north and can be found in increasing numbers carrying everything from tourists' camping gear to golfers' clubs. They are extremely vocal, with a wide range of recognized sounds, and they can spit when annoyed.

They are used as sentries, guarding sheep against dogs and coyotes, and are farmed for their superior-quality wool, which is much in demand.

ALPACA (*Lama pacos*)

SIZE:	Height at shoulders 86–96cm. Weight 50–75kg
DISTRIBUTION:	Peru, Bolivia and Chile. Introduced worldwide
IDENTIFICATION:	Camel-shaped without hump. Smaller than llama but with longer coat of finer hair. Colours range through many shades from white to black

More than 5,000 years ago these 'humming sheep' were kept by the ancestors of the Incas and used as a measure of wealth. Over the next 4,500 years the alpaca became a cornerstone of the Incan economy. Then came the Spanish conquistadors. The alpaca competed with their own sheep for grazing, so they set about eating them. A few prized animals were taken into the mountains by Incan exiles. These developed into a hardier breed and were 'discovered' in the 1800s by European textile merchants who processed and marketed their wonderful wool. Alpaca wool is said to be the finest in the world, smoother than silk, warmer than goose down, finer than cashmere and almost indestructible.

VICUÑA (*Vicugna vicugna*)

SIZE:	Height at shoulder 70–100cm. Length 125–190cm (tail 15–25cm). Weight 35–65kg
DISTRIBUTION:	Andes, South America
IDENTIFICATION:	Slender body, long neck and legs. Long pointed ears, rounded head. Honey brown with yellowish to red-brown head, yellow-red bib. Whitish underside and inner flanks. Silky white 'mane'

The wool of the vicuña, which has been domesticated since pre-Incan times, is hugely valuable. This makes the vicuña, which is endangered in the wild, a prime target for poachers who sell the pelts on the black market. Each year several hundred pelts are confiscated.

Vicuña are shy, alert, graceful animals that graze on open land in family groups, retiring to the mountains at night. When in danger, they give a clear whistling warning call. The vicuña controls its body temperature by exposing bare patches on its inner thighs in hot weather and clamping its legs tight over them in the cold. Some Andean peoples continue to worship the vicuña as a daughter of the fertility goddess Pachamama.

MUNTJAC DEER *(Family Muntiacinae)*

SIZE:	Height from 60–92cm, weight from 11–50kg, depending on species
DISTRIBUTION:	Indigenous to Southeast Asia but introduced and spreading in UK and France. Eight known species
IDENTIFICATION:	Small. Short, soft reddish-brown coat with creamy-white undersides. Forehead and nose black, face pale tan. Males have small, tusk-like canines and small antlers

Muntjac are the oldest of all known deer, yet new muntjac species are still being discovered.

Muntjac will adapt to a wide variety of environments and colonize any area that provides thick cover and food. They are browsing feeders and will eat brambles, fungi and leaves, often bending down saplings to reach them. They will happily enter parks and yards, as they love flowers and fruit, and can be very destructive. The muntjac's willingness to enter built-up areas means it is often involved in road accidents.

Fallow and Roe Deer

Few creatures evoke such tender emotions as baby deer. These large-eyed, large-eared, velvet-coated, gentle animals, vulnerable and gangly-legged as they nuzzle their attentive mother, can melt human hearts.

Among the prettiest are **fallow deer** (*Dama dama*), a widespread species found throughout Europe, South Africa, Australia, New Zealand, USA, Argentina, Chile, Peru, Uruguay and even the Fiji islands. The **Mesopotamian fallow** (*D. mesopotamica*) once found in Lebanon, Syria, Jordan, Israel and Iraq is now endangered and survives only in western Iran.

Fallow deer are mostly found in deer parks or reserves but in the wild prefer mature woodlands, particularly deciduous or mixed with plenty of open areas. They have four main colour variations from the white or cream found in park populations to almost black or very dark brown. More typically they have a back of rich chestnut with characteristic white spots, a pale chest and white rump bordered with a black horseshoe shape. The tail has a central black line. Males, which grow impressive palmate antlers with many points, are up to 1m high at the shoulder and weigh up to 86kg. Females are smaller, without antlers. Fallow deer eat grasses, herbs, leaves, buds, shoots and bark, adding acorns, beech mast and other fruit in autumn. Bramble, holly, ivy and heather supplement grass in winter.

Roe deer (*Capreolus capreolus*) are widespread in Eurasia: from Spain to the Pacific coast, Norway to Italy, Asia Minor to Iran (although absent from Ireland, Corsica, Sardinia and Sicily). The population east of western Siberia is considered a separate species, *Capreolus pygargus*. Roe deer are medium-sized: 60–80cm high at the shoulder and weighing between 27kg for females and 50kg for males. They have a relatively short body and long legs with no obvious tail. The black nose, 'moustache stripe' and white chin are distinctive. In summer the back is reddish-brown, the chest pale and the rump patch creamy buff. In winter the colouring becomes pale olive grey, grey-brown or blackish and the rump patch an almost white inverted heart shape. The males, or bucks, grow sets of upright antlers up to 30cm long with four to six spikes on each side.

Roe deer feed early in the morning or at dusk, eating leaves, buds and shoots of deciduous trees and shrubs, small non-grass plants, fruits and seeds as well as brambles, heather and blueberry. Given the chance they will devastate rose beds, vegetable gardens and even low-hanging baskets.

Fallow deer

Reindeer and Caribou

(*Rangifer tarandus*)

Size:	Male, shoulder height, 1–1.3m, weight 100–140kg. Female smaller
Distribution:	Reindeer: northern Polar circle, Mongolia and a small part of China. Caribou: Alaska, Canada and Greenland
Identification:	Dense coat of varying shades of brown, cream and grey. Facial hair extending down to lips. Both sexes have large, many-branched antlers

The semi-domesticated reindeer and the wild caribou of North America and Greenland are the same species. Reindeer are farmed in many countries. In northern Scandinavia and Russia the herds freely roam over areas up to 8,000 square km. The reindeer herders are dependent on the animal for survival, using it for milk and meat, transport, and clothing. They even use the tendons and sinews for sewing.

The caribou's annual migration is a spectacular 9,000km journey on foot across the vast Canadian tundra, with temperatures varying from 30 °C to –40 °C (86 °F to –40 °F). Its wide-splaying hoofs provide support across snow, act as paddles when swimming, and are essential tools for digging under snow for lichen.

MOOSE *(Alces alces)*

Size:	Shoulder height 1.65–1.95m, weight, male 544–725kg, female 360–590kg
Distribution:	Alaska, Canada, Scandinavia, Russia, Siberia and Poland
Identification:	Coat colour varies from golden brown to almost black. Broad nose, small tail and a dewlap or bell under the chin. The male has large, palmate antlers

The world's largest deer is known as a moose in North America and an elk in Europe, and the biggest of them is the Yukon-Alaska moose. At six or seven years old, the bull carries impressive antlers spanning 1.6m that can weigh up to 32kg. These are shed each winter, growing back in the spring. The Algonquin tribe named the moose: the word means 'eater of twigs' and a moose browses several pounds of leaves, twigs and buds every day.

Calves, often twins, are born in early summer. A moose cow has been known to kill bears, wolves, and even people to protect her offspring. Typically, moose have a lifespan of 16–20 years, but this is often cut short by vehicles colliding with them on forest roads.

GIRAFFE *(Giraffa camelopardalis)*

SIZE:	Height 4.9–5.5m. Weight 1.1–1.9 tonnes. Newborn calves 2m tall
DISTRIBUTION:	Sub-Saharan Africa, mostly in national parks
IDENTIFICATION:	Very tall. Long neck. Brown patches on buff background cover all but belly and inside legs

Although it is the tallest creature on earth, with a kick capable of decapitating a lion, the giraffe is a nervous animal constantly on the lookout for danger. It is vulnerable when splaying its front legs to drink and usually sleeps standing up, napping for a few minutes at a time for a total of about half an hour a day. Despite this its huge, brown eyes always seem bright and, surrounded by long, curling lashes, are one of its most endearing features. Although its neck is nearly 2m long (making tree browsing possible) it contains only seven vertebrae – the same as in a human – but, like the bones in its legs, they are hugely elongated.

BONGO (*Tragelaphus eurycerus*) ▲

SIZE:	Height at shoulder 109–140cm. Weight 210–405kg
DISTRIBUTION:	West Africa
IDENTIFICATION:	Chestnut-red with darker legs. Males darken to brownish-black with age. Narrow vertical white stripes down sides. Long, blackish-brown lyre-shaped horns

The bongo, the most colourful African antelope, relies on clearings in the forest for food and cover. Rainforest with a thick canopy has too little vegetation at ground level. The bongo frequents openings that let in sunlight, encouraging dense growth of bushes, herbs, creepers and bamboo. These clearings might have been made by logging, temporary cultivation or even elephants, which can be fairly destructive eaters. When moving through forest, the bongo rests its huge horns – which can be up to 100cm long – on its back so they do not become entangled, and often has bare patches on its hide where the tips rest. It also uses its horns to break off high branches when feeding. It prefers young, high-carbohydrate, low-fibre leaves and takes garden produce and cereal crops when it can. Being fast and well-camouflaged it is difficult to shoot but is hunted with dogs by local people to provide food.

OKAPI (*Okapi johnstoni*)

SIZE:	Height at shoulder 1.5–1.7m. Weight 200–300kg
DISTRIBUTION:	Zaire, West Africa
IDENTIFICATION:	Dark velvety-brown coat with creamy-white horizontal markings on hindquarters and legs. Long neck and large ears. Males have short (15cm) horns

It was not until Harry Johnston sent two pieces of skin from the okapi's rump to London in 1900 that this member of the giraffe family was found to be a new species. Local people had, of course, known of its existence and hunted it for hundreds of years.

Except at mating time the okapi leads a solitary life, spending its time browsing on forest vegetation, using its long black tongue to pull leaves and buds from the trees and occasionally stooping to graze on grass or fungi. Although nowhere near as long as that of a giraffe, the okapi's neck is used to denote dominance or submission depending on how it is carried. Both sexes rub their necks on tree trunks to scent-mark their territories. The young spend their first two months hiding in a nest until they have grown sufficiently to be able to evade predators.

PRONGHORN *(Antilocapra americana)*

SIZE:	Height at shoulder 81–104cm. Length 100–150cm. Weight 36–70kg
DISTRIBUTION:	Southern Canada, western United States, Mexico
IDENTIFICATION:	Reddish-brown above, white beneath, white rump patch. Males have black mask and patches on neck. Hook-tipped horns, 250mm long. Female horns shorter, not pronged

The pronghorn is a primitive halfway station between antelope and deer, unchanged for at least a million years. It is the fastest mammal in North America and can travel at up to 90kph. Quite why it is so fast is a mystery. There might once have been a predator which could match the pronghorn's speed but if so it has disappeared, leaving the little antelope to charge around the prairies unchallenged. It cannot outrun bullets, though, and a population of 50 million was reduced to just 19,000 by the beginning of the twentieth century. Its intense curiosity makes it easy meat. Conservation has brought numbers back to about one million.

WATER BUFFALO (*Bubalus bubalis*)

SIZE:	Height at shoulder 1.5–1.8m. Length 2.5–3m. Weight 700–1,200kg
DISTRIBUTION:	Wild in India, Bhutan, Nepal, Thailand. Domesticated world-wide
IDENTIFICATION:	Greyish with short, coarse, sparse hair. Long narrow face, small ears. Large hooves. Horns sweep back and inwards, spanning up to 1.2m

Despite its environmental adaptability, the water buffalo is surprisingly susceptible to illnesses. Roundworm is the prime cause of calf death and adults suffer from tuberculosis and pasteurellosis. Many illnesses are transmitted by insects and to escape these pests buffaloes submerge themselves in water or mud with just their nostrils poking above the surface (a coating of dry mud also acts as an insect barrier). However, wallowing also exposes them to waterborne diseases. Despite this there are about 148 million domesticated water buffaloes, mostly in India and the Far East, and the species is not threatened – except in the wild, where numbers are down to 3,000 or so.

YAK *(Bos grunniens)*

SIZE:	Height at shoulder 2m. Length 3.25m. Weight 1 tonne. Domestic animals smaller
DISTRIBUTION:	Wild herds in Qinghai-Tibet Plateau. Domesticated throughout Tibet and Central Asia. Introduced to North America and Caucasus
IDENTIFICATION:	Long, shaggy buff-brown coat, matted undercoat, short legs, pronounced hump at shoulders

For 3,000 years this tough, sure-footed, good-natured animal has been domesticated to pull ploughs, carry loads, and help clothe and feed the people of Tibet. When it sheds its thick woolly coat in summer, the longer hairs are woven to make blankets and tents and the softer wool used for clothing. The yak's rich, low-fat milk is made into butter and cheese. Dried yak dung is the only fuel available on the treeless Tibetan plateau. About 100,000 yak still live wild and can cause problems when they come into contact with domesticated animals. Wild males rush into tamed herds and abduct females on heat, sometimes killing domesticated bulls. Numbers of this endangered species are threatened by illegal hunting.

Wildebeest

(*Connochaetes taurinus*)

Size:	Height at shoulder 130cm. Weight up to 270kg
Distribution:	Eastern southern Africa
Identification:	Antelope with massive shoulders, large muzzle and heavy, cow-like horns. Short slate-grey to dark-brown hair with faint striping on back, black faces, manes and tails

It is late June and beside the Grumeti River in the northern Serengeti National Park in Tanzania, crocodiles await their annual feast. This river is an important watering point – and hazardous crossing – in the annual migration of the wildebeest. Wildebeest herds follow the rains in a 600km round trip circling the Serengeti. They sense rain from 50km away and travel up to 60km a day chasing the new growth it brings. When they arrive at the Grumeti they are in peak condition, fattened on the fertile plains of the south. To reach the next pastures they must cross the river. Hundreds are dragged down by the crocodiles and many more drown in the rush, their stranded bodies picked over by scavengers.

ADDAX *(Addax nasomaculatus)*

SIZE:	Height at shoulder 95–115cm. Length 150–170cm. Weight 60–125kg
DISTRIBUTION:	Sahara Desert
IDENTIFICATION:	Sandy-white in summer, greyish-brown in winter. White mask across nose, white markings on belly, legs and hips. Shaggy mane. Long, rippling horns (72cm) angling back from head

The addax manages to survive without drinking water by extracting all the moisture it needs from the vegetation it feeds on. It is the most desert-adapted of the antelopes and travels huge distances across the soft sand – its splayed feet preventing it from sinking – to find food. It has evolved into a 'short-legged' runner that makes relatively slow progress, falling easy prey to fast predators and hunters. Drought, desertification of savannah land and encroachment by humans have decreased the addax grazing areas and numbers are in serious decline.

Gemsbok (South African Oryx)

(*Oryx gazella*)

Size:	Height at shoulder 120cm. Length 153–170cm (tail 47cm). Weight 180–225kg
Distribution:	Sub-Saharan Africa
Identification:	Buff-coloured body with black striping extending along sides above a paler belly. Dramatic black-and-white mask and short mane. Long, straight, sharp horns angled backwards

The gemsbok, the largest of the oryx family, uses its impressive horns to keep intruders out of its herd's territory but when it comes to establishing dominance within the herd it takes no risks with these deadly weapons. Instead the males will put on a strange, posturing display, standing side by side and pointing their horns over their shoulders at each other in a ritualised fencing match. The oryx is still eaten by native Africans who also use its horn tips as spear points and its hide for shields. Natural enemies include lions, leopards, hunting dogs and hyaenas.

The **Arabian oryx** (*Oryx leucoryx*), which became extinct in the wild but was bred in captivity and reintroduced to the Middle East, has a white coat which reflects heat. It moves and eats mostly at night.

Springbok ▼

(*Antidorcas marsupialis*)

Size:	Height at shoulder 80cm. Weight 33–46kg
Distribution:	South and southwestern Africa
Identification:	Reddish-brown coat darkening on flanks, white beneath. White rump. Fold of skin from mid-back to rump opens into white crest when excited. Black, lyre-shaped horns in both sexes

South African rugby players would no doubt love to have the leaping ability of their nation's sporting mascot, the springbok. This dainty antelope makes vertical leaps up to 4m high with upward-arched back, stiff, downward-pointing legs and feet bunched together. This is called 'pronking'. There were once millions of springbok in southern Africa but they devastated crops during their annual mass-migrations to new pastures and were hunted down to their present number of just 250,000, mainly on reserves and farms. Licensed culls and farmed animals provide high-quality meat, and the skin and horns are used as decorative artefacts, mostly for tourists.

The springbok grazes and browses, seeking out flowers in the dry season as they hold more water.

GREATER KUDU (*Tragelaphus strepsiceros*)

SIZE:	Height at shoulder 100–150cm. Length 120cm. Weight 120–315kg
DISTRIBUTION:	Southern and eastern Africa
IDENTIFICATION:	Colour varying from reddish-brown to blue-grey with faint stripes running down sides of body. Large 'corkscrew' horns

The greater kudu has been a target for hunters for many years, providing excellent meat and one of the most impressive trophies available from the African bush. It is a major prey of lions, leopards, wild dogs and spotted hyaenas. Despite this, the kudu is flourishing. Happy to live near human habitation, it is something of a pest, raiding crops and eating fruit, vines, flowers and herbs.

It prefers to stay where there is some cover, rather than out on the open plains, and in the dry season it is almost always found beside rivers where there is thicker growth.

IMPALA (*Aepyceros melampus*)

SIZE:	Height at shoulder 86–91cm. Weight 45–60kg
DISTRIBUTION:	Eastern and southern Africa
IDENTIFICATION:	Red-brown colouring, paler on sides, with white underbelly, chin, lips, inside-ears and tail. White line over eyes, black stripes down tail, forehead, thighs and ear-tips. Long, elegant horns in male

This graceful antelope is preyed on by lions, hyaenas, crocodiles and vultures but its greatest enemy is the tick. The impala feeds in the zone between open grassland and forest, an area thick with ticks. Blood loss through tick infestation can so weaken an antelope that it becomes diseased or too feeble to evade predators. But the impala has a solution: its mobile incisor and canine teeth are adapted to groom parasites from its skin. The parts it cannot reach are groomed by another impala and it returns the favour.

The impala's scientific name *aepyceros* comes from the Greek meaning 'high horn' and refers to the male's spectacular, ridged, lyre-shaped horns.

Indian Black Buck Antelope

(Antelope cervicapra)

Size:	Height at shoulder 80cm. Weight 32–43kg
Distribution:	India, Pakistan and Nepal
Identification:	Male black above and white below. White highlighting eyes, ears, chin, chest and rump. Long, spiralling horns up to 70cm. Female light-brown and hornless

The Indian black buck is the fastest animal on earth over a long distance. Faced with the challenge of hunting this 80kph beast the Indian princes turned to the only creature that could catch it – the cheetah. But it was brief entertainment. The cheetah can maintain its top speed of 110kph for only 20 seconds and would need to overhaul the antelope within that time – or watch as it disappeared into the distant haze. The black buck, sacred to Hindus and Buddhists, was once found in huge numbers over most of India but has been hunted down to a small population, most of which are in the Velvadar National Park.

CHIRU *(Pantholops hodgsonii)*

SIZE:	Height 90–125cm. Weight 26–40kg
DISTRIBUTION:	Tibetan plateau and Ladakh region of India
IDENTIFICATION:	Beige and grey to whitish with black markings on face and legs. Males with horns up to 60cm, females hornless

At the turn of the last century there were about one million chiru on the Tibetan plateau; now there are 75,000, possibly fewer. Up to 20,000 of this protected species are killed each year by poachers to supply the trade in *shahtoosh* wool shawls which can cost $15,000 each in the West. Chiru hair is 20 per cent finer than human hair and four or five pelts are needed to make one shawl. Each spring the females make a 322km trek north to calve in a barren region of southwest China, possibly to avoid packs of wolves that roam the Tibetan plateau.

CHAMOIS *(Rupicapra rupicapra)* ▲

SIZE:	Height at shoulder 70–80cm. Length 110–135cm. Weight up to 50kg
DISTRIBUTION:	South and central Europe, Turkey, Caucasus and Asia. Introduced toNew Zealand
IDENTIFICATION:	Dark-brown with pale underparts and white rump, face, throat and inner ears. Short horns curved at tip

The chamois is extremely nimble. It can leap and bound, upwards and sideways, at speeds of 50kph on the rockiest of terrain in order to escape its main predators: lynx, wolf and man. When threatened it makes for the most inaccessible spot. This cannot protect it completely from hunters' bullets but it does make recovery of the body difficult, a deterrent in itself. Chamois skin has been used for hat-making for centuries. Stripped of its hair, the soft hide becomes 'chammy leather' for cleaning windows and cars. In winter chamois gather in large groups but stags lead a solitary life, quitting their hideouts in early September to fight other stags for the right to breed.

MOUFFLON *(Ovis musimon)*

SIZE:	Height at shoulder 60–120cm. Length 120–140cm. Weight 25–55kg
DISTRIBUTION:	Originally Corsica, Sardinia and Cyprus. Introduced in USA and Europe
IDENTIFICATION:	Reddish-brown with dark stripe on back, light-coloured saddle patch and underparts. Male has mane and massive, spiral horns

The bigger a male moufflon's horns, the greater his status in the herd. The vast horns arch back and swing round to the front, framing the ram's face. If sheer size does not put off any challengers, a battering contest ensues. The rams leap at each other with a crunching impact of horn on horn. Humans, sadly, covet these impressive appendages and the moufflon has been hunted to virtual extinction in its home islands. However, introduced populations on the European mainland seem to be thriving. The moufflon is thought to be one of the original ancestors of all modern sheep.

ALPINE IBEX *(Capra ibex)*

SIZE:	Height at shoulder 70–94cm. Length 75–170cm. Weight 40–120kg
DISTRIBUTION:	France, Italy, Switzerland, Spain and Austria
IDENTIFICATION:	Brownish-grey with black smudges. Pale belly edged with darker hair. Vertical, backward-curving horns on both sexes, up to 1m long in males

Images of ibex appear in Neolithic cave paintings throughout central Europe. It was hunted almost to extinction until, in 1922, there was a single population left in Italy. Protection, conservation measures and reintroduction to other areas have led to a recovery and there are now about 2,000 in the French Vanoise National Park alone. Alpine ibex are nimble and the young can jump and run after just one day. They live on or near the snowline, moving up the mountain in summer before breeding in the autumn. Males develop huge necks and chests and will fight predators such as wolves, lynxes, bears and jackals.

Bighorn Sheep

(Ovis canadensis)

Size:	Length 150–180cm. Weight 119–130kg (male), 53–91kg (female)
Distribution:	Rocky Mountains. Subspecies in Nevada, California, Texas and Mexico
Identification:	Smooth-coated, mid-brown with whitish rump and pale bands down legs. Male horns huge

The crash of horns as male bighorns battle for breeding rights can be heard echoing through the mountains during the autumn rut. With each contestant charging at full steam the closing speed can be 65kph. This is repeated four or five times an hour until a victor emerges. Horns weigh up to 14kg. Despite these bulky accessories the bighorn is an agile climber and good swimmer, leaping to remote ledges to escape predators such as wolves, bears and bobcats. The bighorn has always been hunted and, despite regulations to prevent its extinction, illegal poaching is a threat.

Musk Ox (*Ovibos moschatus*)

Size:	Shoulder height 1.2–1.5m, weight 227–363kg
Distribution:	Alaska, Canada, Greenland, Norway and Siberia
Identification:	Large, low-slung body with hump on shoulder, long brown hairy coat and downward-pointing horns

The musk ox looks like something from the Ice Age, easily pictured living alongside the mammoth and woolly rhinoceros. Its long hair hangs nearly to the ground and inspired the Inuit name *umingmak*, meaning 'bearded one'.

The musk ox will close ranks with other members of the herd when threatened by predators, circling the young to protect them. With their heads and horns turned outwards, they make a formidable barrier. Unfortunately, this formation made them an easy target for hunters and musk oxen were almost extinct at the beginning of the twentieth century. They are now a protected species in Canada and are farmed in Alaska, where the soft underfur, *qiviut*, is woven and knitted into luxurious caps and scarves.

Sei Whale (*Balaenoptera borealis*) ▲

Size:	Length usually 14–15m but can be up to 21m. Weight up to 30 tonnes
Distribution:	All oceans, particularly temperate, deep offshore areas
Identification:	Dark- or bluish-grey, streamlined body, sometimes with white markings, paler undersides. Small, pointed flippers

In winter the sei whale quite sensibly prefers warm, sub-tropical waters, leaving it later than the blue or fin whale before migrating to polar seas in summer in search of richer feeding grounds. Plankton, small fish or squid are consumed in great quantities as the sei whale swims along with its mouth open. It feeds close to the surface, blowing and diving every 15 minutes or so, but swims horizontally rather than on its side as some other baleen whales do.

The slim, streamlined body of the sei whale makes it an elegant and efficient swimmer. It is known as the fastest whale, reaching speeds of 37kph. Like all whales, the sei occasionally needs to sleep. Sometimes one eye will be closed and the other open; at other times it will sleep on the surface, either bobbing up and down or swimming round in small circles.

Fin Whale (*Balaenoptera physalus*)

Size:	Length up to 27m, weight up to 80 tonnes
Distribution:	All oceans
Identification:	Dark-brown, grey or black body with paler undersides, sometimes with a pale stripe behind the head and from the eye down to the flippers. Distinct ridge along the back

The fin whale is sometimes known as finback or razor back due to the distinct ridge running along its back behind the dorsal fin. This large whale (only the blue whale is longer and heavier) is one of eleven species of baleen whale that feed by swimming along with their mouths open and filtering out food that enters. Plates of keratin in the mouth, known as baleen, act as a sieve allowing seawater to pass through but trapping food. Sometimes called 'whalebone', baleen is not bone but made from the same material as horns or fingernails.

In the fin whale, the yellow or greyish-white baleen is relatively short, just 72cm, but that of the bowhead and black right whale can be over 2.5m. While whales were hunted commercially, baleen was put to a variety of uses from whalebone corsets and umbrella ribs to native carvings, particularly as knife handles.

Minke Whale

(*Balaenoptera acutorostrata*)

Size:	Length 8.5–10.7m. Weight 5–10 tonnes
Distribution:	Worldwide in tropical, temperate and polar waters
Identification:	Black, brown or dark-grey streamlined body, lighter undersides. A diagonal band of white on each flipper. Narrow head and tall dorsal fin

This small whale is the one most often spotted from the shore or a small boat as it frequently enters bays and estuaries. This could be because it often feeds in association with birds that chase shoals of fry into the bay, the whale following to share the bounty. At other times, birds will follow the whale, waiting for it to drive fish to the surface.

Amid great controversy, Iceland resumed whaling in August 2003, catching its first minke whale for 14 years. Japan continues to hunt a few hundred minkes a year for scientific reasons and a similar number are hunted commercially by the Norwegians. Fortunately, this species is not threatened as it is estimated that over 500,000 minke whales still roam our oceans.

Blue Whale ▼

(*Balaenoptera musculus*)

Size:	Length usually 23–27m. Weight 100–120 tonnes
Distribution:	All oceans
Identification:	Broad, blue-grey body, lighter underside. Large blowholes with fleshy splash-guards, small dorsal fin

When man first started hunting whales with sailing ships, the blue whale was too fast to be caught and too strong and powerful to handle so it escaped the fate of many of its cousins. Once steam ships and factory ships came on the scene this mammal was doomed. In 1930 nearly 30,000 blue whales were butchered and it was another 35 years before the Whaling Commission stepped in to stop the slaughter. It is estimated that only a few thousand remain today.

Not only the largest whale, *Balaenoptera musculus* is the largest mammal on earth: its tongue weighs the same as an elephant and, at 33m, the longest recorded animal would only just squeeze into a tournament-sized tennis court. Blue whales feed mostly on krill, taking 3.5–4 tonnes a day from their summer feeding grounds.

Black Right Whale (*Eubalaena glacialis*)

Size:	Length up to 18.3m. Average weight 50–56 tonnes but can reach 100 tonnes
Distribution:	Temperate inshore waters worldwide
Identification:	Dark, rounded body with very large head usually covered with whale lice giving a patchy appearance

According to old whaling records the right whale was a great fighter, resisting capture by thrashing its tail around when harpooned and being able to outmanoeuvre early whaling ships. But the whalers must have persisted because now there are only a few hundred black right whales left in existence. It does not help its own survival by preferring a coastal habitat that is constantly being threatened with development by the oil and gas industry, dredging and sewage discharges. The right whale is particularly vulnerable to collisions with ships as it rests, feeds and socializes on the surface.

The right whale is one of six species to summer in the Antarctic, taking advantage of the abundance of krill. It skim feeds when the krill are near the surface and has been known to hold its tail up like a sail to catch the wind, allowing it to concentrate its energies on feeding rather than swimming.

Humpback Whale (*Megaptera novaeangliae*)

Size:	Length 11.5–18m. Average weight 24–30 tonnes
Distribution:	All oceans, particularly edges of continental shelves
Identification:	Black body, sometimes with white markings. Large, knobbly head, exceptionally long, narrow flippers

The longest and most complicated mating song in the natural world is sung by the male humpback whale. The song is made up of themes and phrases and lasts from 6 to 35 minutes. No sooner has it finished than the whale starts again from the beginning. This can be heard through the water several hundred miles away. Interestingly, different whale populations in different oceans sing different songs.

In the northern hemisphere, the humpback whale spends the summer in its feeding grounds in rich polar seas, heading south in the autumn to spend the breeding season (January to March) in more tropical waters. Sometimes a group might be trapped beneath moving ice packs as winter sets in. If they cannot escape to the open sea, they will eventually die.

KILLER WHALE (*Orcinus orca*)

SIZE:	Length up to 9.5m
DISTRIBUTION:	All oceans but preferring cooler waters and coastal regions
IDENTIFICATION:	Extremely distinctive jet-black bodies with white patches usually over eyes, under jaw, on belly and extending on to sides. Triangular dorsal fin up to 1.2m high

Killer whales hunt in packs to harry and hack to death prey as large as blue whale. But individuals will also tackle easier victims such as seals and penguins, smashing up through the softer pack ice to snatch their quarry. When they catch something small they will often play with it in the same way as a cat toys with a doomed mouse, flicking and tossing the wretched creature about before gobbling it down. This behaviour is exploited by trainers at sealife parks where captive orcas have to perform for their meals. As they are at the very top of the oceanic food chain and have no natural predators, orcas often live to between 50 and 80 years old.

Sperm Whale (*Physeter macrocephalus*)

Size:	Length up to 18m. Weight up to 57 tonnes
Distribution:	All deep oceans
Identification:	Dark-grey or brown wrinkled body, sometimes with paler patches. Very large, square head up to a third of total length

Schools of sperm whales are more than just the usual family group. They can be matriarchal nursery groups with 10–30 mature females and their offspring, juvenile schools of adolescents or even bachelor groups of young males. In the tightly-bonded nursery groups some females share babysitting duties while others hunt for food. They show great concern if one of the group is sick or injured. The group might be spread over a large area and members greet each other when they meet up, rubbing and calling to each other.

Squid is the main food of sperm whales and they dive 400–600m, deeper than most other mammals, in order to feed in the murky twilight zone. Sometimes they co-ordinate the dive with other members of the pod, spreading out to herd the prey and make it easier to catch.

Beluga Whale (White Whale)

(*Delphinapterus leucas*) ▼

Size:	Length up to 4.6m, weight 0.4–1.5 tonnes
Distribution:	Close to pack ice in Arctic, occasionally in European waters
Identification:	Unmistakable pure white with bulbous, melon-shaped head

Belugas are odd-looking creatures. They have flexible necks that can move up and down and side to side, allowing them to nod and turn their heads. The 'melon' on their head becomes bigger as they get older and can change shape.

In the depths of the winter, when the ice cover is almost total, belugas keep breathing holes open by crowding together in one spot to swim in a constant rolling mass. This makes them easy targets for polar bears and they are usually covered with scars from bear attacks. Belugas 'talk' a lot, making all sorts of tweeting, clicking and squeaking noises, earning them the nickname 'sea canary'.

Narwhal

(*Monodon monoceros*)

Size:	Length 3.8–5m, weight 0.8–1.6 tonnes
Distribution:	Close to pack ice in Arctic
Identification:	Mottled-grey with pale blotches. Low hump replaces dorsal fin. Small head, bulbous forehead, flexible neck. One of two teeth forms long tusk in males, occasionally in females. Frequently form large groups

Few treasures brought home from their travels by sailors in ancient times caused more wonderment than the horn of the fabled unicorn. But the sailors' tall tales were eventually found out and the unicorn's horn proved to be the no less extraordinary upper left tooth of the narwhal. The tusk can grow up to 3m long, and is used for fighting other males, usually over a female but often just in a display of strength. Most adult males have battle-scarred heads, and sometimes the hollow tusk breaks. Narwhals, which eat fish, krill and squid, stay close to the pack ice and it is not unknown for them to get trapped beneath it and die.

Dolphins

Mankind has appreciated the playfulness of dolphins for thousands of years. Roman coins show boys riding on their backs and the Greek philosopher Plutarch wrote that the dolphin was the only creature to love man for his own sake rather than for the reward of food. For orientation the dolphin relies on its sophisticated sonar or sound-perception system, which is so highly developed that it can distinguish different materials by the sound rebounding from them. Researchers have also shown that a dolphin can detect a single tiny ball-bearing dropped into the far end of a 20m swimming pool.

The **common dolphin** is widely distributed in all oceans but rarely found in waters less than 180m deep. Its several populations migrate with the seasons. The two forms are the long-beaked *Delphinus capensis* and the short-beaked *D. delphis*. It has characteristic wavy yellow, grey or brown marks on its flanks and an upright triangular dorsal fin. A fish-eater, it grows up to 2.5m long and 110kg in weight, and is very vocal. Its high-pitched squeals can sometimes be heard above the water and are made through its single blow-hole. It is often found in large schools that sometimes join other dolphins or tuna to hunt in the feeding grounds.

Common dolphin

The **spinner dolphin** (*Stenella longirostris*) was one of the first dolphins to be taken into captivity to show off its acrobatic skills, although it does not live long when removed from its home in the Atlantic, Pacific and Indian oceans. Travelling fast, it launches itself as high as 3m into the air and rotates up to seven times longitudinally before smashing back into the water. It is distinguished by its long, slender beak and a black stripe extending from its eye to its flipper. It grows up to 2.1m long and weighs 45–75kg.

The performer most likely to be seen in a sealife park is the **bottlenose dolphin** (*Tursiops truncatus*). It is the most familiar and playful of all 32 species of dolphins, often riding the bow wave of boats and surfing waves. Its arc-like leap is a classic image used the world over to symbolize peaceful harmony with nature. Its playfulness, appallingly for those who see it as a cuddly, intelligent and 'smiling' fellow mammal, extends to its hunting. It will often toy with a fish or even a baby seal, flipping it up in the air and batting it about with its tail, before growing bored and killing it. The size of the bottlenosed dolphin, which is found everywhere except the polar regions, varies greatly depending on where it lives: from 1.9–4m in length and weighing from 150–650kg.

Bottlenose dolphin

Harbour or Common Porpoise

(Phocoena phocoena)

Size:	1.4–1.9m, 45–65kg
Distribution:	Coastal regions of cold temperate oceans in the Northern Hemisphere
Identification:	Short, chunky, tapered body. Small rounded head with no obvious beak. Dark-grey back, paler flanks, white belly

The harbour porpoise is the smallest member of the cetacean family that includes whales and dolphins. But unlike its playful dolphin cousins, the harbour porpoise is a shy creature and is not easily spotted. It stays away from boats and rarely jumps out of the water. You might glimpse one as it rolls, but you are as likely to hear it as it surfaces to breathe with a sharp puff of air – hence one of its names: puffing pig. It eats fish, and will sometimes dive for six minutes, down to depths of 200m, while chasing them. Unfortunately it likes many of the same fish that humans eat, and is often caught accidentally by trawlers as by-catch. This is probably one of the main reasons for the marked decline in harbour porpoise numbers in recent years.

Duck-billed Platypus ▼

(Ornithorhynchus anatinus)

Size:	Length, body, 30–45cm (tail 10–15cm)
Distribution:	Eastern Australia
Identification:	Dense, dark-brown fur, silvery undersides. Elongated snout, flat tail and webbed feet

There is no other creature quite like the duck-billed platypus. Its bizarre appearance once led people seeing it for the first time to believe a duck's bill had been sewn on to a mammal's body. With its streamlined body, flat, beaver-like tail and short legs it is hardly surprising it was thought to be a practical joke. The peculiarity does not end with its looks: the flexible bill is covered in sensory receptors and the platypus is one of only two mammals that lays eggs. The female has no nipples to suckle the young so secretes milk for them to lap up.

The male also has his claim to fame: he is the only mammal to have poisonous spurs. A sharp, hollow spur 15mm long on the inside of each hind leg can deliver enough toxin to kill a dog and inflict considerable pain on a human.

Spectacled Hare Wallaby

(*Lagorchestes conspicillatus*)

Size:	Length, body, 40–50cm (tail 35–45cm)
Distribution:	Northern and central Australia
Identification:	Like a hare-sized kangaroo. Large ears and hind feet, reddish-brown medium-length hair with slightly darker rusty-red patches around eyes. Long tail

The first scientists to see hare wallabies were very impressed by their agility and speed. One, writing in the 1840s, described how a hare wallaby, chased towards him by dogs, 'bounded clear over my head'. There used to be five hare wallaby species of which two are now extinct, two endangered and one – the spectacled – still widespread but vulnerable. It spends the day in a shallow burrow and feeds at night on grass, seeds and fruit. Although its range has diminished over the last 100 years, mainly due to habitat alteration by introduced herbivores, fire and predation, it is widely but patchily distributed across large parts of Northern Territory and Queensland. It has fared better than the other hare wallabies primarily because it can live not only in the arid and semi-arid areas but also in the more tropical parts.

Quokka (*Setonix brachyrus*)

Size:	Weight 2–4kg
Distribution:	Rottnest Island and Bald Island, Australia
Identification:	Small wallaby with rounded body. Short coarse hair, brown above and paler below. Short, rounded ears and hairless nose. Thick, medium-length tail

In the 1600s Dutch explorers sailing round the coast of Australia passed a small island 10km from where the city of Perth is now. The island seemed to be infested with cat-sized rats so they gave it the Dutch name *rotte nest*, or rat's nest, island. But the rats were quokkas. At the time this small, nocturnal marsupial inhabited not only this and other nearby islands but also the southwestern mainland probably for many miles inland. There are now about 10,000 quokkas on predator-free Rottnest with a few small colonies re-establishing themselves around Perth. The young quokka is suckled in the mother's pouch and once it ceases suckling its survival depends on the availability of water and on the nitrogen content of the plants on which it feeds. On hot summer days the males in a family group fight furiously for the best shelter.

KANGAROOS *(Family macropodidae)*

When the British explorer, Captain James Cook, sent his sailors off into the Australian bush in 1770 to find food, they came back with tales of an extraordinary beast: hugely tall with a deer's head, lips like a rabbit, hands like a man, vast hind legs like a mule, a four-foot long mouse's tail and a fur-lined pocket like no other beast. The mariners asked the locals what this creature was. The aborigines spread their hands and said 'Kangaroo'. Roughly translated this means 'It is hopeless to try to tell you'. So kangaroo this strange marsupial became.

The largest of the 50 or more species in the family is the **red kangaroo** (*Macropus rufus*) which lives in central Australia, the most arid part of the continent, and grazes through the night on grass and low herbaceous plants. It moves about in mobs of up to several hundred animals, led by one dominant male. Infant mortality is high in this harsh environment and there are relatively few males. Consequently, the reproductive cycle of the female allows two or three young to develop simultaneously at different stages: a fertilized egg in the womb; a suckling in the pouch and another youngster suckling from outside. The newborn joey, a naked wormlike creature quite unlike its parent and just 2cm long, claws itself out of the cloaca and makes a 15cm journey, lasting three minutes, to the pouch. There it attaches itself to a nipple and milk is pumped to it by the mother.

The **western grey kangaroo** (*Macropus fuliginosus*) is more widespread, found up to and within city boundaries. This greyish-brown animal is often seen early in the morning as it grazes on golf courses. The grey kangaroo competes for grazing with sheep and can damage crops and fencing so it is regularly culled by farmers.

Kangaroos are also killed for their meat and their skins are widely used in the manufacture of sports shoes and other leather goods.

Grey kangaroo

Red kangaroo

KOALA (*Phascolarctos cinereus*)

SIZE:	Length, body, 72–78cm (tail vestigial). Weight 5–11kg
DISTRIBUTION:	Eastern Australia (introduced to Western Australia)
IDENTIFICATION:	Ash grey with white chin and chest. Dense, woolly coat with large furry ears and a broad, flat, leathery black nose. Stout legs with large, long-clawed feet

The koala is not a bear: it is a marsupial. Its brain is exceptionally tiny for an animal of its size: just 0.2 per cent of its bodyweight. This is thought to be an adaptation to its low-energy diet of eucalyptus leaves. It has an extremely specialized diet, preferring only five of the 350 species of eucalyptus. Metabolizing bacteria in its stomach help it to cope with the highly toxic leaves, of which it eats 500g per day. The koala was almost exterminated 100 years ago by fur hunters and burning of the forests. Protected since 1927, it is falling victim to the same mystery virus as is killing the Tasmanian devil and its habitat is still threatened by clearance. The micro-organism *Chlamydia psittaci* also renders it sterile. The koala, which has no sweat glands, cools itself by licking its front legs and stretching out to rest in a tree.

COMMON WOMBAT ►

(*Vombatus ursinus*)

SIZE:	Length, body, 90–115cm (tail vestigial). Weight 22–39kg
DISTRIBUTION:	Eastern Australia, Tasmania, Flinders Island
IDENTIFICATION:	Stocky with short legs and powerful shoulders. Big forepaws with long claws. Broad, blunt, bare muzzle and short, rounded ears. Coarse black, grey or brown coat, often covered with clay or earth

Early settlers called the wombat a badger but its closest relative is actually the koala. Its short tail and legs, waddling walk and cuddly looks make it one of Australia's most loved creatures and it is protected in most states – but not in Victoria where it is classed as vermin. The largest burrowing herbivorous mammal, a wombat can dig a hole 30m long and 2m deep. These burrows bypass rabbit fencing, allowing rabbits in, and are a hazard to large livestock, which step into them. Consequently it is hunted for sport or shot on sight. This, together with food competition from rabbits, habitat clearance, roadkill and poisoning has reduced numbers of this nocturnal marsupial.

Tasmanian Devil

(*Sarcophilus laniarius*)

Size:	Length 53–76cm. Weight 8–11kg
Distribution:	Tasmania
Identification:	Like a small, squat dog. Black with white bib or patch below throat. Pointy, pink ears. Large powerful head with wide jaws and sharp teeth

For a Tasmanian devil life is a struggle from the start. Up to 50 offspring, or 'joeys', are born at the same time, each one the size of a grain of rice, blind and naked. They have to scuttle the 7cm or so from the mother's birth canal into her marsupial pouch and battle for access to the four teats. The four winners remain attached to the nipples for three months until they leave the pouch. After six months they are on their own, but are often killed by adult devils. These noisy carnivores are now threatened with a mystery virus. The illness is spread when these shy, nocturnal scavengers bite each other, which they do regularly when squabbling over food. Scientists estimate that the 150,000 remaining animals will be reduced by 70 per cent within a few years if a cure is not found. The disease, which is new to science, eats away their faces until they cannot feed, and die of starvation.

Numbat (Banded Anteater)

(*Myrmecobius fasciatus*)

Size:	Body length 16–25cm. Tail length 12–15cm. Weight 280–550g
Distribution:	Southwestern Australia
Identification:	Slender graceful body, usually reddish-brown with white banding and pale underbelly. Long, bushy tail. Narrow, pointed snout and a dark stripe across eyes

To us the slow-moving, squirrel-like numbat is a gentle, rather delicate little marsupial. To termites it is a mass murderer. With its long, flickering, sticky tongue it consumes up to 20,000 termites (or white ants) a day from colonies it digs from the soil. The numbat was almost wiped out by habitat destruction, but has been saved through a programme of re-establishment and predator control. It is still endangered but numbers are increasing. The numbat needs open eucalyptus, or wandoo, woodland with plenty of hollow logs to shelter in. If a predator invades the hideaway it uses its rump, which has extremely thick skin, to block the hole and thwart the attacker.

Rabbit-eared Bandicoot

(*Macrotis lagotis*)

Size:	Length up to 50cm plus tail of 29cm (male). Female smaller
Distribution:	West and central Australia
Identification:	Long, rabbit-like ears, pointed snout, bluish-grey fur with lighter underparts. Long, slender tail black, turning to white halfway down its length

Rabbits were introduced into Australia from Europe in the 1800s and have since multiplied in the way rabbits do, destroying crops and competing with native fauna for food. This bandicoot or bilby, as it is popularly known, was once common throughout southern Australia but is now confined to a few isolated pockets as rabbits continue to spread through its former habitat.

The bilby has strong claws to facilitate digging and can shovel fast enough to vanish from sight in about three minutes. Its burrows go straight down for approximately two metres, deterring foxes and other predators from digging it out. Several burrows are dug and used at random, the bilby feeding within a range of 100m from its bolt hole.

Common Cuscus (*Phalanger orientalis*)

Size:	Length, body, 35–55cm (tail up to 42cm)
Distribution:	Australian Oceanic Islands
Identification:	Thick woolly fur, white or grey in males, reddish-brown in females: white underside. Large, forward-facing eyes.

Early European explorers mistook the cuscus for a monkey, probably because of its size, but this marsupial, a member of the same family as possums, is not even distantly related to the primates. The common cuscus is arboreal, rarely coming to ground, and climbs slowly through the trees, gripping with three feet at a time and using its long, prehensile tail to wrap around the branch as an extra precaution. A fairly easy-going creature, the common cuscus is sometimes kept as a pet but in the wild it can be aggressive, especially if it meets up with its cousin, the spotted cuscus. Snarling and barking, it will hit out with its front paws to drive the invader away.

The young (generally twins) stay in the mother's pouch for several months. Usually only the stronger of the two survives.

Bats

On a sultry summer evening in Texas, migrating corn earthworm moths fill the skies over the cornfields around Bracken Cave near San Antonio. From the mouth of the cave erupt 20 million bats, the largest known colony in the world. These are Mexican free-tailed bats and they love eating bugs. By the end of the evening when they return to roost they will have devoured 250 tonnes of insects. They are a boon to farmers.

But bats have not always had a happy relationship with man: far from beautiful, they are creatures of the night, and they live in places which are traditionally associated with fear and superstition – caves, churches, attics – so they have acquired an undeservedly bad reputation.

Bats – or *Chiroptera* – live on all the world's continents except Antarctica and are found everywhere except extremely hot or cold areas and on some remote islands. Most species live in the tropics and rain forests.

They are the only flying mammals, distinct from those that merely glide on membranes. Their wings are long fingers covered by thin skin and they have furry bodies. They give birth to live young and feed them milk. There are about 1,000 different species including fruit-eating bats, frog-eating bats and vampire bats that lap blood, but mostly bats eat insects. They range in size from the endangered **bumblebee bat** (*Craseonycteris thonglongyai*) of Thailand, with a body less than 2cm long, to the golden-crowned **flying fox bat** (*Acerodon jubatus*) of the Sierra Madre mountains in the Philippines, which weighs over 1.3kg and has a wingspan of 180cm.

Bats are divided into two types: *microchiropterans* use echolocation to find insects and small animals, sending out high-pitched sounds (inaudible to humans) that bounce off objects, allowing the bat, with its huge ears, to locate them; *megachiropterans* are larger fruit or nectar eating bats, which use their sense of smell to find food.

Bats will occasionally fly into a darkened room, where their silent, rapid flitting flight might be mistaken for an attack. However, it is a myth that they get tangled in hair. Experiments have shown that they can easily avoid single strands of hair-thin wire in the dark just using echolocation. People think bats spread rabies; although they can carry the disease they also suffer from its symptoms and die.

However, fruit bats are suspected to be the source of a deadly brain virus called Nipah, which has killed hundreds of people in Malaysia, and some scientists believe bats may also be the source of the killer Ebola virus. On the other hand, more than 1,000,000 people die each year of malaria, a virus transmitted by mosquitoes, the very things that bats eat, and therefore protect us from. One bat can eat 600–1,000 mosquitoes in an hour.

Left: Peter's epauletted fruit bat
Right: Wahlberg's fruit bat

AYE-AYE (*Daubentonia madagascariensis*)

SIZE:	Length, body, 36–40cm (tail 50–60cm). Weight 2.8kg
DISTRIBUTION:	Madagascar
IDENTIFICATION:	Black coat with white flecks. Very large ears, large eyes and broad face. Pointed muzzle with prominent incisor teeth. Extremely long, bushy tail. Wire-thin middle finger on front feet

The imminent extinction of this remarkable primate is not purely the result of industrial or agricultural incursions into its habitat or First World rapaciousness. Although logging of Madagascar's rainforest and the increasing land requirements of the island's exploding population are the greatest threats to this mysterious lemur, it is superstition which might ultimately condemn it. It is regarded by many local people as an omen of death and some communities kill it deliberately. Although some animals have been captured and released on protected reserves it may be too late to save the species.

The nocturnal aye-aye uses its large ears to listen for grubs burrowing beneath tree bark then chisels off the outer layer of bark with its incisors before fishing out the larvae with its long middle finger. It eats fruit by gnawing through the skin and using its finger to tear out the flesh.

SLENDER LORIS (*Loris tardigradus*)

SIZE:	Length, body, 18–26cm (tail 4–7cm). Weight 102–285g
DISTRIBUTION:	Sri Lanka and southern India
IDENTIFICATION:	Colour varies from brown to grey or red. Long, pencil-thin limbs with strong hands and opposable thumbs. Large eyes and ears. Long nose with heart-shaped tip

Left alone, this unhurried, gentle primate forages at night for fruit, flowers, leaves and eggs, and sometimes small mammals, birds and reptiles, stalking them slowly before grabbing them with its forepaws. However, its preferred food is insects, particularly noxious or bad-smelling ones that other species find toxic. A particular favourite is the acacia ant, whose bite can paralyse a human arm. The slender loris washes its face, hands and feet with its own urine, which soothes the stings of its toxic meals.

Nevertheless, slender lorises have a struggle to survive. As their habitat is destroyed, they are frequently electrocuted when trying to use power lines to cross from tree to tree, run over by traffic, killed by domestic cats, captured and kept as pets and hunted for use in traditional medicines. Nearly all their body parts are considered to have magical powers.

Red Howler Monkey ▼

(*Alouatta seniculus*)

Size:	Length, body, 46–72cm (tail up to 75cm)
Distribution:	South America from Colombia to Bolivia
Identification:	Deep, chestnut or reddish-brown fur, very long, prehensile tail, deep lower jaw

The howl of the red howler monkey has been likened to the sound of the surf on a distant shore, rather different from that of the black howler monkey, which sounds like a football crowd. These howls are territorial statements made by the males, morning and evening, to warn other troops to keep their distance. The calls can be heard up to 5km away.

Altogether, there are six different species of howler monkey, all living high in the canopy of the rainforests of South America. Like other New World monkeys they can hang from their tails and use them to grab a passing branch to break their fall. The troop is a family group led by a dominant male. When a rival male takes over, he kills his predecessor's offspring to ensure his own lineage, as many pack animals do.

Woolly Spider Monkey

(*Brachyteles arachnoids*)

Size:	Length, body, 78cm (tail up to 78cm)
Distribution:	Southeast Brazil
Identification:	Buff-gold body hair, sooty markings on face, hands and feet. Very long, prehensile tail

The fruit-eating woolly spider monkey could teach the world a lot about the virtue of patience. It camps out close to unripe fruit, eating leaves until the fruit softens and sweetens sufficiently to suit its taste. Living in social groups of 15–25 individuals, these monkeys hurl themselves from branch to branch, often following each other in a line so only the leader has to work out a safe route. The young cling to their mother's side when small, moving to sit on her back after a few months.

Fewer than 500 of these monkeys, also known as muriquis, are known to survive in the wild today and they have been critically endangered since 2000. They used to be hunted for their meat which was considered a delicacy by native Brazilians.

Common Marmoset (*Callithrix jacchus*)

Size:	Length, body, 12–19cm (tail 29–35cm). Weight 300–500g
Distribution:	South and Central America
Identification:	Black and grey fur with black over head and neck. Prominent white ear tufts and white blaze on forehead. Alternating light and dark bands on prehensile tail. Claws on fingers

Not really a neglectful mother, the marmoset will nevertheless take all the help she can get in looking after her young. She normally has twins and her male companions (usually two) and other young (particularly the males) are quick to help. Indeed, this help appears to be essential to the survival of the infants.

The common marmoset's main food is tree sap and gum and it has specialized lower incisor teeth to gnaw holes in tree bark. It has also been seen eating insects, lizards, small animals, birds, eggs and frogs, but only infrequently. Despite its fall in numbers, due to habitat destruction, it can become a pest when it moves near to plantations, feeding on flowers and fruit. However, it is not as threatened as other marmosets and tamarins and it breeds well in captivity.

Golden Lion Tamarin

(*Leontopithecus rosalia*)

Size:	Length, body, 20–37cm (tail up to 40cm)
Distribution:	Southeast Brazil
Identification:	Lustrous golden fur with darker tail and forepaws. Long, silky mane surrounds the face

This strikingly beautiful monkey was once captured for zoos or as an exotic pet, but the main reason for its decline is the loss of 90 per cent of its original Atlantic forest habitat. In 1980, fewer than 100 individuals remained in the wild but captive stock was reintroduced and the oldest conservation project in Brazil has successfully ensured that numbers since then have increased eightfold.

Golden lion tamarins live in social family groups and defend their territory loudly and belligerently, their open mouths and arched backs showing aggressive body language. Not all sounds are threats: tamarins have 17 different calls. Within the group, the females are groomed by the males while the young, usually twins, spend time playing and wrestling.

LION-TAILED MACAQUE

(*Macaca silenus*)

SIZE:	Height 51–96cm. Weight 7–11kg
DISTRIBUTION:	Western Ghats (Sahyardri Mountains) of India
IDENTIFICATION:	Black fur with long, thin, naked tail, tufted at tip. Grey mane surrounding bare, black face. Cheek pouches extending down sides of neck

The squirrel, chipmunk and baboon all store food in their cheeks – but none of them comes close to the lion-tailed macaque for mouth storage capacity. It uses its cheek pouches to gather as much food as possible when danger threatens. When fully extended these pouches can hold as much as the macaque's stomach. This attractive primate is much sought-after by zoos and the pet trade and is also used in medical research. It eats fruit, leaves, stems, buds and flowers and occasionally insects, lizards, small mammals and frogs. *Macaca silenus* moves through the trees during the day, keeping in touch with others in the troop using nearly 20 different vocal patterns as well as distinct body movements. It is unique among macaques in that both sexes communicate vocally and the males use calls to establish territorial boundaries.

Olive Baboon *(Papio hamadryas anubis)*

Size:	Length, body 60–74cm (tail 43–49cm). Weight 14–28kg
Distribution:	Sub-Saharan eastern Africa
Identification:	Greenish-olive agouti coat. Adult males have longer hair on the shoulders than females. Both have a black face and ruffs on cheeks

Big cats are powerful and hyaenas are cunning but mature male olive baboons combine these attributes with viciousness, fearlessness and anger, which enables them to drive most others away from a kill. Males grow up to 74cm in length and can weigh 28kg, so they are not enormous, but it is their attitude – and their vast canine teeth – which make them so formidable.

Olive baboons, which are found in most of sub-Saharan east Africa, are very social animals, living in a matriarchal troop of about 50 individuals who work together for mutual benefit. Grooming, recreation and even apparent friendships play an important part. The troop spirit shows itself when a large adversary needs to be dealt with. The late South African naturalist Eugène Marais once witnessed two baboons attacking a leopard which was threatening their troop. They ambushed the cat as it stalked the main group and although both were killed in the fight, one of them mortally wounded the leopard by puncturing its jugular vein with its long canine teeth. They sacrificed themselves but saved the troop.

Olive baboons are opportunistic feeders eating mainly fruit and grass but also tubers, bulbs, flowers, leaves and seeds as well as insects, eggs, birds and even tree gum. They prey on hares and young gazelle and will take advantage of any kill they come across. They are active during the day and sleep in trees or on cliffs to avoid predators.

Hamadryas Baboon (Desert Baboon)

(Papio hamadryas)

Size:	Length, body, 75cm (tail 55cm). Weight 12–21kg
Distribution:	Somalia, Ethiopia, Saudi Arabia and Yemen
Identification:	Adult male has a long, silvery cape and is larger than female, which is olive-brown. Bright pink face and bottom, long muzzle, heavily hooded eyes and huge canine teeth

Hamadryas baboons have developed a social structure and male-dominated society unique among primates. The smallest unit is the harem of up to 10 females dominated by an adult male. When two or more harems come together with single male followers this is known as a clan. Clans can join to form a band and several bands together make a troupe.

As many as 800 individuals from several troupes sometimes share a sleeping site, often on a cliff face. Males stay in the same clan for life and dominant patriarchs are very touchy about maintaining the cohesion of the group, threatening and biting females that lag behind, wander too far away or fraternize with other units.

MANDRILL *(Mandrillus sphinx)* ▶

SIZE:	Height at shoulder 80cm (walking quadrupedally). Weight 11–25kg
DISTRIBUTION:	West Africa
IDENTIFICATION:	Olive-green coat with paler underparts. Distinctive bright bluish-purple, naked rump. Red stripe down middle of muzzle and round nostrils; sides of muzzle blue. Red patches above eyes and yellow beard

There is no mistaking a mandrill. This highly-coloured monkey is a popular subject for film and cartoon makers and is a favourite at zoos where it can live to a ripe old age. However, a captive mandrill can be a nuisance because it is very skilful at snatching glasses, pipes and jewellery from visitors who venture too close to the bars of its cage. In the wild the mandrill snatches oil palm fruits from plantations and, when food is scarce, raids farm crops – which leads to its being shot. It is also killed for food in many areas and is losing its habitat to mankind. Consequently numbers have declined dramatically in recent years. It eats fruit and seeds, roots, insects, worms and frogs, lizards and snakes, and even small vertebrates. The male does the food finding on the ground while the female and young sit in the mid-level branches.

◀ PROBOSCIS MONKEY *(Nasalis larvatus)*

SIZE:	Length, body, 53–77cm (tail 56–76cm). Weight 7–23kg
DISTRIBUTION:	Borneo
IDENTIFICATION:	Fur varies from brown to cream or cinnamon on the back and creamy-grey on the underside. Bare face with huge nose. Long limbs and long, thin tail. Pot belly

When the Dutch first arrived in the East Indies they must have seemed strange creatures to the native inhabitants. One of the most abnormal features of Europeans must have been their comparatively long noses. Now Westerners are commonplace in Borneo but that first fascination lives on in the local nickname for the nasally super-endowed proboscis monkey: they call it the *belanda,* which means Dutchman. Young proboscis monkeys have a pointed, forward-growing nose. The female's remains like this but the male's gets bigger and bigger until it becomes a pendulous blob hanging down below its mouth. This large, specialized plant eater seems pot-bellied because of its huge, chambered stomachs containing a bacterial soup which digests seeds, leaves and green fruits. It is under extreme threat from habitat destruction by agriculture, settlement, drainage, mining, hunting and shrimp farming. Fewer than 8,000 remain.

Western Gorilla (*Gorilla gorilla*)

Size:	Males 1.7–1.8m high, weighing up to 275kg. Females 1.4–1.5m high, weighing up to 100kg
Distribution:	Equatorial Africa
Identification:	Short legs, long arms, wide chest and large head with overhanging lip. Black skin covered with coarse, dark hair except on face, hands and feet

The gorilla is the gentle giant of the jungle, generally behaving peacefully. When threatened, however, a male will put up a show of strength by standing tall, growling and beating his chest. If this does not frighten his attacker, he will sometimes charge – but swerve at the last minute to avoid actual contact.

Family groups of 5–15 comprise the dominant male – known as a silverback because of his greying hair – his mates and their offspring. The silverback leads his family, deciding when and where to eat and sleep and constantly guarding them from other males trying to take over the group.

Gorillas are intelligent, have good memories and can be taught problem-solving. In the 1970s, researchers taught one gorilla, Koko, sign language and he was able to communicate using more than 1,000 signs.

Orang Utan (*Pongo pygmaeus*) ►

Size:	Length 1.5m. Armspan 2.2m. Weight 30–90kg
Distribution:	Borneo and Southern Sumatra
Identification:	Dark, blue-grey skin with thin, shaggy red-brown coat (more maroon in Bornean sub-species). Hairless face (except in Sumatran sub-species) with, in male, large cheek pads. Short legs, strong arms and hands

The orang utan has the least humanoid general appearance of all the great apes yet the face of a mature male, with its bushy moustache, long beard and general demeanour of calmness and grandeur, is suggestive of a wise old man. Orang utan means 'wild person' or 'man of the woods' in Malay and Indonesian and early explorers thought the animal was indeed a strange human.

The orang utan moves through the forest following the ripening of different species of date, its favourite food. It also eats leaves, bark, buds and flowers, the occasional insect, egg or small vertebrate, and mineral-rich soil. It is protected but poaching goes on, mainly to supply the pet and zoo trade, and both numbers and range are declining. Deforestation for the planting of palm-oil trees is a major threat.

A captive animal has been known to live to the age of 59, the oldest non-human primate recorded.

Common Gibbon (*Hylobates lar*)

Size:	Length 42–58cm. Weight 4.4–7.6kg
Distribution:	Southern and Southeast Asia
Identification:	Fur colour ranges from cream to reddish-brown to black. Face, hands and feet are white

The gibbon is blessed with arms longer than its legs, making it practically impossible for the animal to walk on all fours. Fortunately, it does not need to, for almost its entire life is spent in the trees. Its long arms are much more useful for swinging hand-over-hand from branch to branch, bridging gaps of up to 10m. The common, or white-handed gibbon, one of the best known gibbons, is now endangered as rainforests disappear at an alarming rate.

Gibbons mate for life and stay together in the same territory of 12–53 hectares. Their morning duet, started by the female and joined by the male, is primarily a territorial call but singing together is also thought to strengthen their pair bond.

◄ BONOBO *(Pan paniscus)*

SIZE:	Height (standing bipedally) up to 119cm. Weight up to 43kg (male), 37kg (female)
DISTRIBUTION:	Congo south of Zaire River
IDENTIFICATION:	Like a chimpanzee but lighter in build with pinkish lips, smaller ears and wider nostrils. Flatter, more open face with higher forehead. Graceful mover. Very passive

If humans were more like the bonobo and less like the chimpanzee, the world would be a more peaceful place. Where chimps are aggressive and quarrelsome, bonobos, or pygmy chimpanzees, are great appeasers. This might be because the females are in charge. A chimp clan is ruled by a (usually temperamental) alpha male given to dangerous displays of machismo. In bonobo groups males are kept in their place by the alpha female and her sister animals who not only get the pick of whatever food is available but who are looked to by all – including males – for defence and security. Much of the interaction between bonobos is erotically tactile and they spend a great deal of time mating, apparently not simply for procreation but as a social activity, to resolve disputes and avoid confrontations.

CHIMPANZEE *(Pan troglodytes)* ►

SIZE:	Height (standing bipedally) up to 120cm. Weight up to 60kg (male), 47.5kg (female)
DISTRIBUTION:	West and Central Africa
IDENTIFICATION:	Smooth black skin covered in black hair. Hairless face, ears and feet. Prominent brow, depressed nasal bridge and flattened nostrils. Protruding, mobile lips

Millions of hours have been spent studying the chimpanzee for one major reason: chimpanzee and human genes are 98 per cent alike. The chimp is cunning, aggressive, inquisitive, strongly hierarchical but also inventive and capable of learning. Like *Homo sapiens* it also makes war. The legendary primate researcher Jane Goodall recorded one instance in the Gombe National Park, Tanzania, of a conflict between two chimp communities which ended with the annihilation of the smaller group.

One hundred years ago there were probably about a million chimps in Africa. Now there are about 200,000, due mainly to land clearance for agriculture and logging, killing for meat and capture for zoos. The chimp uses tools (sticks to dig out ants, stones to break open nuts, leaves to carry water) and can be taught to communicate with humans – and other chimps – using rudimentary sign language.

Birds

OSTRICH *(Struthio camelus)*

SIZE:	Height 1.75–2.75m. Weight up to 150kg (male), 90–110kg (female)
DISTRIBUTION:	Southern and eastern Africa, small populations in north and west Africa. Farmed worldwide
IDENTIFICATION:	Rounded bodies, fluffy plumage and long, powerful legs and neck. Huge claws. Males black with light wing and tail tips, females grey-brown

The Book of Job (chapter 39, verse 16) says of the female ostrich: 'She is hardened against her young ones as though they were not hers'. Job puts this down to stupidity but the real reason is safety in numbers. The senior female in a group is the first to lay her 1.5kg eggs, whereupon other females are attracted to the nest and lay their own eggs in it. The lead pair in a group then raises the resultant brood of 10–15. They kidnap young birds until they have a family of up to several hundred. This may make donor parents look uncaring but individual chicks are vulnerable to predators and a group can protect itself.

The ostrich is the largest living bird and the world's fastest two-legged animal, running at up to 70kph. It was reduced to tiny numbers in the eighteenth century due to demand for its feathers. Nowadays, ostrich farming provides enough meat, leather and feathers to meet consumer demands and wild birds are left to flourish.

Southern Cassowary

(*Casuarius casuarius*)

Size:	Height up to 1.8m. Weight up to 60kg. Female larger than male
Distribution:	Northern Australia
Identification:	Glossy-black plumage. Naked blue neck and head, red wattles. Large keratinous protuberance on top of head. Stout scaly legs, large feet and claws

The flightless cassowary plays an essential part in maintaining the plant diversity of the wet tropics of Queensland, Australia, by dispersing the seeds of the fruit it eats. Of the 150 trees and vines which depend on the cassowary, 70 have seeds too large for other creatures to eat and 80 produce toxic seeds which only the cassowary can safely consume, thanks to its rapid digestive system. Without the cassowary, seeds would only germinate near parent trees and species would become confined to pockets, changing the structure of the forest. The double-wattled cassowary, as it is also known, is under threat from habitat destruction, traffic and dog attack (especially near residential areas where it becomes tame through hand feeding). There might be as few as 900 left although some estimates put the figure at 1,500. The casque protects the bird's head as it runs through the forest undergrowth.

EMU (*Dromaius novaehollandiae*)

SIZE:	Height 1.5–2m. Weight up to 45kg (female larger)
DISTRIBUTION:	Throughout Australia in desert, scrubland, grassland and woods
IDENTIFICATION:	Long legs and neck, rounded body and thick, shaggy, brown to grey-brown feathers. Pointy beak, large eyes and sometimes a bluish throat

Severe drought conditions sometimes drive hungry, thirsty emus into urban areas where they can create havoc – wrecking gardens, running into traffic and getting into scraps with pet dogs. One reason why these flightless birds are so difficult to deal with is that they run so fast. In open countryside they can cover the ground at up to 50kph, with a swaying, bouncing motion. Emus eat insects such as grasshoppers but feed mainly on green herbage like grass and flowers – which is why they should be kept out of gardens. Although wild birds are protected in Australia, emus are farmed throughout the world, yielding low-cholesterol, low-fat meat, highly penetrating non-toxic oil (used in cosmetics), soft and supple leather and exotic feathers for the fashion industry.

Penguins

Although 11 of the 17 penguin species live in warmer waters on the coasts of Australia, South Africa, Peru and the Galapagos islands, we tend to think mainly of those inhabiting the freezing waters of the Antarctic. Penguins have heavy bones that help them stay submerged and are by far the best swimmers in the bird world, 'flying' underwater and steering with their feet. Travel on land is more difficult – they either stomp along slowly or toboggan on their front. Despite this, an Emperor penguin might travel up to 960km on a feeding trip.

Macaroni penguins (*Eudyptes chrysolophus*) are named after an eighteenth-century men's fashion of putting feathers in caps. In mid-October, the southern spring, they assemble in colonies of 200,000 or more on the island of South Georgia. The males arrive first and the females follow a few days later to lay eggs in simple scraped nests. The pair take turns to incubate the eggs, which hatch after just over a month. For 60 days the parents feed the young until they are ready for the sea.

acaroni penguins

Emperor penguins (*Aptenodytes forsteri*) endure the harshest conditions of any warm-blooded creature. They reproduce during the long, dark, unimaginably cold winters. Courtship begins in April, and lasts three to five weeks during which time the pair learn each other's call. The egg is laid in late May or early June. The male tucks it away in a warm, feathery fold of skin above his feet and his mate heads back to sea to feed. So begins the male's bitter vigil through a winter where winds reach 200kph and temperatures fall below −20 °C (−4 °F). Huddled in a slowly shifting mass, their heads bowed to lock out the weather, the males slowly waste away until they have lost 40 per cent of their body weight.

While the females are away the ice grows out into the sea at over 3km a day so by the time they return, they might have to plod and slide 160km to reach the breeding site. Pairs recognize one another by their calls. The female regurgitates the first meal for their chick. The male gives up the young and begins his own trudge to the sea – and his first meal for four months. A month or so later the males return, and the females go off to eat. This goes on until the chicks fledge at 150 days. The parents then stop feeding them and the whole colony starts its slog back to the sea. They have just over three months before they start the whole process again.

Adélie penguins (*Pygoscelis adeliae*), the archetypal 'waiter-in-a-suit' penguins, are one of nature's victims. They face, among other predators, one of the most efficient killing machines: leopard seals. Adélies (45–55cm tall and weighing 3.6–4kg) breed on the Antarctic pack ice and by late summer the young are ready to leave the rookery. The parents feed them closer and closer to the water's edge and then stop feeding them altogether. Now a tense drama plays out.
The hungry young penguins edge nearer to the sea, bunching up in their hundreds on the lip of the ice. Finally they leap. The lucky ones dodge under the ice and swim to freedom. For the patient, patrolling seals it is a time of plenty.

Adélie pengui

mperor penguins

Wandering Albatross ▲

(*Diomedea exulans*)

Size:	Wingspan up to 3.45m
Range:	Throughout the southern oceans
Identification:	White body and head, wings white beneath, dark above. Pink bill with yellow, hooked tip. Grey legs and webbed feet. Unmistakably huge wingspan

These vie with condors as the largest flying birds in the world. For most of the year they glide in solitude over the vast southern oceans, covering up to 480km a day, and staying aloft on thin, low-drag wings that lock into position to save energy. They need the wind to allow them to take off and, once airborne, can glide for hours at speeds of up to 70kph, resting only occasionally at night. In the breeding season they come together on sub-Antarctic islands, perform their bobbing, groaning courtship display and build perfectly round nests of mud on the high, windswept cliffs.

These open ocean hunters feed mainly on squid and carrion. They sometimes pluck prey from the water while in flight. Sadly, they also plunge-dive to take the bait on longline fishing tackle, particularly the sort used to catch tuna, and get snagged on the hooks and drowned. Many thousands die in this way each year.

Slavonian or Horned Grebe

(*Podiceps auritus*)

Size:	Length 30–38cm
Distribution:	Eurasia and United States, breeding in north, wintering in south
Identification:	In summer, long orange-gold ear plumes, reddish flanks and white in wing. In winter, white neck and cheeks, dark crown

This pretty little grebe is a superb aquanaut, able to swim and dive immediately after hatching and capable of staying under water for up to three minutes once fully grown. It can swim submerged for 200m or so but pays the price for this proficiency when it comes ashore. Its legs, which give it such paddling power and agility in the water, are set too far back to be of much use on land where it is virtually helpless. Consequently it spends most of its time in the water and even its nests are floating structures, made of plant material anchored to standing vegetation. In a striking breeding display a pair make synchronised dives to fetch weed from the bottom and then charge almost upright along the surface side-by-side carrying the greenery in their bills. The slavonian grebe eats insects, crustaceans, fish, molluscs, salamanders and occasionally plants.

Southern Giant Petrel

(*Macronectes giganteus*)

Size:	Wingspan 175–195cm
Range:	Throughout the Southern Oceans
Identification:	Most individuals flecked grey but species has wide colour range from black, brown to almost white. Long hook-ended bill with tubular nostrils along top edge

If you bother a southern giant petrel you will discover why its nickname is 'stinker'. It has the unsavoury skill of projecting a large blob of nauseating oil and stomach contents with great force and accuracy. This master scavenger will eat virtually anything it comes across, from a rotting seal carcass to a live penguin chick. However, its gluttony could also be its downfall. Like the wandering albatross it duck-dives for the bait of fishermen, becoming tangled in the lines and drowned. By the start of the century the global population had fallen by 17 per cent, largely through drowning but also from predation by feral cats and rats on the breeding islands. On some islands, hunting has brought about huge population decreases and even local extinction.

American White Pelican *(Pelecanus erythrorhynchos)*

Size:	Wingspan up to 3.5m. Weight 5–9kg
Distribution:	North America
Identification:	White plumage with black primary feathers. Long, flattened orange bill with bright-orange pouch beneath. Breeding male has fibrous horn sprouting from top of bill. Flies with neck tucked in. Short, orange legs

White pelicans may not seem to have a lot in common with lionesses – until you see them hunting. Just like the queens of the savannah, these huge, graceful sovereigns of the coastal waters work in teams. A group of up to a dozen lands on the water and adopts a horseshoe formation. Then they swim slowly forwards, occasionally flapping their wings and jabbing the surface with their huge bills in perfect unison, herding fish before them. Finally they close ranks, encircle their prey, and simultaneously plunge into the trapped shoal. Their net-like pouches gather up fish – and gallons of water. They get rid of the water by holding their bills vertically, letting it drain out before swallowing their catch. Human activity is the greatest threat to the white pelican. Secure breeding areas have been set up in the north of its range to ensure its survival.

Northern Gannet

(*Morus bassanus* or *Sula bassanus*)

Size:	Wingspan 180–190cm.Weight 3–3.5kg
Distribution:	North Atlantic
Identification:	Large white bird seen diving into sea to fish. Yellowish head and nape, black wing tips, long bill, black legs

Tourists visit Bonaventure Island, Quebec, and St Kilda, off the west coast of Scotland, to see the huge gannetries where hundreds of thousands of these large birds nest on the sheer sea cliffs. An impressive sight it is, too: the birds wheel in the sky in such huge numbers that they block out the sun. Gannet numbers generally are increasing but this has not always been the case. They declined drastically in the 19th century, particularly in Canada, through egg collection and slaughter of the adult birds. The gannet is now protected everywhere, with one exception: each September young gannets, known as gugas, are harvested by special permit on the Scottish island of Sulisgeir by men from the Isle of Lewis in the Outer Hebrides. They are considered a delicacy locally and are even posted around the world to expatriates to give them a (rather fishy) taste of the old country.

Blue-footed Booby

(*Sula nebouxii*)

Size:	Wingspan 150–155cm. Weight 2.5–3kg
Distribution:	West coast of Central and South America
Identification:	Pale, streaked head. Dark upper parts with white nape and rump patches. White beneath. Blue legs and feet. Large, dark, pointed bill

During his courtship display the male blue-footed booby struts back and forth like a soldier showing off his blue feet in a high-stepping march. If a female appears unmoved he takes to the air dangling his legs and flapping his feet so she can get a better look. This performance, together with the bird's curiosity and clumsiness, led Spanish sailors to call it the 'bobo', meaning clown. Boobies have no fear of man and will walk up to people to investigate. They spend almost all their time at sea, diving from great heights for fish in the same way as gannets, which are closely related to them. They can also judge when flying fish are about to leave the water and will snatch them in mid-air. The masked or blue-faced boody is the largest of the family and strongly resembles the gannet.

Common Cormorant

(Phalacrocorax carbo)

Size:	Length 80–100cm. Weight 1.8–2.8kg
Distribution:	Eurasia, Africa, Australia, New Zealand
Identification:	Browny-green upper parts, black below, black neck and head with white cheek-patches and chin. Long yellow bill. White thigh-patch when breeding

Cormorants were being used to catch fish by Ukai fishermen in Japan 1,300 years ago. This is still done, at night, by the light of flaming torches that attract fish to the boat. The fisherman fastens his birds to leads and they dive to snatch their quarry in their hooked bills. Thin twine around their necks prevents them swallowing large fish, which are regurgitated once the bird returns to the boat. A team of eight birds can gather about 36kg of fish in a night.

The cormorant has an unjustified reputation for greed. It eats no more than any seabird of its size but has long been persecuted for stealing fish. Most people first see a cormorant standing on a rock, its wings spread out to dry. They also haunt power station outlets, looking for mashed fish from the cooling systems, and take the occasional unguarded trout from a farm.

GREY HERON *(Ardea cinerea)*

SIZE:	Wingspan 155–175cm. Length 84–102cm
DISTRIBUTION:	Widespread in Europe, Africa and Asia
IDENTIFICATION:	Grey with long yellow-orange bill, white underparts and wispy crest. In flight long neck drawn back, large wings arched. Long legs. Harsh, crawking call

People put plastic herons next to their fishponds to keep away the real thing (theoretically deterred by competition) but sometimes it is hard to tell the two apart as the heron can stand so still for so long. It waits until a fish or eel swims beneath its feet and then extends its curled neck in a lightning-fast movement, jabbing the prey with its sharp bill. Sometimes it will wade slowly as it searches for food which might include frogs, snails, mice and rats and even quite large birds like water rail. The heron suffers in harsh winters when the waters freeze over. It makes a huge nest, 2m or more across, which it returns to each year. In flight, its slow-beating wings and unmistakable silhouette are a stunning sight.

The heron used to be hunted with hawks but earned a reputation as a coward for flying high and avoiding the fight. Those killed were often eaten.

American Bittern *(Botaurus lentiginosus)*

Size:	Length up to 35cm
Distribution:	Breeds mid-USA to northern Canada; winters southern USA, Mexico
Identification:	Stout body, short legs. Speckled-brown above, brown and white below lighter neck. Black patch from eye down side of neck

Like the other 12 bittern species, the American bittern is famous for the male's deep, resonant, booming mating call which can be heard 5km away across the reedbeds and wetlands where it lives. This sound, more mechanical than natural, has led to nicknames such as thunder-pumper, mire-drum, slough-pumper, and stake-driver. The strange call and the bird's liking for desolate, creepy wetlands has led to it being associated with evil. According to the author C. H. Merriam, one Sunday in 1786 the men in a Connecticut town gathered together to rid nearby swamps of bitterns thought to be having a malevolent influence on the townsfolk.

The bittern eats insects, amphibians, crayfish, small fish and mammals, waiting patiently and unmoving for the victim to pass by then stabbing it with its long bill. The population is declining through habitat loss and degradation.

Great Frigate bird

(*Fregata minor*)

Size:	Wingspan 86–100cm
Distribution:	Tropical Pacific and Indian Oceans
Identification:	Very large, black bird, with long pointed wings and deeply-forked tail. Males have inflatable red throat pouch. Females have white breast and throat

The male great frigate bird knows exactly what attracts a female of the species: a well-waggled red balloon. At mating time he forces air into the patch of slack red skin at his throat until it is fully inflated. Then he waits, usually as part of a large group, until a female flies overhead. This is the signal to him to waggle his balloon, flap his wings, and give his gobbling, turkey-like call. It must be a seductive sight for the females because laying the single egg that sometimes follows and raising the chick is quite a commitment. The process takes 18 months, for most of which the female is left with sole responsibility – a single mother.

The frigate bird is a notorious pirate. Though capable of snatching fish from the water with its long, hooked bill, it often harasses other birds and steals their catch before they can swallow it.

SHOEBILL *(Balaeniceps rex)*

SIZE:	Height 110–140cm
DISTRIBUTION:	East central Africa
IDENTIFICATION:	Slate-grey plumage, darker-grey head, lighter underparts. Enormous, yellowish, clog-shaped bill with curved hook

With such a vast, cumbersome bill it is not surprising that the shoebill's fishing method is clumsy. This heron-like bird stands motionless in shallow water or wades slowly and when it spots its prey – anything from a frog to a young crocodile – it simply collapses onto it. If it isn't successful it has to rearrange itself and get back on its feet before it can try again: an ungraceful procedure. It eats mostly lungfish and watersnakes and usually emerges from a collapse with its bill full of prey, mud and vegetation. It sways its head to eject the weed before swallowing the prey – usually after decapitating it.

Many zoos want shoebills, paying up to $20,000 per bird (making them the most expensive zoo-trade birds) and creating income for local people who also catch it for food.

HAMERKOP

(Scopus umbretta)

SIZE:	Length 50cm
DISTRIBUTION:	Widespread in sub-Saharan Africa
IDENTIFICATION:	Chicken-sized stork with dumpy body, shortish neck and legs, stout bill and distinctive large, horizontal backward-pointing crest. Generally brownish with faint light stripe through eye

The hamerkop (its name means 'hammer head' in Afrikaans) is a master builder and creates one of the largest nests of any individual bird, usually in a tree near a marshy area where it feeds on frogs, tadpoles, fish and insects. The nest-building process takes about six weeks. First the pair lays down a platform of stout sticks. Then they build walls – leaving a gap for the doorway – and finally erect a roof by stabbing inward-leaning sticks into the walls and piling material on top. The interior and doorway are plastered with mud. The nest can be as much as two metres from floor to rooftop and weigh more than 45kg.

The hamerkop is considered an unlucky bird and some Africans throw stones at it to prevent it flying over their homes or settling on their rooftops – events that supposedly presage death to one of the inhabitants.

Scarlet Ibis

(*Eudocimus ruber*)

Size:	Wingspan 96cm. Length 53–59cm
Distribution:	Northern South America
Identification:	Vivid scarlet plumage with long, curved bill. Long neck and legs

The most startlingly coloured and arguably most beautiful of the 33 ibis species, the scarlet ibis is one of the national birds of Trinidad & Tobago, where it is protected. Its colouring comes from the synthesis of carotene in its food – mostly fiddler and aratus crabs, algae, shrimp and other aquatic insects. The ibis lives in big colonies in the mangrove swamps, estuaries, mudflats and lagoons and nests are built in treetops overlooking the water. The young are brown with a white rump and belly but become scarlet by the time they are mature at two years old. Fossil records for the ibis go back 60 million years and the ancient Egyptians venerated the old world species, often mummifying birds and burying them with their pharaohs. Ibis are found all over the world, the most widely distributed being the glossy ibis.

Lesser Flamingo

(*Phoenicopterus minor*)

Size:	Wingspan 94–100cm. Height 100cm. Weight 2.2–2.8kg
Distribution:	Salt lakes of southern Africa
Identification:	Smallest flamingo. Pinky-white plumage with black feathers on wings and pink legs. Downward-curved purple-pink bill with black tip

Lesser flamingos have pale pink plumage, with black feathers on their wings, although the chicks hatch with grey legs and feathers and a straight bill. They form large, sociable colonies and pairs mate for life.

Flamingos rely on their acute eyesight and hearing for protection, calling and flashing their black wing feathers to communicate with one another. Eggs and chicks are the prey of marabou and vultures but adult birds are regular targets of lions, cheetahs, leopards, jackals and even pythons.

A flamingo eats by holding its bill upside-down and swinging it backwards and forwards in the water, filtering up to 20 litres of water a day. Lamellae (or spines) in the bill catch filtered food particles.

Marabou Stork

(Leptoptilos crumeniferus)

Size:	Wingspan 260cm. Height 152cm. Weight 6.8–9kg
Distribution:	Throughout Africa, usually between Sahara and South Africa
Identification:	Largest stork. Upper parts black or grey, underparts white. Neck and head bare. Long, 'meat cleaver' bill. Long reddish pouch hanging from neck

The marabou stork is ugly but its soft, fluffy undertail feathers, known simply as marabou, are beautiful and were once used to trim hats and gowns and to make scarves. Few if any of the women wearing these fripperies could have known they came from a carrion eater with a scabby, blood-encrusted head and a habit of squirting its legs with its own excrement.

The marabou has two large inflatable air sacs under its skin, one on its back and one below its throat. The male puffs these up at mating time and is aggressive to all-comers – including his prospective mate. She is submissive and, once pairing is established, will also inflate her sacs and be equally offensive to intruders. Often found near fishing villages, rubbish dumps, camps and abattoirs, marabous will become quite tame and feed within a few feet of people.

Tundra Swan

In North America the tundra swan is the **whistling swan** (*Cygnus columbianus ssp. columbianus*) and in Europe it is the **Bewick swan** (*C. columbianus bewickii*). These are two races of the same swan but they are sufficiently different to be considered separate species. Both birds are all-white with black legs and feet although where they have been feeding in iron-rich waters the neck and head may have a reddish hue. The whistling swan's bill is almost always completely black with perhaps a small yellow or orange spot on the upper mandible, while the Bewick swan's bill has a large yellow patch, the pattern of which is unique to each bird. Both have a wingspan of 1.2m.

The name whistling swan comes from the noise made by the bird's wings – a rhythmical *whoo-whoo-whoo*. Observing a skein of these graceful birds with their wingspan of 120cm and sleek profile whispering their way across a moonlit sky is one of the great nature-watching experiences.

The 140,000 whistling swans breed high in Arctic Alaska and Canada and winter 5,900km away on the west and east coasts of the USA. Bewicks, of which there are about 60,000, breed in the Russian Arctic tundra along the northern shores of Eurasia. The western population migrates to winter mainly in the Netherlands and Britain,

Bewick swan

with smaller numbers wintering in Germany, Denmark, Belgium, and Ireland. An eastern contingent winters in Japan, China, and Korea. A third small population winters on the Caspian Sea. The Wildfowl and Wetlands Trust website shows daily satellite tracking of Bewicks along their migration routes from Russia to the WWT site in Slimbridge, Gloucestershire, England.

Tundra swans pair for life and breed in wetlands, their cygnets staying with them all winter. They begin to nest in late May or early June before the snow has left the tundra and while many of the lakes are still frozen. They select islets in ponds and lakes and are solitary nesters with each pair defending a territory of 1.9 square km or more. The cream-coloured eggs average 107mm long and are incubated for 30 to 32 days. A clutch of four is normal, although in exceptionally warm springs the female often lays five or six eggs. On the other hand, an unusually cold spring might prevent nesting and, if the eggs are destroyed or fail to hatch, the swans do not nest again that year.

ndra swan

GIANT CANADA GOOSE

(*Branta canadensis maxima*)

SIZE:	Wingspan up to 2m. Length 110cm. Weight up to 6.5kg
DISTRIBUTION:	Eastern and midwestern USA
IDENTIFICATION:	Greyish-brown with black head, long black neck, white cheek-patch

There are 11 sub-species of the Canada goose in North America and *B. c. maxima* is the largest of them all. It is also the most pestiferous. This huge bird was considered extinct until a small colony was discovered in the early 1960s. A breeding and reintroduction programme was rather too successful and it is now to be found in great numbers in many town and city parks, golf courses and other urban open spaces where water is nearby. Of all Canada geese it has the highest tolerance for people. It is also the only non-migratory species so once a flock has found a suitable location it stays put and increases. It feeds on aquatic plants, grass, roots, seeds and berries and a flock will graze a grassy area like sheep, neatly trimming right down to the ground. They can also devastate a grain field in no time.

Greater Snow Goose

(*Anser caerulescens atlantica*)

Size:	Wingspan 150cm. Adult males up to 3.5kg
Range:	Nests throughout eastern Arctic including Baffin Island, Bathurst Island, Ellesmere Island and northwest Greenland. Overwinters in New England
Identification:	Almost entirely white with black primaries at wing tips. Heads often stained rusty-orange from traces of iron, in mud dug in for food. Narrow, rather high pinkish bill

By the turn of the twentieth century, hunting had reduced the population of these striking birds – mythologized by the native population of Canada, Alaska and Greenland – to 3,000. Shortly after, the United States and Canada banned most hunting of migratory birds, including snow geese. By the 1990s they were so plentiful that subsistence hunting by the Inuit people was allowed. Now there are more than 800,000 birds and they are so over-abundant that numbers are culled in spring hunts.

Mandarin Duck ▲

(*Aix galericulata*)

Size:	Length 43–51cm. Weight 444–550g
Distribution:	Siberia, China and Japan. Small feral populations in Britain, Europe and North America
Identification:	Spectacular multi-coloured plumage in male including twin 'sail' of orange and cream feathers on back. Female duller-greyish

Chinese and Siberian mandarin ducks are migratory and have been known to cover 800 km in 24 hours. The mandarin eats water plants, rice and grains and prefers wooded ponds and fast-flowing streams. Habitat destruction is a major threat in Asia where numbers are much reduced. The mandarin courtship display is impressive and once a pairing is established it lasts for years. This is why in the ancient Chinese practice of *Feng Shui* mandarins are the most popular symbol of love. Having a pair – either in the flesh or in ornamental form – is supposed to emit *chi* or energy which is conducive to love and harmonious marriage. For the *chi* to work effectively, the ducks should be in the south west corner of the room, something easier to achieve with porcelain models than with the real thing.

Ancient Murrelet

(*Synthliboramphus antiquus*)

Size:	Length 20cm
Distribution:	Northern Pacific
Identification:	Black above with greyish shoulders, white below with white throat and pale white line behind eye. Pale bill

The ancient murrelet spends almost all of its life at sea, diving and swimming in search of fish. But it must come ashore to breed – and waiting in the trees above the breeding burrow are peregrines and eagles. Unfortunately for the murrelet its stubby wings are designed for swimming, not controlled flight, and its legs, so good at steering it in water, are virtually useless on land. Consequently it comes roaring in to its island retreat at high speed and, after a crash landing, staggers about trying desperately to shuffle to its burrow. Easy pickings for a pair of peregrines which might catch 1,000 murrelets in a season. After hatching in the burrow the chicks must run a similar gauntlet and the lucky ones dash across the beach into the sea with such determination that, if picked up, their little legs carry on scurrying like a clockwork toy.

MALLARD (*Anas platyrhynchos*)

SIZE:	Length 38–58cm. Wingspan 89cm
DISTRIBUTION:	Almost anywhere in the world other than polar regions
IDENTIFICATION:	Male: green iridescent plumage on head and neck; curled black tail feathers. Female: drab brown

This is the quintessential duck: the one that quacks and has water roll off its back, and inhabits numerous park and village ponds. It is the most abundant and widespread of all waterfowl and despite being hunted in its millions each year it continues to thrive. It is the female that quacks, usually to call her young to her, and the familiar sound travels many kilometres. Mallards winter in the warmer south and travel north in the spring to breed. Their arrival time for breeding depends on average air temperatures during the trip – the warmer, the earlier – hence the regard in which country folk and hunters hold them as harbingers of good or bad weather. The mallard eats a wide variety of food: the bread thrown by countless park visitors is probably a staple for some.

EIDER *(Somateria mollissima)*

SIZE:	Length 50–70cm. Weight 1–3kg
DISTRIBUTION:	North America, northwest Europe, Iceland
IDENTIFICATION:	Male with white upper parts, breast and head. Breast has rosy tint. Black cap, green nape. Black belly, rump and flight feathers. Greenish bill with yellow along top. Female mottled brown

Iceland took the lead in protecting the eider in the wild and now runs a multi-million dollar eider down industry based on farmed birds. The female lines her nest with down that she plucks from her breast and the olive-brown eggs snuggle into one of the lightest and warmest insulation materials known. Eider down commands a high price and is used in top quality duvets, sleeping bags and parkas. The bird is protected throughout its range and numbers are increasing. It is often seen in flocks of thousands and in harsh weather these gather in compact groups to conserve energy.

Eiders nest on small islets, often benefiting from the aggression of neighbouring terns that keep predators at bay. Eider eggs and chicks are taken by gulls, ravens and crows and occasionally foxes and polar bears. Eiders dive for molluscs or crabs and are happy in the roughest of seas.

CONDOR (*Vultur gryphus*)

SIZE:	Wingspan 3.7m
DISTRIBUTION:	Andes mountains of South America. Up to 5,500m
IDENTIFICATION:	Black plumage, white on upper wings and thick white ruff round neck. Male has fleshy comb on forehead and pale-red face

According to the Embera Indians of Colombia's Choco forest this is how mankind multiplied: for some time the first men, called *Jiti*, had seen condors 'from the land above', with bodies like women, come to a river, take off their condor's clothing and bathe, before getting dressed and flying away. One day the *Jiti* stole the clothing of one of the condors so she couldn't return home. This bird stayed on earth and bore many children with the *Jiti*, eventually populating the world. That is how important this 'messenger of the sun' – one of the largest flying birds – is to the people of the Andes. Nevertheless, it is shot and poisoned as a pest (it takes newborn livestock as well as sick animals and carrion) and its numbers are in serious decline.

OSPREY *(Pandion haliaetus)*

SIZE:	Wingspan 145–170cm
DISTRIBUTION:	Worldwide except Antarctica
IDENTIFICATION:	Dark-brown above with white underparts, slightly speckled breast, crested head with dark eye streak. Large wingspan. Long, hooked talons

Anglers occasionally catch a very large fish, usually a pike, which has several lines gouged into its back. These are most probably marks left by the sharp talons of an osprey which found the fish too big to haul from the water. The osprey feeds only on live fish and catches them by swooping from 20–30m high and plunging its legs – and sometimes its whole body – deep into the water. It has spiny projections on its feet which help it hold its prey. In flight it holds the fish head first, with one leg in front of the other, to reduce drag. But if the fish is too large there is a danger it could drag the bird under and drown it – so it lets it go for another type of fisher to catch.

Where fish are scarce an osprey will eat small mammals, reptiles, amphibians and even insects.

BALD EAGLE AND GOLDEN EAGLE

Eagles hold a very special place in many cultures. They symbolize power and dominate the skies; their piercing, hooded gaze commands respect and their mighty hooked beak and talons strike terror.

The state of New York used a **bald eagle** (*Haliaeetus leucocephalus*) in its coat of arms in 1778 but it was not until 1782 that it was chosen to adorn the Great Seal of the United States. This choice was famously much against the desire of Benjamin Franklin who wrote: 'I wish that the bald eagle had not been chosen ..., he is a bird of bad moral character, he does not get his living honestly, ... he is a rank coward [and] by no means a proper emblem for the brave and honest of America.' Franklin wanted the turkey, but was out-voted.

Having plumped for the bald eagle the nation could have been more caring towards it. Settlers blamed it for killing livestock and it was shot indiscriminately. By 1967, when it was officially declared an endangered species, only 400 breeding pairs were left in the lower 48 states. The pesticide DDT was banned in 1972 and this, with other measures, led to a resurgence in numbers to the present 6,000 breeding pairs. The bald eagle is found only in North America.

The **golden eagle** (*Aquila chrysaetos*), which is more widespread throughout Eurasia, North America and Northern Africa, has also been shot and poisoned by landowners and farmers. Working in open countryside, the golden eagle has to be a canny hunter. It patrols at enormous height and, once it has spotted its prey, it flies off, gradually losing height. It then roars in at high speed, almost at ground level, to hit its unsuspecting victim. It can reach a speed of 300kph.

Bald and golden eagles are similar in size with wingspans up to 210cm and 250cm respectively and can be difficult to tell apart when young. The bald eagle does not develop its white head and tail until it is two or three years old but during that time it does not have 'booted' or feathered legs like the young golden eagle. They both eat rabbits, hares and other small mammals, birds up to the size of geese and cranes, and carrion.

olden eagle

Bald eagle

Steller's Sea Eagle

(*Haliaeetus pelagicus*)

Size:	Wingspan up to 2.3m. Weight up to 6–9kg. Female larger than male
Distribution:	Eastern Asia
Identification:	Large. Dark-brown to black plumage with white tail, shoulders, thighs, forehead and crown. Yellow, deep, strongly arched bill. Yellow eyes and legs

The Steller's sea eagles of eastern Russia are the largest of all eagles and rely heavily on the summer and autumn run of salmon in the coastal waters and rivers. The sea eagle spies for fish from an overhanging tree or ledge or patrols on its vast wings. When a salmon is spotted it dives like an osprey, snatching the prey from the water with its talons. It is protected by law and in Japan it has the status of National Treasure. Feeding groups of 700 birds have been reported and total numbers are stable at about 3,200 pairs, despite persecution by fur trappers. As its biggest threat is lack of food in winter, it has to eat whatever is available, including hare, ermine, sable and fox – sometimes taken from hunters' traps. In February many sea eagles feed on the cod that escape from the nets of commercial trawlers off Hokkaido.

White-tailed Sea Eagle ▲

(*Haliaeetus albicilla*)

Size:	Wingspan 180–240cm
Distribution:	Iceland, Greenland, northern Europe and Asia. Near sea coasts, valleys of large rivers and inland lakes
Identification:	Very large bird with enormous wingspan. Uniformly brown in colour but with lighter head and white tail feathers. Feathered legs with yellow talons. Fiercely hooked yellowish bill. Hooded, bright yellow eyes. Young uniformly dark in colour

The white-tailed sea eagle has been much persecuted over the years and numbers have been greatly reduced. The Faroese believed sea eagle claws cured jaundice and the Anglo-Saxons thought its bones possessed remarkable curative properties. Mostly, though, the bird was killed because it preyed upon other useful wildlife such as wildfowl and fish. It spends a great deal of time perching motionless in trees, only occasionally taking to the air to sweep across its huge kingdom. A breeding pair needs up to 250 square km to supply the 0.4–0.6kg of food each bird needs daily. A pair remain in their territory all year, except in areas where the winters are so harsh that they have to leave. The biggest concentration of population is in Norway where there are well over 350 pairs.

Harpy Eagle (*Harpia harpyja*)

Size:	Wingspan 2.2m. Weight 7–9kg (female), 5–8kg (male)
Distribution:	Lowland forests of Central and South America
Identification:	Black chest and white underside. Plume of grey feathers on greyish head. Very long talons

Other eagles might have bigger wingspans but none has the armoury of the harpy eagle's fearsome talons – up to 18cm long in some fully-grown females. The harpy uses these to grasp its prey of large, tree-dwelling animals such as sloths, green iguanas and birds. It has been wiped out across much of its historical range – from southeast Mexico to northern Argentina and southern Brazil – through destruction of nesting sites (it nests a dizzying 40m high in trees), forest fragmentation and shooting. Recovery is hampered by the fact that it has the longest breeding period of any raptor: sometimes three years pass between the production of a chick and the next nesting attempt. Captive breeding and release programmes have had limited success although a handful of birds reintroduced in the Chiquibul Forest of Belize have prospered.

LAPPET-FACED VULTURE (*Torgos tracheliotus*)

SIZE:	Wingspan 3–3.6m. Length 114cm
DISTRIBUTION:	Throughout Africa (except extreme south), Arabia and Israel
IDENTIFICATION:	Very large with bare pink head and neck, powerful hooked beak and broad wings. Black and brown with white underbelly. Flaps of skin (lappets) on sides of head

These huge birds will attack live prey, although usually only small mammals. Other vultures often rely on the lappet-faced vulture to rip open a carcass. The lappet-faced lets nothing go to waste. It will eat all the parts other raptors cannot tackle, such as skin, ligaments and bones. Its naked head and neck are an adaptation that prevents infection by putrid carrion. Vultures are generally in decline in southern Africa due to shooting, poisoning and electrocution by high-voltage pylons. The steady elimination of hyaenas has also had a detrimental effect on vulture numbers as hyaenas crush carrion bones which vultures feed to their young, providing essential calcium.

Cape Griffon Vulture

(*Gyps coprotheres*)

Size:	Wingspan 2.7–3.4m. Length 110cm. Weight 9kg
Distribution:	Southern Africa, isolated pockets
Identification:	Pale-buff above, cream to light-tan below. White down surrounding brown crop. Head and neck covered with sparse white down with buff-grey ruff. Bluish-grey skin on face

One day in 1996 a Namibian farmer killed more than 200 of these endangered birds through careless use of poison. His was a dreadful mistake but other farmers, believing vultures transmit disease to cattle by sharing drinking water, poison Cape griffons on purpose and numbers have been reduced to just a few thousand. The Cape griffon is the second largest of African vultures. It lives in the highland crags and descends to the grassland to feed on carrion. Like the lapped-faced vulture, it has been hit by a decline in the number of hyaena which, by breaking up carcasses and leaving bone fragments, supply the birds and their chicks with their calcium needs.

African witch doctors traditionally wear vulture skins (a practice outlawed in South Africa) and use their body parts for *muti* or medicine. Eating vulture brains is supposed to confer clairvoyance and a dried Cape griffon foot is thought to bring gamblers luck.

Swainson's Hawk

(Buteo swainsoni)

Size:	Wingspan 120–145cm. Length 48–56cm. Weight 0.8–1.1kg (female heavier)
Distribution:	Western US and southwest Canada. Overwinters in Argentina
Identification:	Dark-brown with white patches on head, throat and belly, or entirely dark-brown with small white patch under tail

Most hawks are seen either on their own or in twos and threes but Swainson's hawk gathers in flocks of 100 or more to make its 8,000km migration to Argentina. Unfortunately, uncontrolled use of pesticides by Argentinian farmers has killed more than 20,000 of these versatile and opportunistic predators. During the breeding season it eats mostly birds and small mammals, but during migration more than 90 per cent of its diet is made up of insects like grasshoppers and crickets. It is an important controller of vermin and pests and often follows the plough. Breeding pairs return each year to a previous nest site in a tree or shrub, on the ground or at the top of a utility pole.

GYRFALCON (*Falco rusticolis*)

SIZE:	Wingspan 120–130cm
DISTRIBUTION:	Circumpolar nesting in Arctic regions of North America, Europe, Asia, Greenland, and Iceland
IDENTIFICATION:	Polymorphic: dark type almost black; white type usually almost pure white with some markings; grey type typically two tones of greyon the body, most easily seen on flight feathers

The common name for the gyrfalcon probably comes from the old High German *giri*, meaning greedy, and *valke*, meaning falcon. The tundra and taiga are not the ideal habitat for a greedy animal, as food is hard to come by. The gyrfalcon tackles prey as large as ptarmigan (its staple food) and grouse, as well as hares and waterfowl. It also eats ground squirrels and lemmings.

Gyrfalcons are admired for their raw power, and are highly valued for falconry. In the Middle Ages, only a king could hunt with a gyrfalcon and it was a favourite hunting bird of the Mongol leader Genghis Khan. It is the official bird of Iceland.

SECRETARY BIRD *(Sagittarius serpentarius)*

SIZE:	Wingspan 2.1m. Body length 150cm. Height 1m
DISTRIBUTION:	Sub-Saharan Africa
IDENTIFICATION:	Dove-grey above with black on wings, thighs and long central tail feathers. White beneath tail and at top of thighs. Long legs covered in black feathers halfway down. Distinctive black crest

The secretary bird, although a raptor, has virtually given up flying and become a proficient ground-based predator. It uses its long legs to stamp its victims to death and is best known for killing snakes. It also eats insects, rats, amphibians, tortoises and lizards, plodding up to 32km a day as it hunts.

The secretary bird is such an efficient pest killer that it is kept in captivity for just such a task. If alarmed it relies on its running speed to escape and only flies if extremely hard-pressed. Secretary birds mate for life and usually stay in the same nest, adding to it year by year to create huge bundles of sticks commonly seen in acacia trees.

The bird probably got its common name because of its crest feathers, which are thought to resemble the quill pens habitually carried in the wigs of nineteenth-century British legal secretaries.

Blue Grouse

(*Dendragapus obscurus*)

Size:	Wingspan 71cm. Length 43–53cm. Weight 1–1.4kg
Distribution:	Western North America from southern Alaska down to New Mexico
Identification:	Male dark brown with mottled upper parts, yellow-orange comb over eyes, yellow neck sac surrounded with white. Female brown, mottled underparts

The blue grouse is widespread in the forests of the Sierra Nevada and Rocky Mountains. It has many local names including sooty grouse, mountain grouse, dusky grouse, dusky blue grouse, grey grouse, pine grouse and fool hen. The males courtship display involves puffing up his brightly-coloured throat sac, emitting a series of loud, hooting 'harrumphs', and charging up and down in front of the female with his head down and tail fanned out.

The blue grouse winters in coniferous forests, feeding on pine needles, and spends summer in deciduous forests eating seeds, fruit, buds, insects, berries and leaves.

WILD TURKEY (*Meleagris gallopavo*)

SIZE:	Length up to 86cm, weight varies according to season and food availability but can be several kg
DISTRIBUTION:	Widespread throughout North America in a variety of woodland habitats
IDENTIFICATION:	Very large. Small bluish head, unfeathered, reddish throat. Iridescent bronze and green rounded wings. Barred primary feathers. Dark, fan-shaped tail with brown or buff band at tip. Adult male more iridescent, larger head with wattle at throat, caruncled forehead and projection behind bill

Turkey hunting generates millions of dollars for national and local government, and public and private groups are introducing the already widespread bird to new areas. Hunters work to preserve habitat and are among the keenest conservationists. Consequently, the turkey has been introduced to almost every state outside its original range.

There are six subspecies distinguished by colour, size, and distribution: eastern, Florida, Gould's, Merriam's, Rio Grande and Mexican. Turkeys eat fruit, seeds, tubers, bulbs, and greenery of common plants. They also eat small creatures such as snails, spiders, grasshoppers, millipedes and salamanders. In turn they are the prey of a wide variety of animals. Turkeys have suffered from urbanization, intense farming and conversion of native forest to pine plantations. They are also susceptible to the same sort of poultry diseases that affect domestic birds.

Greater Prairie Chicken

(*Tympanuchus cupido*)

Size:	Length 42–46cm. Weight 700–900g
Distribution:	South Dakota, Nebraska, Kansas; isolated pockets in Oklahoma, Wisconsin, Missouri, Minnesota
Identification:	Strongly barred black, tan and white. Legs feathered to toes. Long tuft of feathers on side of neck. Orange air sacs and eyebrows in breeding male

Plains Indians dance round the campfire to a thumping drum rhythm. Crouching low in their feathered costumes, their pounding feet stamp clouds of dust from the vibrating soil. This is a love dance and the steps, the booming song, the fiery intensity are all drawn directly from the spectacular but increasingly rare breeding display of the male prairie chicken. The prairie chicken once ranged over millions of square km in North America. Like the buffalo, it was hunted in huge numbers then driven from its habitat by agriculture. Most threatened of all is the Attwater's sub-species (*T. c. attwateri*), which is down to about 50 birds in two Texas refuges: the loss of just one or two birds to predators, disease or starvation could bring extinction.

Common Pheasant (Ring-necked Pheasant)

(Phasianus colchicus)

Size:	Wingspan, male 75–90cm, female 48–72cm. Weight up to 1.7kg
Distribution:	Originally Black Sea area. Introduced widely in Europe, North America, Africa, New Zealand, and elsewhere
Identification:	Male distinctive with flecked russet plumage, red face, dark-green head, white collar and long, pointed tail. Female mottled-buff

When we see our roads littered with the corpses of pheasants, it is hard to believe that the indigenous populations of these birds are in danger of extinction in some parts of the world. Non-indigenous species, introduced to satisfy sportsmen, and the use of pesticides, are threatening these birds in the wild.

Pheasants are mostly ground feeders, scratching in the earth for their food, like chickens, although they will jump to reach berries and occasionally feed in trees. They sometimes form breeding pairs although one male is likely to mate with several females. Eggs are often laid in other birds' nests.

Willow Ptarmigan *(Lagopus lagopus)*

Size:	Weight 0.45–0.8kg
Range:	All lands ringing North Pole: Alaska, Canada, Scandinavia, Finland, Russia. **Rock ptarmigan** (*Lagopus mutus*) also Scotland and northern Eurasia. **White-tailed ptarmigan** (*Lagopus leucurus*) exclusive to North America as far south as New Mexico
Identification:	Chunky body, short tail and legs, short, rounded wings. Feathered feet. Inflatable red comb above eyes. In winter, all ptarmigan, both sexes, basically white.

Ptarmigan chicks must be able to move with the migrant flocks as they wander the snowy wastes and mountains seeking food. They can fly expertly within eight weeks. The survival rate of young and the availability of food might be factors in the ptarmigan's well-known population fluctuations, swinging from superabundance to virtual absence and back again in the space of a few years.

Ptarmigan have three seasonal plumages that keep the birds well camouflaged all year. Their feathered feet improve their ability to walk in snow but make them easy prey to hunters. In Alaska they are an important winter food source and are deeply woven into the folklore.

PEAFOWL (*Pavo cristatus*)

SIZE:	Length, body, 76–135cm (tail of male up to 153cm). Weight up to 5.9kg
DISTRIBUTION:	Pakistan, India, Sri Lanka. Introduced worldwide
IDENTIFICATION:	Male extremely colourful with long, ornate, iridescent tail, royal-blue neck and breast. Female mostly brownish-grey with white throat, greenish neck and breast and pale underside

We are so used to seeing only the extravagant male of this national bird of India that we habitually refer to the species as the peacock. The poor, drab female is a peahen and the offspring a peachick. Peafowl strut on the lawns of parks and large gardens throughout the world but, as in the wild, prefer to spend the night perched high in trees. In its native lands it is very wary, being both conspicuous and a food source, and scuttles into the undergrowth at the slightest sign of danger.

The male's splendid tail is fully formed by the time he is 3 years old. It continues growing for a further 2–3 years but is lost through moulting every summer. Throughout the history of most of the world's major civilizations, peacocks have been valued for their plumage and presented in offerings along with gold, silver and precious stones.

SIBERIAN CRANE

(*Grus leucogeranus*)

SIZE:	Wingspan 195cm, height 150cm
DISTRIBUTION:	Eastern flock summers in northeastern Russia, winters in eastern China. Western and central flocks summer in western Russia, winter in India
IDENTIFICATION:	A large, elegant, long-legged bird, all white above and below with black wing tips. Vivid red 'face mask', yellow eyes and very long, greyish bill

There are only about 3,000 Siberian cranes left, making them arguably the most seriously endangered crane species. The western and central flocks number just 10–20. An internationally co-ordinated recovery effort persuades captive cranes to breed, by artificially replicating 24-hour Siberian summer daylight, fostering spare eggs with other cranes, and training juvenile chicks to fly along their migration paths by following hang gliders.

Videos have been distributed to people living along crane migration routes, asking them not to hunt the cranes or damage their habitats. Cranes are also threatened by the massive hydroelectric scheme on the Yangtze River, which affects water levels in their wintering area.

TAKAHE (*Porphyrio mantelli*)

SIZE:	Height 50cm. Weight 3kg
DISTRIBUTION:	New Zealand
IDENTIFICATION:	Hefty, rounded body with green, turquoise and blue plumage. Huge, stout scarlet bill extending above eyes. Short, flightless wings

If you pull a stem of tussock grass out of its clump and chew on the soft, whitish base it tastes slightly sweet. It is these comparatively sugary portions which are eaten – all day long – by the takahe, a large, flightless water rail found only in the wild, unspoilt Fiordland area of South Island in New Zealand. The takahe leaves a trail of nibbled stems as it feeds and it was just such a trail that led to the discovery in 1948 of 400 takahe in the Murchison Mountains, after years of assumed extinction. Even so, numbers fell further with the spread of introduced red deer which grazed out the tussock grass. The remaining 190 birds are now protected and breeding programmes are increasing numbers on several offshore island sanctuaries. Recovery is slow, however, because 80 per cent of eggs are sterile, probably as a result of genetic non-diversity.

KNOT (RED KNOT) *(Calidris canutus)*

SIZE:	Length 25cm
DISTRIBUTION:	Breeds in the Arctic. Winters further south, all over the world, including north and south America, west Africa, Great Britain, Australia
IDENTIFICATION:	Medium-sized wader, thick bill. Plumage drab in winter. Rusty red underparts in breeding season

It is said that King Canute, who ruled England in the 11th century, was fond of this bird. Some people have thought that the knot resembles him – standing at the edge of the sea, as the king is supposed to have done to prove to his courtiers that he did not have the power to turn the sea back. Canute is certainly remembered in the bird's scientific name: *canutus*. It is likely that the bird got its English name from its low-pitched call of '*knut*'.

The knot is a long-distance migrant, from the Arctic tundra where it breeds to places as far south as Tierra del Fuego, at the tip of South America. It likes marshy flats and estuaries, where it can probe the mud or sand to find crustaceans, molluscs, worms and insects. Knots are sometimes seen flying in large flocks, as if one creature, flashing white then black as they twist and turn – a wonderful sight.

TURNSTONE *(Arenaria interpres)*

SIZE:	Length 23cm
DISTRIBUTION:	Breeds in Arctic fringes. Winters further south, in coastal areas from western Europe to Africa, India, southeast Asia and Australia
IDENTIFICATION:	Ruddy tortoiseshell upper parts in breeding season, duller in winter; white belly; orange legs; short black bill

The turnstone gets its name from the way it finds the sand-hoppers and other small creatures that it eats: probing along the shoreline, turning over stones, seaweed and shells with its bill to find the goodies underneath. In its breeding plumage, with chestnut-coloured back and wings, distinctive black bands and white patches on the head, the turnstone is a very handsome bird. In the winter the colours fade and the head turns brown. Then it is most easily spotted when it takes off, showing its harlequin black-and-white wing pattern and giving its twittering call. The turnstone is a long-distance traveller. It migrates from its Arctic breeding grounds to spend the winter as far south as Tierra del Fuego, at the tip of South America and can be found turning its stones along coastlines all over the world.

BUFF-BREASTED SANDPIPER
(Tryngites subruficollis)

SIZE:	Wingspan 45cm
DISTRIBUTION:	Breeds in northern Alaska and northwest Canadian Arctic. Winters in South America.
IDENTIFICATION:	Mottled light-brown upper parts, paler buff underparts, white underwings.

Unlike many male birds, the male buff-breasted sandpiper is fairly drab. So he makes use of his only impressive feature – his armpits – to attract a mate. He waits in his lek, or courtship area, until some females pass by. Then he lifts a wing and flashes the white feathers beneath. If a female is taken by this she will stop and wait for another performance. If he gets very excited he will flash both underwings at once, perhaps attracting a small crowd of females from which he will take his pick.

In some areas the buff-breasted sandpiper is now uncommon because of decades of hunting. It prefers raised and grassy terrain, sometimes by streams, and nests in a shallow cavity in dry, mossy or grassy tundra, eating insects and weed seeds.

SNOWY SHEATHBILL (*Chionis alba*)

SIZE:	Wingspan 75–78cm, length 40–42cm
RANGE:	Antarctic Peninsula and the islands of the Scotia Arc, through the South Orkneys and South Georgia
IDENTIFICATION:	All white plumage, 'naked' pinkish face with stout bill embedded in pink, fleshy sheath. Black legs and feet. Wings short for size of body

The snowy sheathbill is not a very likeable bird. It will eat anything and survives quite happily on penguin droppings. It steals penguin eggs and sneaks off with their hard-won food. It devours the weakest young seals and enjoys nibbling a nice rotting carcass. And when it gets together to socialize with other sheathbills it spends most of its time fighting. Antarctica's only permanently land-based bird, the snowy sheathbill, also known as a paddy, will sometimes make long flights, even over sea, but is usually found on the ground. Sheathbills from the extreme south of the range migrate north in winter, but those on sub-antarctic islands usually stay there.

IVORY GULL (*Pagophila eburnea*)

SIZE:	Wingspan 100cm
RANGE:	Across Canada, Greenland, and Arctic Western Europe
IDENTIFICATION:	The only gulls with completely white feathers. Distinguished from other white-winged gulls by black feet and bill. Young birds have black faces and chins with black spots on their wings and tail

For most of the year, these beautiful, angel-like gulls are found along the borders of the pack ice. They wait until the receding ice allows them access to food in the summer before moving on to land to breed. They must then wait until the ground is sufficiently thawed to build a nest. The gulls are extremely susceptible to disturbance during breeding and will leave the nest if alarmed by a low-flying plane, for instance. They are also a favourite meal for polar bears and Arctic foxes; predators have been known to wipe out all the colony's young in a single visit. Fortunately, ivory gulls choose some of the most inaccessible and remote sites to breed.

Arctic Tern

(*Sterna paradisaea*)

Size:	Wingspan 34cm
Range:	Antarctic in southern summer, northern Atlantic and Arctic regions in northern summer
Identification:	White below, grey-white above with black forehead and cap, all-red bill, short, red legs, forked tail

Arctic terns are the ultimate sunseekers, getting more exposure to its warming rays than any other creature. To achieve this, of course, they have to travel a long way. Each August they leave their northern quarters and head south. Those from Arctic Canada and Greenland meet the groups from Arctic Russia in western Europe and travel down the African coast to the Cape of Good Hope. Some re-cross the Atlantic to join another group from northern Canada at Cape Horn. Then they all fly across the Southern Ocean to Antarctica to enjoy their second summer of the year with 24-hour daylight. Terns can be extremely aggressive at nesting time, 'dive-bombing' intruders and screaming raucously. Anyone coming a little bit too near will be punctured by their sharp red beaks. Other birds like to nest near them to benefit from their protection.

Sooty Tern (*Sterna fuscata*)

Size:	Length 41–45cm
Distribution:	Tropical and subtropical regions. Coastal and oceanic islands during breeding season; open ocean at other times
Identification:	Black above with white forehead; white below. Long, narrow wings and deeply-forked tail; thin black bill

In the breeding season, sooty terns gather in huge numbers on tropical islands in their best black-and-white plumage and make a lot of noise. Their harsh, high-pitched call is said to sound as if they are saying 'wide-awake', which is what you will be if you are anywhere near them. It also gives them one of their common names.

The rest of the sooty tern's life is spent wandering the warmer oceans of the world. It feeds mainly on fish, which it swoops down on and plucks from near the surface of the sea. Sometimes it will follow shoals of migrating tuna, snatching the small fish that the tuna drive to the surface. It travels far and wide across the open oceans, and is sometimes found many hundreds of miles from its normal range, blown by the hurricanes and tropical storms that rage there.

ATLANTIC PUFFIN *(Fratercula arctica)*

SIZE:	Wingspan 30cm
RANGE:	Greenland and Northern Canada, Gulf of St Lawrence, Nova Scotia, Iceland, Northern Scandinavia, Northern Russia, Ireland, and northwest coast of France
IDENTIFICATION:	Distinctive. Huge, multicoloured bill, stocky build, white face with black forehead, cap and nape. Black back and white underparts. Orange, webbed feet on short legs

The puffin, a consummate swimmer and diver, is uncomfortable on land and is so vulnerable to predators that it does the only thing possible to get away from them: it goes underground. Puffins dig burrows up to 1m long in soft cliffs on headlands and islands. Sometimes they requisition old rabbit burrows. Here they lay their eggs and the chick spends its first seven weeks below ground being fed on the sand eels or other small fish that its parents carry, up to 30 at a time, in their huge, colourful bills. The parents then abandon the chick and, after a few days, it creeps by night to the sea.

The islanders on St Kilda off the west coast of Scotland used to hunt the puffin, among other seabirds, and make a nourishing dish of whole puffin cooked in porridge oats.

ECLECTUS PARROT (*Eclectus roratus*)

SIZE:	Length 35cm. Wingspan up to 71cm. Weight up to 454g
DISTRIBUTION:	Lesser Sunda, Solomon and Molluccan Islands, New Guinea, northeast Australia
IDENTIFICATION:	Male: glossy-green plumage with red flashes on sides and underwings. Female: red head, throat and wings, brilliant-blue chest, purple underwings

It is not surprising that this strikingly beautiful bird is a big favourite with aviarists. Indeed it is thought to have been introduced to many Pacific Islands by people who kept it as a pet. It is noisy and sociable, gathering in flocks of up to 80, and when not flitting between trees or flying above the forest canopy, it scrambles through the branches using its bill and feet to hold on. It eats fruit, nuts, nectar and leaf buds and while feeding gives a mellow, flute-like call or a wailing cry. Its flight call is a harsh screech. The sexes are so different in colouring that they were once thought to be separate species. The chicks are different again, hatching with a covering of short, thick bristles, replaced by fluffy, grey down after a few days. Another reason why the parrot is a popular cage bird is its long lifespan of 40–50 years – frequently outliving its keeper.

Scarlet Macaw

(*Ara macao*)

Size:	Length, body, 50cm (tail 30-40cm)
Distribution:	Mexico, Central and South America
Identification:	Scarlet on head and shoulders, yellow on back and mid-wing, blue on wing tips and tail. White around yellow eyes. Bill light above, dark below. Black legs

The brightly-coloured macaw eats fruit, nuts – and clay. It needs the clay to aid digestion and absorb toxins from many of the seeds it eats. The virulent poison strychnine, from liana seeds, is one of many found in jungle plants and the macaw specializes in eating toxic seeds which would sicken or kill other animals. It also eats unripe fruit which contains high levels of tannin. Just as humans turn to kaolin (or china clay) to settle an upset stomach, so the macaw uses the clay it finds on river banks and flocks can be seen gobbling down mouthfuls after a feeding session. The macaw, like most parrots, is left-footed, using the right foot to support itself as it manipulates its food with the left. Although protected, it is a target for illegal traders who sell either the feathers or the live bird, worth $1,000 to an unscrupulous collector.

EURASIAN CUCKOO (*Cuculus canorus*)

SIZE:	Wingspan 58cm
DISTRIBUTION:	Common throughout Europe, north coast of Africa, Asia, Iran, Himalayas and southern China. Western populations overwinter in Africa. East Asiatic birds migrate to the Philippines
IDENTIFICATION:	Generally grey with underparts lighter and heavily barred. Long tail with rounded end and white patches. Small head with thin bill. Legs yellow

It is hard to believe that adult reed warblers are unaware that the monster bird they are feeding is not their own. Perhaps they resign themselves to filling the gaping maw of the cuckoo chick in the absence of anything else to do, the imposter having ejected their own brood from the nest. A cuckoo lays up to 12 eggs in different nests and some resemble the eggs of the host bird.

Cuckoos are found in all continents except Antarctica. There are 136 different species and 45 of these lay their eggs in the nests of other birds. The cuckoo is declining, probably due to loss of habitat and food, as well as colder, wetter springs and summers.

HOATZIN (*Opisthocomus hoazin*)

SIZE:	Length 61–66cm. Weight 816g
DISTRIBUTION:	South America
IDENTIFICATION:	Bronze-brown back, wings and tail feathers with dull yellow streaks, mottling and tail tips. Dull-yellow chin, breast and underside. Bright red eye. Long, spiky yellow crest

The peculiar swamp-dwelling hoatzin looks like a survivor from prehistory and does indeed have a strong link with the fossil archaeopteryx. Like the ancient bird-like creature, young hoatzins have strong wing claws which they use to haul themselves about in the trees before they can fly. But the hoatzin is odd in other ways: it digests fibre, produces cow-like dung and defies classification. It eats the leaves of the moka-moka, stuffing its massive crop and then perching with its distended pouch resting between its feet. The leaves ferment as the muscular crop pummels them into a fatty, foul-smelling soup from which all the goodness is extracted. The excreted remains give the hoatzin its nickname – stinkbird. Classified over the years with both fowl-like birds (*Galliformes*) and cuckoos, the hoatzin has been placed by recent genetic research with the turacos (*Musophagiformes*) of sub-Saharan Africa.

ROAD RUNNER (*Geococcyx californianus*)

SIZE:	Height 25.5–30.5cm. Length 51–61cm. Wingspan 43–56cm. Weight 227–680g
DISTRIBUTION:	Nevada, Utah, New Mexico, Arizona and Colorado
IDENTIFICATION:	Black and white with mottling, long white-tipped tail, ruffled crest. Bluish patch of skin circling eyes. Long, stout, bluish legs with strong feet

This lightning-fast ground cuckoo is a master hunter. It is quick enough to catch a hummingbird or dragonfly in flight and is one of the few animals that can out-manoeuvre a rattlesnake. It dances around the rattler using its wing like a matador's cape then snatches the snake's tail, cracks the reptile like a whip and slams its head on the ground until it is dead. It swallows the snake whole and will go about with the tail protruding from its large bill, digesting its meal slowly over several hours. It also catches scorpions, lizards, rodents and other birds. The road runner can run at up to 30kph but takes short flights when it needs to escape danger or when travelling downhill.

wny owl

Owls

Owls have been around for at least 60 million years and their relationships with humans have been mixed. Some cultures see them as good omens, some as bad; some as kindly and wise, some as evil. In India and the north of England, owl broth was thought to cure a variety of ailments, and in Algeria it was believed that putting the right eye of an eagle owl into the hand of a sleeping woman would result in her telling you all you ever wanted to know. To the Greeks the sight of an owl on the battlefield spelt victory; to the Romans defeat. English folklore alleged that a child given an owl's egg to drink would be forever protected against alcoholism. And the custom of nailing an owl to a barn door to ward off evil persisted well into the nineteenth century. Many cultures believe owls to be the souls of the newly-dead, which isn't surprising, given that their stealthy, ghostlike night-time travels are utterly silent due to the peculiar design and arrangement of their wing feathers.

The call of the **tawny owl** (*Strix aluco*) rivals that of the cuckoo as the best known bird song. The famed *to-whit-to-woo* is actually three short *hoos* followed by a long one, and is heard throughout Europe, North Africa, Iran, Siberia, northwest India, the Himalayas, southern China, Korea, and Taiwan. The tawny owl is distinguished by its large size (females up to 45cm long, weighing 0.8kg with a 100cm wingspan), and its dark face and eyes.

The concept of the wise owl probably has its origins in the association of the **little owl** (*Athene noctua*) with the Greek goddess of wisdom, Athene. This small bird (just 20cm long) is found right across Eurasia and into North Africa. It can sometimes be seen during the day perching on a tree stump or fence post with its distinctive 'frown' framing yellow eyes. Like other owls it preys on mice and insects but, unusually, will also eat vegetation.

The **barn owl** (*Tyto alba*) is one of the most widespread land birds, found on all continents except Antarctica. It nests in tree hollows, old buildings and caves and breeds at any time of year, sometimes twice if there is a glut of small rodents, its main prey. The female is slightly larger than the male, with a wingspan of up to 109cm and weighing 0.5kg. The barn owl is generally light grey with buff markings but has a distinctive white, heart-shaped facial disc with a brown rim line. It is the most mythologized of all owls and usually seen as a harbinger of death.

A medium-sized owl with a very flat face and deep, moth-like wing beats is sure to be a **short-eared owl** (*Asio flammeus*). It will sometimes roost in dense clumps of conifers but prefers open spaces where it can patrol the meadows or prairies, looking for voles. It is widespread across Eurasia, North America, and South America and is highly nomadic, migrating up to 1980km and crossing high mountain passes. Its long wings are pale below and dark with strong barring above, and it has distinctive 'wrists' on both upper and lower surfaces. The Inuit believe a young girl was turned into the short-eared owl and originally had a long bill but, frightened, flew into a building and flattened her face.

Weighing up to 4kg with a wingspan of 109cm the **eagle owl** (*Bubo bubo*) has no natural enemies. It is a fearsomely efficient predator, taking victims as large as foxes and young roe deer. Its most common meals are voles and rats but it also kills hares, ducks, grouse, crows, seabirds, and other birds of prey, including owls. Snakes, lizards, frogs, fish and crabs are also on its menu. With 14 or so subspecies, it is found across Eurasia, the Middle East and into North Africa. Its main danger of death from anything other than old age is the hazard of flying into power lines, aircraft or cars. In captivity it has been known to live for more than 60 years.

Barn owl

SNOWY OWL *(Nyctea scandiaca)*

SIZE:	Wingspan 135–150cm
DISTRIBUTION:	Circumpolar in Scandinavia, Russia, Alaska and Canada, north of the tree line but south of permanent snow and ice. Hugely mobile throughout range
IDENTIFICATION:	Unmistakable large, almost pure-white owl with golden-yellow eyes and heavily feathered feet. Females and juveniles have grey-brown banding on body and upper parts of wings, adult males have up to three tail bands

When lemmings have a bad year, so do snowy owls. The lemming population has a direct effect on how many owls reproduce and how many young they raise. Nestling owls need about two lemmings a day and a family of owls might eat as many as 1,500 lemmings before the young disperse. In peak years an older, highly aggressive male might establish two nests with two different mates, hunting for both, and protecting two territories. In bad feeding years the owls move south, with sightings as close to the equator as southern Texas and the Azores.

These day-flying owls will, however, take a large variety of prey, from voles to birds the size of geese. They will also prey on other raptors such as short-eared owl, peregrine, gyrfalcon, and buzzard, and when desperate will eat fish and carrion. When food is very scarce, snowy owls can live off reserves of fat for almost six weeks. They rarely seek shelter, even from roaring winds, and their plumage protects them so efficiently that adults can endure temperatures as low as –40 °C (–40 °F).

The owl is protected throughout much of America and in the UK but in Alaska it is legal for residents to kill an unlimited number for food or clothing.

Other names for this charismatic bird are Arctic owl, ghost owl, tundra ghost, ookpik, Scandinavian nightbird, and white terror of the north. In Romania it is said that the souls of repentant sinners fly to heaven as snowy owls.

Burrowing Owl

(*Athene cunicularia*)

Size:	Length 22–28cm. Wingspan 50–60cm. Weight 170–210g
Distribution:	Throughout Americas except in Amazon rainforests and eastern North America
Identification:	Small owl with long legs, short tail and no ear tufts. Brown with white speckles, lighter breast and white surrounding face. Yellow eyes

Many Native American tribes thought the burrowing owl was a link with the spirit world. The Hopi called it *ko'ko*, meaning 'watcher of the dark' and thought it was a favourite of Masauu, god of the dead and guardian of fire and all growing things. The Gosuite tribe of Nevada and Utah thought it protected warriors and wore its feathers and shook rattles made of its skin to frighten the enemy.

This daytime-hunting owl nests and roosts, often in colonies, in the disused burrows of prairie dogs and ground squirrels but is becoming more scarce as its habitat is destroyed. Insecticides have also contributed to its decline. It catches a variety of prey including small insects, scorpions, reptiles, small mammals and birds and, unusually for a raptor, it will eat fruit and seeds.

Great Grey Owl

(*Strix nebulosa*)

Size:	Wingspan 127–167cm, length 62–80cm
Distribution:	Extensive across middle of Northern hemisphere, from Scandinavia across to Asia and throughout Canada and northern USA, in forested areas, hunting mainly in clearings, and near meadows and bogs
Identification:	Very distinctive large, strongly lined, facial disc with bright yellow eyes. Large speckled-grey body. Heavy-looking but bulk made up of feathers as protection against cold

The great grey owl can pick up sounds completely inaudible to human beings – like the faint rustling of a vole nibbling a leaf 50m away beneath 50cm of snow. This makes it a formidable hunter, particularly through the long winter months when the Arctic forests are in partial or total darkness. It can also locate sounds accurately. The large ruffs on either side of its head and its asymmetric ears achieve perfect stereo and pinpoint detection.

Males and females defend nests aggressively and have been known to drive off predators as large as black bears. Among other threats, ravens and great horned owls prey on both eggs and nestlings.

Other names for this owl are spectral, spruce, bearded, or sooty owl, the great grey ghost, and phantom of the north.

Common Swift (*Apus apus*) ▲

Size:	Wingspan 44cm
Distribution:	Widespread throughout western Palaearctic, east to 120°E, south as far as Iran and the northwest Himalayas
Identification:	Distinctive sickle-shaped wings, generally black plumage, grey throat, short, forked tail

From a nest tucked away in a barn roof somewhere in Europe, a young swift tumbles out to make its first flight on an August day. It is off to spend the winter in tropical Africa. Its tiny feet will probably not touch down again until it returns to nest the following year. A swift spends almost its entire life in the air, feeding, drinking, sleeping, and even mating on the wing. Its feet are no more than clusters of four needle-thin claws and if it lands on the ground it has enormous difficulty moving about or taking off. A swift has been recorded living for 18 years during which time it is estimated to have flown 6.4 million km – to the moon and back eight times. Most swifts build nests by cementing together with spittle feathers and dried grass found floating in the air – but some cave-nesting swiftlets of Borneo use nothing but spittle. It is these creamy white nests that are used in birds' nest soup.

Whippoorwill (*Caprimulgus vociferus*)

Size:	Length, including tail, 23cm
Distribution:	Breeds from Manitoba east through southern Canada and south to Arizona, Texas, Arkansas, and South Carolina. Winters from southern USA to Costa Rica
Identification:	Upper parts heavily mottled with grey, black, and brown. Underparts pale with grey and black mottling. Black throat, wide mouth fringed with bristles, very short bill. Medium length tail. Song sounds like *whip-poor-will*

No bird marks the fall of night quite so persistently and clearly as this otherwise secretive little nightjar. Song is essential to the whippoorwill, which depends almost entirely on voice to locate mates and rivals. Its song is easily recognized, travels clearly over vast spaces, and is extremely repetitive. Little wonder that its scientific name is *vociferus*, meaning 'noisy'. It feeds exclusively on insects, mostly moths, which it catches on the wing, scooping them into its wide mouth. Its reproductive cycle is synchronized with the lunar cycle so young hatch out when the moon is full, allowing the adults more light by which to forage for insects.

Hummingbirds

There are 340 species of hummingbird, all found in the Americas, many of which inhabit the rainforest where they feed on the nectar of the profuse tropical flowers. These usually small (about 7cm) and, in the males at least, brightly-coloured birds are well known for hovering as they feed, with wings flapping at about 80 beats per second to produce the 'hum'. They can fly backwards, have ultra-violet vision, high metabolic rates, nocturnal hibernation and relatively large brains. Recent research on three Brazilian species, the **rufuous-breasted hermit** (*Glaucis hirsuta*), **sombre** (*Aphantochroa cirrochloris*), and **white-throated** (*Leuchocloris abicolis*) hummingbirds, has shown they have another unusual trait: vocal learning, or the ability to acquire songs through imitation rather than instinct. Humans can do this, of course, and so can birds such as the lark, starling and mynah but it now seems that the hummingbird is a member of this select club.

The **bee hummingbird** (*Mellisuga helenae*) is, at just 2.2g, the smallest bird in the world.

Rufuous-breasted hermi

Resplendent Quetzal

(*Pharomachrus mocinno*)

Size:	Length, body, 35cm (male tail feathers up to 90cm)
Distribution:	Guatemala, Nicaragua, Costa Rica, Mexico, Honduras and Panama
Identification:	Male has long, iridescent tail plumes. Generally metallic-green with bright crimson breast and underside and golden-green crest. Female similar but more muted

In ancient Mayan times killing a quetzal was punishable by death and the bird's feathers were so valuable they were used as currency. The Spanish conquistadors, however, killed this exquisitely beautiful bird in its thousands until doing so was outlawed in 1895. Now greatly reduced in numbers, Guatemala's national bird is again a source of wealth – through eco-tourism. In Costa Rica about a million people a year visit the 28 national parks specifically to see a quetzal, paying a total of $21 million for the privilege. This makes the 1,000 or so quetzals left in Costa Rica worth about $21,000 each. In Guatemala the bird's cloud forest habitat is being cleared by peasants claiming their traditional *milpas* plots to raise maize. Ecologists estimate that this, together with killing for feathers bought by collectors, will doom the avocado-eating quetzal to extinction within a few years.

Common Kingfisher *(Alcedo atthis)*

Size:	Length 17–19cm. Beak 4cm
Distribution:	Europe (except far north), north Africa and Asia
Identification:	Brightly coloured. Mostly iridescent greenish-blue plumage with orange underparts and white bib. Orange in front and behind eyes. White on sides of head

The kingfisher has extremely keen eyesight with built-in polarizing filters to eliminate water surface glare. From its perch beside a river it can easily spot a minnow, gudgeon, stickleback or similar small fish as it passes across the stones on the bottom. But when the bird dives into the water, arrowing down with its long, sharp bill, it can no longer see what it is doing and has to rely on memory to catch its prey, which is why it occasionally misses its target and emerges with a pebble in its bill. If it catches a fish it takes it back to its perch, beats it against the branch until it is dead and eats it head first.

Red-billed Hornbill ▲

(*Tockus erythrorhynchus*)

Size:	Length 51cm
Distribution:	Sub-Saharan Africa
Identification:	Thin red bill and pale head with dark-grey crown and nape, whiteneck and face, sooty-brown back with central white stripe, white underparts and black primary feathers and tail

No mother likes to be shut up in the house with the kids all day but the female red-billed hornbill fares worse than most. After mating she enters her nest – a hole in a tree – and is sealed in with mud by her partner. There she stays for three months. First she lays 3 to 5 eggs, then she incubates them and when the chicks are about 22 days old she breaks out of her prison (whereupon the youngsters immediately re-seal the gap with droppings and food scraps). Throughout this time the male brings food, mostly insects and larvae, for her and the chicks, poking it through a narrow hole. The hornbill gets most of its food on the ground and only takes to the air occasionally to snatch flying termites. It also eats geckos, birds' eggs, nestlings and dead rodents.

Greater or Black-throated Honeyguide (*Indicator indicator*)

Size:	Length 20cm
Distribution:	Sub-Saharan Africa
Identification:	Largest of the honeyguides. Drab plumage, short bill with raised rims round nostrils, long pointed wings, sturdy toes with long, hooked claws. Flashing white tail-patch

Thanks to this dull-looking little bird, Theodore Roosevelt had honey for breakfast while on safari in 1909–10. The US president wrote: 'Several times we followed the birds, which in each case led us to bee-trees, and then perched quietly by until the gun-bearers and porters got out the honey – which we found excellent eating.'

The honeyguide is said to lead ratels (honey badgers), baboons, mongooses and humans to bees' nests. The larger animal breaks in to get the honey and the bird (which is the only vertebrate that can digest wax) gets any leftover wax and larvae. However, the 15 honeyguide species of Asia do not display this behaviour and there are some researchers who doubt that the two African species do, claiming that the birds actually follow the honey-hunting animals, rather than vice versa.

Toco Toucan (*Ramphastos toco*)

Size:	Length 64cm. Bill 19cm long
Distribution:	Eastern South America: Guianas to northern Argentina
Identification:	Black plumage with white throat and rump. Huge, golden-orange, black-tipped bill. Orange around eye. Long, narrow, feather-like tongue. Stout, scaly legs. Long, square-ended tail

The bright colours, spectacular bill and perky appearance of the toco toucan catch the eye, making it a favourite icon for many advertising campaigns. However, in the forest it blends with its surroundings, its black and white body lost in the shadows and its gaudy bill easily mistaken for a flower or fruit. When sleeping it is even less conspicuous: turning its head to rest its bill along its back and folding its long tail up and over to cover the bill it becomes a mere bundle of feathers. The bill is a honeycomb construction which means that it is light and of no use as a weapon. It helps the bird reach for fruit at the tip of branches and is also used to chip into wood and probe about in mud as the toucan searches for insects to eat. It will sometimes also eat lizards, young birds and eggs. The toucan has a loud and insistent call and in some tribal traditions is associated with evil.

Acorn Woodpecker ►

(*Melanerpes formicivorus*)

Size:	Wingspan 38–40cm
Distribution:	Northwestern Oregon, California, the American Southwest, western Mexico, the Central American highlands and northern Andes of Colombia
Identification:	Black upper parts, creamy-white underparts, white patch on forehead with pale yellow collar and red skull-cap. Sharp black bill. White wing-patch in flight

A huge oak tree towers into the deep blue Californian sky. It has been dead for many years yet it is covered with thousands of acorns. How can this be? The answer lies with the acorn woodpecker. This industrious bird drills perfectly round little hidey-holes in the trunks of oak trees in which to stash its hoard of acorns. Where there isn't a suitable tree, a telephone pole is used. The birds spend all summer chiselling out the funnel-shaped holes and when the acorns are ripe, they are brought one at a time and tried out in several holes until a perfect fit is found – too tight and the shell gets damaged in the effort and the nut rots; too loose and it falls out. Even when a snug fit is found there is work to do later. As the acorns dry they shrink and have to be re-housed. With some stores numbering up to 50,000 nuts, the task is too much for a lone bird or even a pair and has to be carried out by a whole family group.

Northern Three-toed Woodpecker (*Picoides tridactylus*)

Size:	Length 19cm
Distribution:	Northern parts of North America and Eurasia
Identification:	Mostly black with white 'moustache', throat, breast, belly and flanks. White back barred with black. Wings have white dots on primary feathers, tail has white outer edge. Adult male has yellow cap

The northern three-toed woodpecker is one of the most important birds in the fight against woodland insects, particularly elm bark beetles which are the carriers of Dutch elm disease. Over the year some 65 per cent of its diet is made up of these beetles. It also eats ants, caterpillars, wood-boring larvae, nuts, fruits and shoots. It hacks its nest out of standing dead trees – usually a conifer or aspen – or in dead branches on live trees, usually 1.5–4m above the ground. It has been known to nest in utility poles but it prefers areas where fires have left large stands of dead trees.
The black-backed three-toed woodpecker occupies a similar range and has a plain black back.

WATER PIPIT (*Anthus spinoletta*) ▲

SIZE:	Length 17.5cm
DISTRIBUTION:	Breeds in mountains of southern Europe and southwest Asia. Winters near water throughout Europe
IDENTIFICATION:	In winter olive-brown above; underparts whitish, lightly-streaked; pale wing-bars. Thin black bar through eye. In summer chin, throat and sides of neck pinkish

In most bird species song repertoire and song rate or duration affect how successful the male is in finding a mate. With the water pipit, however, it is one particular element of his song, a strange rasping, grating noise known as a snarr, which is the key to success. Research has shown that males who include double the number of snarr phrases in their songs are four times more likely to mate and have offspring. More usual factors such as age, territory size, food gathering ability, paternal performance or appearance make no difference.

Pipits are ground-dwelling and nesting. Unusually, the young leave the nest before they can fly.

MELODIOUS LARK

(*Mirafra cheniana*)

SIZE:	Length 12–14cm
DISTRIBUTION:	South African highvelt, localized and fragmented populations
IDENTIFICATION:	Small brown bird with white outer tail feathers and marked upper parts. Distinguishing white throat, breast markings and buff belly and flanks. Rapid wingbeat in display flight and characteristic song

There is no songster in nature as versatile as the male melodious lark. During the breeding season he shows off a stunning range of imitative calls. He hovers between 25m and 50m, wings beating furiously, for up to 25 minutes and down float the songs of the plover, pipit, starling, waxbill, guinea fowl, swift, fulvous duck, greenshank, stonechat, mousebird – and many more. The melodious lark has been recorded imitating 57 identifiable species and can probably mimic many others. Its own call is a fairly unexciting trill. The males expend a huge amount of energy in this display flight and the females favour those with larger repertoires. The male is also responsible for feeding the chicks which, like the adults, eat seeds and insects such as ants and termites.

ROBIN *(Erithacus rubecula)*

SIZE:	Length 14cm
DISTRIBUTION:	Widespread throughout Europe though restricted to hills and mountains in some southern regions
IDENTIFICATION:	Brown back and crown, red face and breast, white underside. Melodious song of trills and warbles with *tic-tic-tic* alarm call

The American robin is a large thrush, while the British robin is a dainty little bird the size of a chickadee. Both are a boon to gardeners, admired for their boldness and their aid in consuming insect pests.

For millennia the British robin relied on large beasts like the wild pig to grub about in the woodland soil, turning up the worms and bugs it loves. Then along came man and, later, the garden fork. From then on there existed a happy relationship between horticulturalist and bird. Whenever you break the ground the bold little redbreast appears, ready to hop into the hole and recover a morsel. Some are so tame they will eat from the hand. In continental Europe, where small birds are hunted for food, it is understandably shy and retiring.

WREN (WINTER WREN)
(Troglodytes troglodytes)

SIZE:	Length 9cm
DISTRIBUTION:	Widespread across Eurasia and North America
IDENTIFICATION:	Tiny, mouse-like bird. Rich-brown, finely-barred plumage, fat body, spiky tail held cocked up. Smallest North American wren. Loud complex song

Often seen in gardens, the wren is also a woodland dweller, scurrying through ground cover or ivy-covered trees. Fairly solitary during the day, wrens will gather to roost at night, especially in cold weather, when extraordinary numbers will squeeze together in nesting boxes or holes in walls.

As if to compensate for its tiny size, the wren sings astonishingly loudly throughout the day and sometimes into the night. They are quarrelsome birds and can be seen tumbling and arguing in large groups. Despite their diminutive size, wrens will travel widely: one bird ringed in Sweden was found in southern Spain.

GOLDCREST (*Regulus regulus*)

Size:	Weight 4.5–7g, wingspan 13.5–15.5cm
Distribution:	Widespread
Identification:	Very small with dull greenish upper parts and pale underparts. Distinctive crest stripe, orange in male, yellow in female, bordered with black

The goldcrest is most at home in coniferous woodland where it flits about in treetops snatching insects and spiders from twigs. Its extremely high-pitched song is often the only evidence most people have of it as it is so small. During the warm breeding season, the females breed furiously, often starting a second nest and clutch before the first one has fledged. They lay up to 13 eggs. Goldcrests are very vulnerable to the cold. A poor winter can deplete a regional population by as much as 80 per cent. Goldcrests do not like crossing open spaces. Where development breaks up forests, they might be deterred from living and breeding, reducing numbers further.

COMMON NIGHTINGALE
(*Luscinia megarhynchos*)

Size:	Wingspan 23cm
Distribution:	Breeds in summer throughout Europe. Up to 5 million breeding pairs across Europe. France, Italy and Spain have largest populations. Rare around the Alps, southern Germany and Austria. Winters in African savannah
Identification:	Brown upper parts, pale below with buff tinge to breast. Longish chestnut tail. Like a large robin in shape and stance. Beautiful song, mostly at night, during breeding season

The nightingale's song is unlike any other bird song heard in Europe. It has varied and highly tuneful phrases and repetitions, with deep, low sustained notes. It does sing through the night, as its name suggests, but in wooded cover will sing loudly throughout the day, its song carrying far across the fields. Strangely, once its chicks have hatched, it loses its singing voice and calls harshly to its young.

Many traditional tales are told to explain the nightingale's nocturnal singing, and all relate that the bird sings with its breast pressed against a sharp thorn, in order to stay awake. It is said that the nightingale originally only had one eye and that it stole the single eye of the slow worm. Ever since, the slow worm has been searching for the bird in order to get its eye back. So the nightingale sings all night to keep itself awake.

Sunbirds

Size:	Most less than 15cm long
Distribution:	Mainly found in Africa but species also in southern Asia and northeastern Australia
Identification:	Male has iridescent plumage until end of breeding season, females brown or grey. Thin, downward-curving bill is characteristic of many species

Old World sunbirds, of which there are over 100 species, are often compared with American hummingbirds, although the groups are not related. Sunbirds rival hummingbirds in their diversity of brilliant colours but not in form. Both groups feed on nectar and insects but the sunbird prefers to eat while perched, although they can feed on the wing. Many species, such as the golden-winged sunbird, inhabit Africa's montane forests. The greater double-collared sunbird (*Nectarinia afer* or *Cinnyris afer*), **below**, is commonly found in South Africa. Its preferred habitat are coastal and montane forests and coastal and valley bush.

Snow bunting

(*Plectrophenax nivalis*)

Size:	Wingspan 16cm
Distribution:	Circumpolar, breeding throughout tundra regions, wintering further south in northerly regions of Europe, Asia and North America
Identification:	Distinctive long, black and white wings, with flashing white wing-patches.

The snow bunting breeds further north than any other perching bird. It certainly seems to prefer the cold as, even in its winter journey south, it seeks out snowy areas and cooler coastlines. In winter the male is a fairly unremarkable light brown but in summer he has striking black and white plumage and flaunts it during courtship. The name bunting comes from the German word *bunt*, meaning mottled, and refers to the bird's multicoloured plumage. Snow buntings flock in large numbers and often tumble to rest in a great flurry, giving rise to one of their common names, the snowflake.

Baltimore Oriole

(*Icterus galbula*)

Size:	Wingspan 30cm
Distribution:	Breed in summer throughout North America and winter primarily south of the US–Mexico border
Identification:	Male flame-orange with a black head. Female dull- or olive-green on the top and mostly yellow underneath

Orange and black were the family colours of the Baltimores, English gentry who ruled the American colony of Maryland in the seventeenth and eighteenth centuries. It seemed natural that a common and well-loved orange and black bird should be named after them. It is now the state bird of Maryland. Orioles sing loudly and sweetly and build purse-like nests that dangle from branches, with an entrance near the bottom to one side. They eat insects, seeds and fruit.

Sociable Weaver (*Philetairus socius*) ▼

Size:	Length 14cm
Distribution:	Southern Africa centred on northern Cape Province and southern Namibia, particularly Kalahari Desert
Identification:	Sparrow-sized. Brown bodies, black face masks with bluish bills, neatly-patterned backs and wings and bold, black-speckled sides

The giant nests of these small birds are assembled straw by straw by the whole weaver colony. Some are more than a century old, have 90 or so entrances, weigh over a tonne and house up to 500 birds. But for the sociable weaver there is always the danger that somewhere in the building lurks a deadly killer. Other creatures also make their home in these massive thatches: falcons, chats, lovebirds, finches – and snakes. Somewhere, slithering through the myriad tunnels, might be a boomslang (*Dispholidus typus*) or Cape cobra (*Naja nivea*), both predators of the weaver. Nests eventually grow so big that the host tree dies or collapses under the weight.

Red Crossbill (*Loxia curvirostra*) ▲

Size:	Length 14cm
Distribution:	Europe to southeastern Asia and Middle America
Identification:	Male has dull-red head and body, blackish wings and tail. Female dull-grey with dull-yellow crown, breast and rump. Large bill with crossed tips

The crossbill's build, odd beak and sidling movement along branches are all very parrot-like. It holds on to a pine cone with one foot while it pecks away, just like some exotic jungle bird. It harvests pine seeds before the cones ripen, working with astonishing speed and agility, tilting its head and inserting its weird bill between the scales of one cone after another. The tip of the lower mandible pushes each scale apart so the crossbill can either scoop out the seed with its tongue or hook it out with the upper mandible. The crossbill is becoming more widespread in parts of Europe. It breeds in coniferous forests, often at high levels.

Yellow-billed Oxpecker

(Buphagus africanus)

Size:	Length 21–22cm
Distribution:	Sub-Sahara excluding forests of west and central Africa
Identification:	Slate-grey upper parts, head and neck, creamy underparts and rump. Distinctive yellow-based bill with red tip. Bright orange eye

This tick-eating bird is now being reintroduced to South Africa where it became extinct in 1910. It was eliminated because its preferred host species – buffalo, rhinoceros and giraffe – were hunted out and the cattle to which it transferred its services were treated with chemicals that eradicated ticks. However, game farming is on the increase and it is costly and difficult to dip semi-wild animals, so farmers want it back. It is an extraordinarily efficient parasite destroyer. A female tick lays 18,000 eggs but a single oxpecker eats 150,000 ticks a year so just a few birds have a huge effect on tick numbers. Unlike dipping, oxpeckers leave a few ticks on each animal, which ensures immunity to parasite-borne diseases.

Vogelkop Bowerbird

(*Amblyornis inornatus*)

Size:	Length 23cm
Distribution:	Arfak Mountains, Western New Guinea
Identification:	Drab brownish plumage, lighter beneath

The male vogelkop, which looks like a fairly dreary thrush, is the plainest of all the bowerbirds but compensates by building the most remarkable structure. Not only does he build a hut large enough for a man to crawl into, he lays out a colourful garden and spends up to nine months of the year tending the whole assemblage. His bower, designed to attract as many females as possible for him to mate with, is usually made from bent-over saplings or twigs thatched with dried grasses and other plant stems. It can be as much as 2.2m tall and 2m across. Laid out on the front garden of moss might be flowers, fruits, stones, bones or beetles as well as man-made objects like keys, gun cartridges, mugs, buttons and scraps of material. He cannot afford to leave the bower for too long or neighbouring birds will help themselves to his choicest treasures.

Birds of Paradise

(family Paradisae)

Male birds of paradise gather in display territories called leks, where they dance and show off their colours to lure a mate. They perch on branches and sway about or lean at acute angles, clash their wings together overhead, crouch, fan their tails, stand erect, even hang upside down: whatever it takes to attract a female's attention. Count Raggi's, or the Raggiana, bird of paradise is famed for its frenzied dance, hopping and quivering as it spreads its ornamental plumes above its back, while the others in the lek put up a loud, wild chorus of singing. Spectacular plumes on each flank help to identify the male lesser bird of paradise. After mating, the male is solitary while the female nests and rears the young birds alone.

There are 43 bird of paradise species, all of which are protected by inter national conventions, which control trade in the birds and their beautiful feathers. Although illegal for non-nationals, Papuan citizens are allowed to possess both birds and feathers.

Lesser bird of

Blue Jay (*Cyanocitta cristata*)

Size:	Wingspan 40cm
Distribution:	Southern Canada south to Texas and Florida
Identification:	White-faced with blue crest, back, wings, and tail. Strongly marked with black and white. Crest raised when angry or excited

The vivid cobalt or azure of a blue jay feather is instantly eye-catching but in fact there is no blue pigmentation in birds' feathers and the colour is a result of light refracting in the feather's peculiar inner structure. Squash the feather and the colour goes.

The call of the blue jay has been described as an 'unrelenting steel-cold scream', rather unkind but very near the mark. This perky, popular bird, often caricatured in books and cartoons, is the sentinel of the woods and forests, calling out its raucous *jay-jay* warning when it spots an intruder. Its elegant appearance is exposed as a sham at the bird feeder where it pushes and shoves others out of the way. An omnivore, it performs a great service by devouring the pupae of the pestiferous tent caterpillar, each pair feeding hundreds to their nestlings in the early summer.

STELLER'S JAY (*Cyanocitta stellari*)

SIZE:	Length 30–34cm
DISTRIBUTION:	Southern Alaska, California and Rocky Mountains in North America and as far south as Nicaragua in Central America
IDENTIFICATION:	Black head, crest and bill. White eyebrows. Iridescent blue body

Understandably quiet in the vicinity of its nest, the Steller's jay can be quite bold and noisy around camp sites and picnic areas, quickly becoming accustomed to the presence of people. It is probably hoping for scraps although it usually feeds in the tree tops readily consuming seeds, nuts, acorns and berries, even taking other birds' eggs or nestlings. It can generally be found at altitudes from 900–3,000m and those living at higher levels move lower in winter.

The prominent crest makes this jay easy to identify. The male and female are similar in appearance, but some regional variations occur.

Clark's Nutcracker

(*Nucifragra columbiana*)

Size:	Length 28cm
Distribution:	Rocky Mountains of United States and Canada
Identification:	Pale-grey with white around base of long, sharp, sturdy bill, white undertail, black wings with white patch on secondary feathers, black tail with white outer feathers

In summer the Clark's nutcracker eats about 82 pine cone seeds a day. In the depths of the winter its energy needs double, but the trees are bare. Fortunately, it has planned ahead. From mid August until late November or December it stocks up a network of food stores across the mountain. A single bird might stow away 150–200,000 seeds per year. Caches are usually 10–100cm apart and near the harvest tree but the nutcracker has been known to fly 20km to a cache site. It starts to retrieve the seeds in February, finding the stores using highly developed spatial memory. It supplements its diet with insects, spiders, carrion, nestlings and eggs, small mammals and frogs.

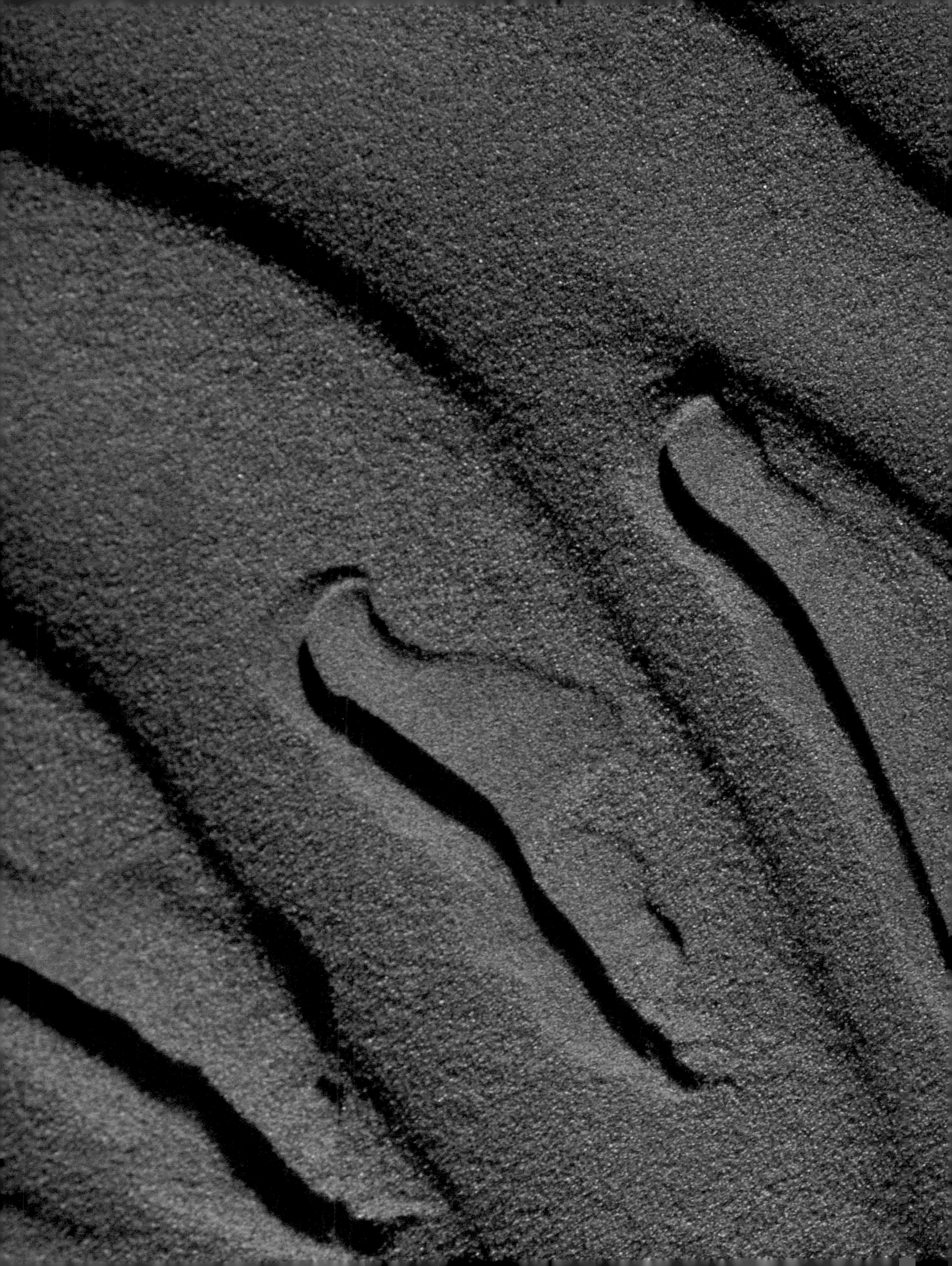

Amphibians and Reptiles

Boreal Chorus Frog

(*Pseudacris triseriata*)

Size:	Length 2–5cm
Distribution:	North America
Identification:	Reddish-brown, olive or grey with paler underside. Three dark stripes running down the back. White or cream stripe along the upper lip

Run a fingernail down the teeth of a fine tooth comb and you will get an idea of the mating call of the boreal chorus frog. These breeding songs increase in speed and pitch and are usually heard soon after the spring thaw. The male, which is usually smaller than the female, has a yellow vocal sac and, when this is not puffed up during calling, it hangs as a loose flap of skin.

Small clusters of eggs are laid before the end of May and the grey or brown tadpoles metamorphose in 8–10 weeks. Newly-formed western or boreal chorus froglets feed on midges and similar tiny creatures, moving on to ants, beetles, moths and caterpillars as they reach adult size.

Common Toad

(*Bufo bufo*)

Size:	Length 8–15cm, males smaller than females
Distribution:	Widespread in Europe, northwest Africa and Asia. In damp, deciduous woodland, scrub, gardens, parks and fields. Breeding in ponds, lakes and ditches
Identification:	Broad, squat body covered in warts. Colours vary. Short toes, webbed hind feet, rounded snout. Orange eyes with horizontal pupils. Dry to the touch. Crawls rather than hops. Mainly nocturnal

Nowadays we mostly see toads squashed on the roads as they move to their breeding ponds. Females lay up to 4,000 eggs in long strings that lie like necklaces tangled in water plants. Although larger specimens will swallow harvest mice or small grass snakes whole, most toads eat insects, larvae, spiders, slugs, and worms. One insect gets its revenge. The flesh fly (*Lucilia bufonivora*) lays its eggs on the toad's skin where they hatch into maggots that crawl into the nostrils and eat the toad from within.

Common Frog (*Rana temporaria*) ▲

Size:	Length up to 10cm
Distribution:	Throughout Europe and northwestern Asia, as far north as Arctic Circle in Scandinavia. Any moist habitat but commoner in cooler woodland and wet meadows
Identification:	Small, squat, solid body without tail. Wide, flat head with prominent eyes and large, gaping mouth. Moist to the touch. Colours variable

Frogs have been around for 150 million years. Because they arrived with the life-giving annual floods, frogs were seen by the Ancient Egyptians as symbols of abundance. They were also the symbol of the goddess Heqit, the midwife, and women wore frog amulets for luck in childbirth.

The common frog breeds in early March, the female laying copious amounts of spawn in a pond over ten days. The young frogs leave their pond in June and all frogs go into hibernation before the first frosts.

Edible Frog (*Rana esculenta*)

Size:	Length up to 11cm, usually shorter
Distribution:	France eastward through central Europe to western Russia; north to Sweden and south to Italy and northern Balkans. Introduced to southern Britain
Identification:	Slim-waisted body with fairly smooth skin, long legs and large, prominent eyes with horizontal pupils. Colour of back variable. Legs barred dark green

The edible frog is aquatic in habit and is often active during the day, sometimes basking in the sun. It will live up to 14 years or so, if it can elude its three main predators: heron, pike and French people. Properly prepared and very fresh, frog's legs are delicate, tender and lightly sweet, like a very young chicken. The French are not the only race to eat frogs. In the Philippines frogs are stuffed with pork and garlic, dried in the sun (usually on the washing line) and then deep-fried until golden brown.

Golden Poison Arrow Frog (*Dendrobates auratus*)

Size:	Length 40–50mm
Distribution:	Central and South America. Introduced to Hawaii
Identification:	Small, brightly coloured frog, usually metallic-green or blue and black, sometimes brownish-gold or yellow

One of the most deadly poisons from the animal kingdom comes from the skin of this tiny frog, a fact long known to the indigenous people of the Amazon rainforests. One frog would yield enough poison to coat fifty arrowheads, providing formidable weapons to paralyse and kill their quarry. Today, scientists are investigating using this poison as a painkiller, as experiments show it is more than 200 times as effective as morphine.

Perfectly at home on the forest floor, the poison frog or dart frog does not need to hide from predators: they recognize the brilliant colours and leave well alone. These frogs have an elaborate mating ritual and, after the batch of 6–8 eggs are laid in a small pool, the male keeps an eye on them. After hatching, he carries the tadpoles on his back to a lake or stream.

Pygmy Marsupial Frog ▼

(*Flectonotus pygmaeus*)

Size:	Length 25–50mm
Distribution:	Brazil, South America
Identification:	Adaptable colouring. Open pouch on back of female

Most frogs lay their eggs in ponds or streams but the pygmy marsupial frog carries her fertilized eggs around with her in an open pouch on her back. There they remain in the early tadpole stage until she finds a suitable pool of water near a stream where she can release the tadpoles. As an adult, this tree frog spends most of its time climbing in bushes or trees, using suction pads on its toes to keep it from falling. Living high above ground keeps it safe from most large mammals but it is often preyed upon by birds and snakes of the Amazon rainforest. Hunting and feeding are done at night, spiders and insects making up the major part of its diet.

Goliath Frog (*Conraua goliath*)

Size:	Body length 30.5cm, overall length 91cm. Weight up to 3.2kg
Distribution:	Cameroon and Equatorial Guinea, western Africa
Identification:	Very large frog with mottled-brown or olive-green skin, paler, golden undersides. Long back legs with webbed feet

The swift-moving rivers in the dense rain forests of western Africa are the home of this enormous frog but commercial logging has reduced its original habitat by half and the goliath frog is in danger of becoming extinct. Loss of habitat is not all it has to contend with. The goliath frog has also suffered from hunting by zoos and private collectors and continues to be hunted for food. The Bayele, a pygmy tribe, not only eat the frogs but collect their thigh bones as a symbol of good luck. The meat is sweet and reputed to be good for pregnant women as it is associated with clean water spirits. Local restaurateurs will pay approximately five dollars for a frog for the table but American collectors have been known to pay as much as $3,000 for this rare amphibian.

Great Crested Newt (*Triturus cristatus*)

Size:	Length up to 15cm including tail, females sometimes 17cm
Distribution:	Britain, northern and central Europe north of Alps, east to Russia and central Asia. Absent from Ireland and much of Scandinavia
Identification:	Large, dark, coarse-skinned with dark spots and white stippling along flanks. Belly yellow or orange with dark spots or blotches. Dark throat. Moist skin. Serrated crest running length of back. Vertically flattened tail, broad in the centre and tapering at each end

Newts, like salamanders, were once thought to suckle resting cows, rendering them incapable of producing more milk. The myth probably arose because a crested newt, when disturbed, will exude a whitish liquid (which is noxious) and twist itself round a handy object – perhaps the teat of an udder, if it happens to have been disturbed by a cow. To the cowherd this would look pretty much like being caught red-handed in the act of milk theft.

The great crested newt is fairly aquatic but outside the breeding season can be seen several hundred metres from water, particularly in broad-leaved woodland. After hibernation, usually on land but sometimes in the mud at the bottom of a pond, the male inseminates the female by depositing a small packet of sperm and then encouraging her to move over it, allowing the sperm to enter her cloaca (reproductive opening). The eggs are laid underwater, wrapped in the leaves of plants.

FIRE SALAMANDER (*Salamandra salamandra*)

SIZE:	Length 16–29cm, sometimes longer
DISTRIBUTION:	West, central and southern Europe. Typically in cool, moist broad-leaved forest. Similar animals in northwestern Africa and southwestern Asia are separate species
IDENTIFICATION:	Largest salamander. Shiny black body with bright yellow or orange markings. Underside dark grey. Stout legs. Body longer than tail

It is from the Arabic term meaning 'lives in fire' that we get the name salamander for these fiery-coloured, nocturnal amphibians that like to creep into a cool, moist, hollow log during the day, often ending up on a fire in the evening, justifying their name.

The salamander's defence is its toxicity. Vanilla-scented alkaloids are secreted from its skin and are present in its saliva. These have a burning taste and can cause muscle convulsion and death in small mammals. Salamanders eat worms, slugs, flies, millipedes, centipedes and beetles.

STARRED TORTOISE

(*Geochelone elegans*)

SIZE:	Length up to 20cm (male) and 30cm (female)
DISTRIBUTION:	Indian subcontinent and Sri Lanka
IDENTIFICATION:	Greyish-brown with golden radiating star pattern on carapace (shell)

Zoos often feature a star, or starred, tortoise because its carapace markings are so striking but in the wild these markings are not for attracting attention: quite the reverse. In its dry grassland habitat, where sunlight flickers through tussocks of grass, this pattern is excellent camouflage. The centre of each star is in the middle of a pyramid-shaped bump and the female is usually bumpier than the male. One explanation for these raised bumps is that they help the tortoise to roll back over after being stranded on its back – never an easy job for a creature with such short legs.

The young hatchlings could also do with longer legs, or at least mole-like feet. The female covers her eggs with soil and the hatchlings have to wait for a rainstorm to wash enough soil away for them to leave the nest.

WESTERN PAINTED TURTLE

(*Chrysemys picta bellii*)

SIZE:	Length 9–18cm
DISTRIBUTION:	Canadian boreal forests
IDENTIFICATION:	Dark shell with network of yellow streaks or stripes, rectangles on the marginals outlined in orange-red. Black skin with bright-yellow stripes on head and legs

Any permanent area of water with a muddy bottom and a suitable basking site will be inhabited by these colourful turtles. Painted turtle are found across North America but in the Canadian boreal forests, the western painted turtle has made itself at home. This remarkably hardy turtle can be seen swimming beneath the ice in winter and is one of the last reptiles each year to go into hibernation, waiting until late October to do so.

Courtship begins shortly after waking in the spring. The male uses his long front claws to stroke the female's face. She might accept his advances by touching his feet. After mating, she finds a sunny nesting site to lay her clutch of 7–10 eggs. The young are mostly carnivorous but older turtles will browse on aquatic vegetation. All the turtle's food must be found and eaten in water as its fixed tongue cannot cope with swallowing dry food.

Common Snapping Turtle ▲

(*Chelydra serpentina*)

Size:	Shell length up to 47cm. Weight 4–16kg
Distribution:	North, Central and South America
Identification:	Brown, olive or black shell, long yellowish tail. Yellowish neck and legs with tubercles

This is the turtle most commonly used in the famous turtle soup and stews but despite this the population remains fairly stable. It is not difficult to see how it got its name: it can be ferocious on land, striking out with its long neck at blinding speed. Small prey are eaten whole; larger creatures torn to pieces with its claws, usually after being dragged into the water and drowned. Even other snapping turtles are not safe, although aquatic vegetation also features largely on the menu. The snapping turtle is more docile in the water and poses little threat to swimmers who are more likely to see its long tail as the turtle escapes to the muddy bottom.

In Asia more than 60 freshwater turtle species are threatened due to an increasing harvest for food and medicinal uses.

European Pond Turtle

(*Emys orbicularis*)

Size:	Length 14–20cm
Distribution:	Spain, France, Italy, Germany, Poland, Turkey, Iran, Russia, Morocco and Algeria
Identification:	Colours vary but generally a dark carapace and skin with pretty, bright yellow or gold speckles. Bright yellow ring around iris. Prominent thin tail

The European pond turtle is protected in Europe and cannot be kept as a pet. It will eat plant matter but prefers small lobsters, fish, worms, amphibians, and slugs. In America, where keeping and breeding pond turtles is permitted, owners feed the turtles proprietary fish and turtle products supplemented with plenty of earthworms. In the wild, European pond turtles lay about 10 eggs per clutch although they may not lay at all if the weather is too cool.

TURTLES

Marine turtles can grow to more than 900kg and have a lifespan of over 100 years – if they are left alone. Humans and their activities have driven all large sea turtles to the edge of extinction and some scientists predict that without a huge worldwide conservation effort there might be no turtles left on the planet by 2010. Loss of habitat, entrapment in long lines and shrimp trawling nets, beach sand extraction and even artificial lighting along coasts (which disorients nesting females) all play a part in reducing numbers of these ponderous but serene behemoths. Where sea turtles are protected by law poaching is rife.

The **leatherback turtle** (*Dermochelys coriacea*), which has swum all the oceans for 100 million years, is the largest of them all with a span of up to 2.7m across its front flippers. Its numbers fell from 91,000 in 1980 to fewer than 5,000 in 2002. Some shrimp trawlers have incorporated special turtle

Leatherback tur

Green sea tur

escape hatches into their nets but these only work with smaller animals. Larger openings have been called for by conservation organisations but governments have been slow in implementing legislation. The leatherback, as its name suggests, does not have a hard carapace. Its favourite food is the Portuguese man-of-war jellyfish but when it tucks into one of these giants the debris sometimes attracts sharks – which eat the leatherback. Nesting females and eggs are regularly taken for food and its unhatched eggs raise about $5 each on the black market. In 2000 an American woman was jailed for six months for importing 2,900 eggs from El Salvador.

The huge head of the **Atlantic loggerhead turtle** (*Caretta caretta*) houses not a large brain but giant jaw muscles. This turtle, found from Argentina to Nova Scotia and growing to 100kg, eats crabs, clams and oysters (as well as jellyfish and sponges) and its powerful jaws crush the shells easily. As with other large sea turtles, the females come ashore at night to lay their eggs in the sand. After a 60-day incubation the hatchlings – just 6cm long – emerge to make a desperate scramble to the sea, preyed on by crabs and birds. Only one in every 1,000 survives into adulthood. The loggerhead is a major food source in rural Caribbean communities where its meat commands a high price. Its eggs are used to make cakes and in Cuba are dried in the oviduct and sold like sausages. It is also the source of a varnish-like oil and its carapace is used in Honduras to make paddle boats.

Most threatened of all is the **green turtle** (*Chelonia mydas*) which is found in all warm tropical waters. The green flesh for which it is named is a delicacy in many countries where it is sometimes made into soup. Trade in green turtle products is banned by international treaty, however. This means there is a thriving black market with poachers selling live turtles off the boat for up to $20 each, despite the threat of huge fines and imprisonment for up to five years. By the time its meat reaches the table and its carapace reaches the souvenir stall, each turtle is worth possibly thousands of dollars. The green turtle, which grows up to 200kg, sometimes nests on public beaches and conservationists have to move the eggs to safe havens.

oggerhead turtle

Thorny Devil ▶

(*Moloch horridus*)

Size:	Length up to 20cm including tail
Distribution:	Throughout Australia's interior desert
Identification:	Scaly-skinned lizard with prominent spines and a knob or false head on its neck. Colour varies yellow, red, or olive-green

The thorny devil belies its name, moving slowly round the Australian desert harming only the ant population which makes up its sole diet. Huge numbers of ants are consumed, however, between 600 and 3,000 per meal, and the remarkable thing is that the thorny devil eats them one at a time.

The thorny devil can change colour to blend in with its surroundings and will freeze in mid-stride to avoid detection. If it is spotted, it can puff itself up to appear larger. If attack cannot be avoided, the lizard will tuck its head between its front legs, the large spiny bump at the base of its neck presenting a false head to its assailant.

Common Sandfish

(*Scincus scincus*)

Size:	Length 13–15cm including tail
Distribution:	North Africa and the Middle East
Identification:	A small yellow or tan lizard with horizontal brown bands, medium-length tail, long pointed nose

The common sandfish is a lizard that moves like a fish. It is actually a skink with a streamlined body and scales so close together that it is smooth enough to glide through sand. A burrow provides a bed for the night, an escape from the heat of the day, a place to hibernate and a refuge from predators. The sand-coloured body provides excellent camouflage but, if capture is inevitable, the sandfish can break free and leave its tail behind with its assailant.

Common sandfish, and their more colourful cousins the Arabian sandfish skinks (*Scincus mitranus*), are sometimes sold as pets but they are not easy to care for as they need live food such as crickets and constant heat for the sand in the tanks.

TOKAY GECKO (*Gekko gecko*) ▲

SIZE:	Length 35cm
DISTRIBUTION:	From northeast India to the Indo-Australian archipelago
IDENTIFICATION:	Cylindrical grey body with brownish-red spots, large prominent eyes

The tokay gecko is adept at avoiding predators. It can lighten or darken the colour of its velvety skin to blend in with its surroundings and has the ghostly ability to prevent itself from casting a shadow. It does this whilst resting on the branch of a tree by opening up folds of skin to blend completely with the bark. If it is unfortunate enough to be caught the tokay gecko can cast its tail which will continue to move for several minutes and distract the predator for long enough for the gecko to escape. Three weeks later, a new tail will be completely regenerated.

Regarded as a sign of good luck or fertility, these geckos are sometimes sold as pets. They do not take kindly to attempts to domesticate them and are likely to bite when handled.

COMMON LIZARD (*Lacerta vivipara*)

SIZE:	Length up to 14cm including tail
DISTRIBUTION:	Most of Europe and east through northern Asia to Pacific coast
IDENTIFICATION:	Long body with short legs and rounded head. Thick neck and tail. Dry, scaly skin. Variable colouring. Yellow or orange spotted belly. Swelling at base of tail in male during breeding season

The common lizard emerges from hibernation in mid-February and spends as long as it can soaking up the sun before starting to mate in April or May. It is mostly seen in grassland, hedgerows, woodland edges and the embankments of roads and railways, where it hunts insects. It is ovo-viviparous, usually producing live young but sometimes laying eggs, particularly in mountainous areas. In some traditions, lizards used to be regarded as protectors for unborn children: expectant mothers wore lizard charms in the hope of having a happy, healthy baby.

FRILLED LIZARD (*Chlamydosaurus kingii*)

SIZE:	Length, head and body, up to 28cm (tail 42–67cm)
DISTRIBUTION:	Northern Australia and southern New Guinea
IDENTIFICATION:	A large, greyish-brown lizard with a long, slender, tapering tail and a distinctive frill around the neck

During the 1980s this lizard shot to fame in Japan when it starred in a car commercial on television. Such was its popularity that Australian two-cent coins which featured the frilled lizard sold for one dollar each in Japan. Throughout the rest of the world, it is famed merely for its amazing neck frill. Made of thin skin and cartilage, the frill settles round the shoulders like a cape when the lizard is relaxed. But when it is alarmed, the frill opens like an umbrella and the lizard gapes its mouth wide, hoping its bright pink or yellow tongue and mouth lining will frighten its attacker. If this does not work, the frilled lizard will stand on its hind legs, hiss, thrash its tail and leap towards its predator. This display is little more than a bluff and if it fails the lizard will dart up the nearest tree where it is usually well camouflaged.

Green Iguana

(*Iguana iguana*)

Size:	Length 1.2–2.1m, including tail
Distribution:	Central and South America, Caribbean Islands
Identification:	Rough, scaly skin in varying shades of green. Long tail, long fingers and claws

High up in the branches of mangrove trees, well camouflaged by leaves, the green iguana feels fairly well protected and browses on leaves, flowers and fruit. If it is threatened, this large lizard will dive from the tree into a swamp or river and swim to safety. It can fall 12–15 metres to the ground unhurt if the water is too far away to break its fall. Not all of its time is spent climbing or swimming: the cold-blooded iguana also lies on rocks basking in the sunshine.

The green iguana has long been hunted for food by South Americans, who call it 'bamboo chicken', although some say the taste resembles rabbit. Many wild iguanas have been captured for the pet industry but iguana farms now cater for this trade and laws protect it from over-hunting.

Jackson's Chameleon

(*Chameleo jacksonii*)

Size:	Length 15–35cm
Distribution:	Kenya and Tanzania, east Africa. Introduced to Hawaii and California
Identification:	Yellowish-green skin, long tail and protruding eyes. Male has three horns on its head

Chameleons are best known for their ability to change colour to blend in with surroundings and the Jackson's chameleon is no exception. This master of camouflage can darken its drab green skin to almost black in less than two minutes. Apart from the obvious advantage this provides when hiding from predators, colour change is used to threaten rivals and to attract their prospective mates.

The long, prehensile tail and feet with toes pointing in opposite directions help the Jackson's chameleon to grip branches and spend most of its time in trees, coming to ground level only to mate and lay eggs. After basking in the morning sun it lies in wait for insects or spiders, each eye looking in a different direction. A quick flick with its long, sticky tipped tongue will take the prey by surprise and bring it back to be chewed and swallowed.

Crocodile Monitor Lizard

(*Varanus salvadori*)

Size:	Length up to 4.5m including tail
Distribution:	Papua New Guinea
Identification:	Long, slender body and lengthy sturdy tail, black skin with white flecks. Long forked tongue

The upper jungle canopies of Papua New Guinea are the only places to find the rare crocodile monitor lizard, the longest lizard in the world. Well-developed claws help it to climb trees in search of the smaller reptiles on which it feeds. Fresh meat is not essential, though, as this lizard also eats carrion. Local tribesmen are wary of this large creature, believing it to be a man eater, but a blow from its tail is a more real danger than being eaten. Monitor lizards are inclined to flee rather than confront an attacker. Because of their relative docility, some monitor lizards are kept as pets, becoming tame enough to eat out of their owner's hand.

The crocodile monitor lizard is hunted mainly for its smooth skin which is used to cover Kundu drums.

Gila Monster (*Heloderma suspectum*)

Size:	Length 46–60cm including tail
Distribution:	Deserts of southwestern United States and south into Mexico
Identification:	Sturdy lizard with short, fat tail. Scales are black, pink, orange and yellow patterned with broken blotches, bars and spots

There are only two species of venomous lizard in the world and the gila monster, named after the Gila River Basin of the southwestern United States, is one of them. The painful bite is rarely fatal to humans but can cause nausea, fainting, vomiting and excessive thirst. Unlike snake bites, the toxin is not injected but flows from glands down two grooves in the teeth and onto the wound as the lizard chews on its victim. Not surprisingly, the first piece of advice offered to anyone bitten is to flush the wound with copious amounts of fresh water – after removing the lizard of course.

Boa Constrictor (*Boa constrictor*)

Size:	Average length 3m
Distribution:	South and Central America
Identification:	Colour varies from donkey-brown through olive-green to silver-grey or cream with oval and diamond markings

The stories of huge boa constrictors crushing people to death are gross exaggerations. The boa is only the world's fifth or sixth largest snake and, on average, only half the size of an anaconda. But, like the anaconda and python, the boa kills by wrapping its coils around the victim's chest and squeezing. As the unfortunate creature exhales, the snake tightens its grip until its prey can no longer breathe and is ready to be swallowed.

Bats make a favourite meal and the boa constrictor hangs from a branch near the entrance to a cave and catches the bat as it flies by. Under the snake's upper lip, heat sensors help it to locate warm blooded mammals. Because of its penchant for rats, it is sometimes kept as a house snake to control rodents.

Green Anaconda *(Eunectes murinus)*

Size:	Length up to 9m
Distribution:	South America, east of the Andes
Identification:	Dark-green with oval black spots. Dull yellow-centred spots along the sides of the body

Anacondas got their name from a Tamil word meaning 'elephant killer'. Although this is probably an exaggeration, anacondas are one of the largest snakes in the world and have been known to prey on crocodiles and small deer. One advantage (to the snake) is that a meal of this size will last for months as, although the victim is swallowed all in one go, the anaconda's slow-acting digestive system will work its way through it while the snake basks in the sun.

This nocturnal snake spends a lot of time in slow-moving rivers or swamps and is sometimes known as the water boa. It will remain almost submerged whilst waiting for suitable prey, breathing easily as its nostrils and eyes are on the top of its head. Its victim is usually dragged into the water to drown, but larger prey are squeezed with its coils until breathing stops.

MANGROVE SNAKE (*Boiga dendrophila*)

SIZE:	Length 1.8–2.4m
DISTRIBUTION:	Malay peninsular, Sumatra, Singapore
IDENTIFICATION:	Bluish-black body with narrow yellow bars. Short, broad head

In mangrove swamps and lowland jungles, this strikingly coloured snake coils itself up in branches overhanging rivers or streams and waits until dusk. Twilight is the best hunting time for the mangrove snake, allowing it to slither silently after birds or rodents, almost unseen. This is one of the back-fanged or rear-fanged snakes which work their prey to the back of their mouths and chew their food rather than swallowing the catch whole. The venom in the saliva penetrates the victim through the chewing wounds rather than being injected via fangs; because of this, and its docility, the mangrove snake is not regarded as particularly dangerous to man.

The mangrove snake's colouring is similar to the deadly banded krait (*Bungarus fasciatus*), but the krait's black and yellow bands are of equal width.

Grass Snake (*Natrix natrix*)

Size:	Length 70–150cm
Distribution:	Europe, North Africa, central Asia
Identification:	Vertical bars mark the sides of the greenish body. Yellow or cream collar behind the head

This harmless snake is a strong swimmer, gliding along with just its head above water. It will dive if disturbed and can stay underwater for up to an hour hunting for small fish and newts. Frogs and toads feature largely in its diet and the prey is swallowed whole and alive. Like other snakes, it derives its body heat from external sources and needs to lie and bask in the sun.

The grass snake, or water snake as it is sometimes known, will puff up its body and hiss in an attempt to frighten predators. If this doesn't work, it will play dead – lying on its back completely still with open mouth and tongue lolling out. Often the aggressor will lose interest and walk away. But not always.

ADDER OR VIPER *(Vipera berus berus)*

SIZE:	Length up to 62cm, exceptionally 90cm. Females larger than males
DISTRIBUTION:	Most of Europe up to 68°N, south to northwestern Spain and northern Italy, east to Pacific coast of Russia. Absent from Ireland
IDENTIFICATION:	Thick body with triangular head bearing characteristic V mark. Zig-zag stripe along spine. Males pale with stark black markings; females brownish with brown markings. Vertical pupil in copper-coloured eye

Fatalities from an adder's bite are rare but not unknown. It is certainly the snake most likely to sink its teeth into a European, as it is so widespread, being found further north than any other snake in the world. But it only attacks when alarmed and is usually encountered slumbering in the sun. It is a fairly slow-moving, bulky snake, preferring to ambush its prey of lizards, mice, voles, shrews and frogs. Rarely for snakes, it is truly viviparous, the female giving birth to up to 18 young, along with a placenta.

The adder is the only snake indigenous to the British Isles and so it has been laden with superstition and folklore.

Sumatran pit viper

PIT VIPERS

Most of the 140 species of pit vipers are ground-dwelling though some are tree-dwellers and a few are semi-aquatic. They are widely distributed throughout the Americas, Europe, Asia and Africa. The most famous pit vipers are undoubtedly the 30 species of rattlesnake. The other main group is the genus *Gloydius* (formerly *Agkistrodon*) and its relatives, found in North and Central America and Asia. Pit vipers have earned their name because they have a pair of heat-detecting pit-shaped organs between the eyes and nostril. These are exceedingly sensitive, able to monitor temperature changes as small as 0.2 °C (0.36 °F), and by comparing messages from left and right sides allow the snakes to locate warm-blooded prey. They can strike with deadly accuracy even in the dark. Their usual prey is mountain lizards and skinks but they will strike at a human if alarmed or pestered. Pit vipers frequent rocky, wooded hillsides, living in caves and crevices, and hibernate from October to April. They are fairly sluggish and are usually seen basking in the sun. They are found at higher altitudes than any other snake.

BUSHMASTER SNAKE *(Lachesis mutus)*

SIZE:	Average length 2.1m, maximum 3.7m
DISTRIBUTION:	Southern Central America and northern South America
IDENTIFICATION:	Tan or yellowish-brown, slightly flattened body with dark, diamond-shaped blotches. Wedge-shaped head

The venomous bushmaster's Latin name means 'silent fate' but it is such a shy and retiring snake that the fate is seldom suffered by humans, whether silently or otherwise. Well camouflaged on the leaf-strewn rain forest floor, the bushmaster is more interested in small, warm-blooded mammals which it locates with two heat-sensitive pits on the side of its head. These are so sensitive that when an animal gets within 50cm, the snake can detect its position accurately enough to strike, even in the dark.

In the Americas, the bushmaster is the only pit viper to lay eggs rather than bear live young. Eight to twelve eggs are laid in another animal's burrow which the female adopts for this purpose. She coils herself round the eggs and remains with them constantly until they hatch about eleven weeks later.

Alligators and Crocodiles

Spanish explorers in Florida in the 1700s sent word home of 'terrible lizards' – up to six metres long – which were so abundant and tightly packed in some rivers that the more adventurous could consider walking across their backs from bank to bank. There is no record of anyone having performed this feat and it would be impossible today as there are just not enough alligators (which is what these 'terrible lizards' were) left. They were slaughtered in their millions, mostly for their skins, until protection came in the 1940s. The **American alligator** (*Alligator mississippiensis*) seldom grows larger than 4m long but that is enough to make it a dangerous adversary and occasional mankiller. It is found in the swamps and rivers along the coastal plain from Virginia and North Carolina down through Florida and west to the Rio Grande in Texas. Its range seems to be spreading thanks to the increasing number of cattle water holes which it frequents. 'Gators are a big tourist attraction and can be seen sunning themselves on riverbanks beside busy highways.

Most things that go into the mouth of the **Nile crocodile** (*Crocodylus niloticus*) never come out again. Not so its young. This consummate killer, which grows up to 5.5m long and can easily bite a man in half, is amazingly gentle with its offspring. The female lays up to 50 eggs in a hole, which she

American alligator

Nile crocodile

covers with soil and guards for 90 days. When she hears high-pitched noises from below she knows it is hatching time and she digs away to help the hatchlings – which look exactly like miniature adults – emerge from their shells. Then she catches them all up in her mouth and, peering out from between the bars of her huge teeth like tiny crocodilian convicts, they are carried to a river to clean themselves. Found throughout sub-Saharan Africa, Nile crocodiles have few enemies other than man but they do occasionally get into fights with hippopotamuses. In a one-to-one clash the hippo will invariably be victor but more often other crocodiles join the fray and win an unequal battle.

At the other end of the scale comes **Cuvier's dwarf caiman** (*Paleosuchus palpebrosus*), the smallest crocodilian in the New World at just 1.5m long. It inhabits flooded forests around big lakes in the Amazon river system and streamside forests to the north and south of the Amazon. Unlike the other three caiman species – all of which are found only in South America – its head is dog-shaped with a high, smooth skull and a short snout. It eats fish and invertebrates. Caimans have an unusual way of coping with extreme cold: they turn themselves black. Melanin cells in their skin expand when the temperature drops and the darker pigment absorbs more heat.

Cuvier's dwarf caiman

Saltwater or Estuarine Crocodile

(*Crocodylus porosus*)

Size:	Length up to 6m (male), 3m (female), occasionally larger. Weight up to 1 tonne
Distribution:	India and Australasia
Identification:	Large-headed, with heavy jaws and marked ridges from eye sockets to snout. Young pale yellow with black stripes and spots, adults darker

The saltwater crocodile is not a fussy eater. Waiting patiently submerged, eyes and nostrils showing, it will lunge at any animal foolish enough to come too close to the water's edge. It is the largest living reptile and the bigger it is, the bigger its prey. It will take animals as large as buffalo, dragging them underwater to drown them. For this it has a useful valve at the back of the throat that seals off the mouth and prevents it from swallowing water. It will kill and eat unwary humans too, although the chances of being a victim are slim: more people die from bee stings each year than from crocodile attacks.

It does have its caring side. A mother crocodile stands guard over the mound where she has laid her eggs for 100 days then carries the young to the water one by one in unexpectedly gentle jaws.

Fish, Crustaceans and other Aquatic Life

Great White Shark

(*Carcharodon carcharias*)

Size:	Length up to 6m. Weight up to 3 tonnes
Distribution:	Temperate and subtropical oceans, especially coastal waters
Identification:	Torpedo-shaped body, with a grey back and white belly. Conical snout, with triangular serrated teeth. Large first dorsal fin and crescent-shaped caudal tail

The great white shark has a fearsome reputation, thanks largely to Peter Benchley's novel *Jaws* and the series of films based on it. It is the largest predatory fish around, though reports of 10m monsters are probably just sailors' yarns, and it accounts for about 5–10 human deaths every year. However, the shark has far more to fear from us. We catch it for the prize of its awesome teeth and jaws, we turn its fins into soup and its skin into handbags, squeeze its liver for oil, and use the carcass for fish meal.

Considering its renown, remarkably little is known about the great white shark. Its reproductive system is not fully understood, we do not know how long it lives, and we cannot be sure why it occasionally attacks humans. One thing is certain – it is not interested in eating us. It does not make a meal of its human victims, preferring fish and marine mammals with plenty of nutritious blubber.

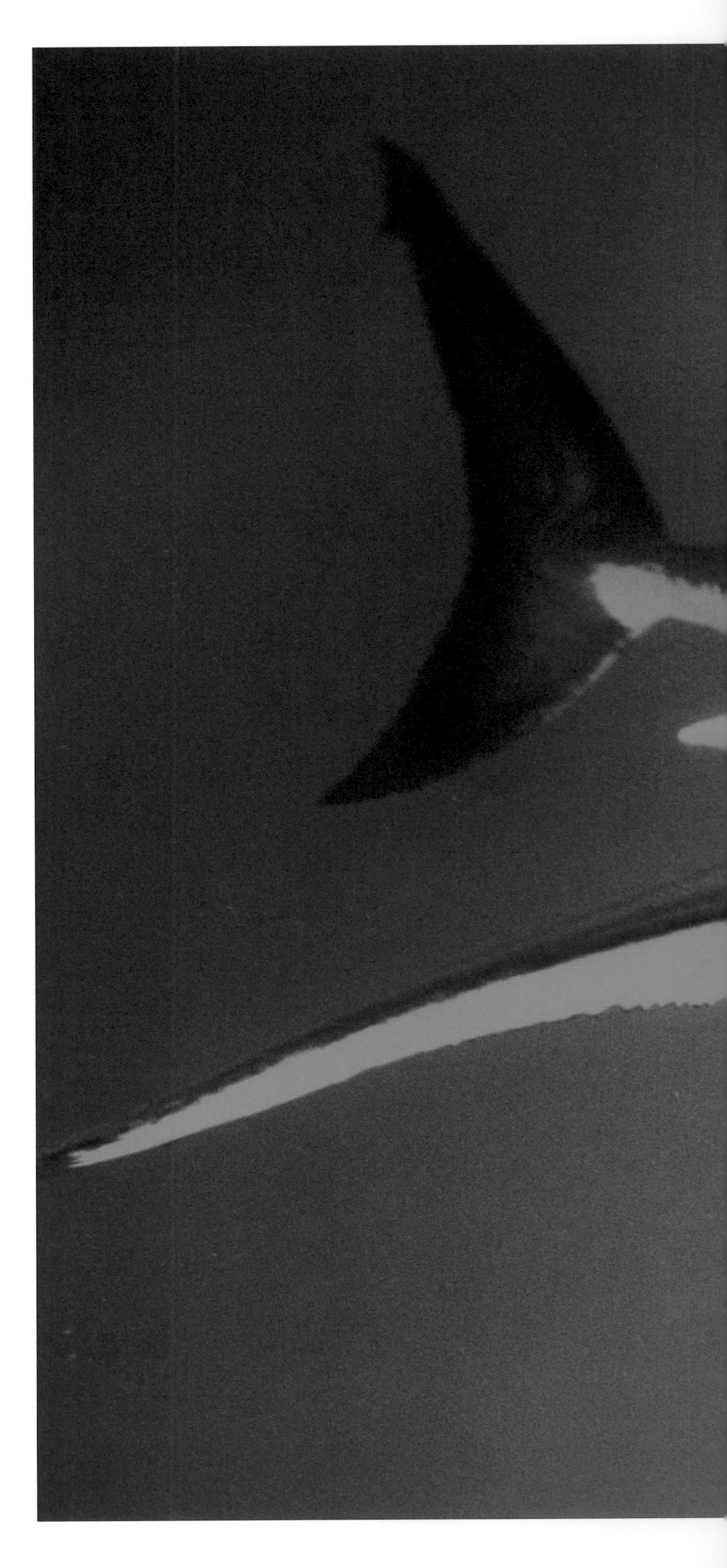

White-tipped Reef Shark

(Triaenodon obesus)

Size:	Length up to 2.1m
Distribution:	Tropical and subtropical oceans, especially near coral reefs in Indian and Pacific Oceans
Identification:	Dark-grey with conspicuous white tips on first dorsal fin and caudal fin. A small, relatively slender shark with a broad flattened head

Although the white-tipped reef shark is a placid creature, and will only bite humans if harassed, you might be forgiven for imagining much worse. A down-slanted mouth and prominent brow ridges give this shark a permanent look of disgust or disdain. In fact, that mean mouth is specially adapted to chasing its favourite prey – squid, octopus, lobster and crab – into crevices at the base of reefs. In its pursuit of food it will often jam itself into small caves made by coral and during its feeding frenzy thick membranes cover and protect its eyes.

This shark does most of its hunting at night. During daylight hours, it often lies near its chosen caves in groups, which sometimes appear stacked up like a pile of logs. It likes to stick to the bottom, and is capable of lying motionless for long periods of time.

Manta Ray

(*Manta birostris*)

Size:	Disc width 4–7m. Weight up to 1.4 tonnes
Distribution:	Warm temperate and tropical oceans, especially near coasts, between 35° north and 35° south
Identification:	Huge triangular wings (pectoral fins) and horn-like projections at front of head. Grey-blue to green-brown above, white below. Whip-like tail

The manta is the largest species of ray in the world. Though normally a solitary creature, large groups of these gentle giants sometimes congregate in food-rich waters, swimming in slow looping somersaults to concentrate the plankton they are feeding on. It is a sight that attracts divers from all over the world. During the mating season, a huge fish may be seen to jump clear of the water, then flop back with a loud slap. A sharp-eyed observer will also see the remora fish clinging to the underside of the manta, feeding on scraps it misses and the parasites on its skin.

The manta is usually quite happy to be watched. It is thought to like the feel of the divers' air bubbles, and enjoys being touched – but touching is not encouraged. Sores can develop where there is damage to the layer of mucus protecting the ray's skin.

Northern Bluefin Tuna

(*Thunnus thynnus*)

Size:	Length up to 4.6m. Weight up to 684kg
Distribution:	East and west Atlantic, Mediterranean and Black Sea
Identification:	Bluish-black above with yellowish or bluish dorsal fin. Lower sides and belly silvery-white with pale transverse lines. Black beneath near tail

A huge, fast, killing machine, the bluefin tuna, with its torpedo-shaped body, is built for speed and endurance. It can swim at more than 80kph and feeds on anchovies, hake, squid and red crabs. When young it moves in schools of many hundreds but when it grows larger – the average size is about 230kg – it forms smaller groups of up to 40. A monster fish of 500kg or more tends to be solitary. Tuna meat has always had a high reputation for flavour and texture and this has led to a very high demand, despite its high price. The result has been overfishing and, in the case of the northern bluefin, a depletion in stocks to the point of rarity. Other tuna species are also suffering a similar fate, particularly since the popularization in the west of Japanese dishes such as *sashimi* which use fresh tuna.

Atlantic Mackerel *(Scomber scombrus)*

Size:	Length up to 66cm (average 30–40cm). Weight up to 3kg (average about 680g)
Distribution:	North Atlantic, North Sea and Mediterranean
Identification:	Iridescent greenish and blue-black backs with distinctive dark wavy lines. Silvery-pink beneath. Torpedo-shaped with smooth scales

The mackerel is a fast mover, both when hunting and when being hunted. Its streamlined shape, powerful, meaty muscles and lack of a swim bladder allow it to achieve a speed of 32kph and dive to great depths in an instant. Luckily for rod fishermen it is also greedy and stupid. It will snatch at any shiny or bright object – feathered or even bare hooks are commonly used – and allow the most unskilled of anglers to make a bumper catch in no time. When mackerel are chasing schools of sprats or other baitfish they often erupt from the water in a feeding frenzy, frothing the surface in a scrum of fish and, having devoured their prey (together with a few smaller fellow hunters) will as quickly disappear, leaving nothing but a sparkle of scales shimmering down through the water as evidence of the carnage. Mackerel themselves make excellent eating.

Atlantic Herring *(Clupea harengus)*

Size:	Length up to 43cm
Distribution:	North Atlantic down to northern France and Chesapeake Bay
Identification:	Silvery fish with a single dorsal fin and protruding lower jaw

The botanist Linneaeus referred to herring as '*copiosissimus piscis*' meaning most prolific of fish, and so they remain. Schools of awesome dimensions migrate across the Atlantic in search of zooplankton. Called 'silver darlings' by Scottish fishermen, herring spend daytime in the safety of the depths as the sunlight catching their shiny scales makes them an easy target. The school usually swims in perfect unison – each fish with its own personal space – but when threatened masses together to form a bait ball, swirling in all directions to confuse the attacker.

In British coastal towns and villages herring fishing was once a thriving industry and many country recipes have survived. One is stargazy pie where the herring are placed in the pie dish like the spokes of a wheel with their tails in the centre and their heads on the rim uncovered by pastry, so they can gaze up at the stars.

Arctic Cod (*Boreogadus saida*)

Size:	Length up to 37cm
Distribution:	Circumpolar as far as 42° north. Seas off northern Russia, Alaska, Canada and Greenland
Identification:	Elongated body tapering markedly towards tail. Distinguished from other members of the cod family by more slender build, deeply-forked tail, projecting lower jaw and small barbel under jaw. Generally brownish with black dots over back and upper sides, dark fins with narrow pale edge. Pale lateral line. Very small scales

No fish has been found as far north as the Arctic cod. It has been caught in waters below freezing and likes to hide in cracks under the ice sheets. It prefers to stay near the surface but has been found as far down as 870m. It plays a key role in the diet of marine mammals, seabirds and other fish and although not harvested commercially on a large scale, it is rated as an excellent table fish by the Russians and some are caught for fishmeal. One of the most recent uses for the Arctic cod is as a source of oil for homeopathic treatments. Exaggerated claims have been made of its powers. According to one supplier, Arctic cod oil is supposed to promote brain development and visual function, increase and enhance learning and achievement, create a positive mood, ease pain and promote healthy skin!

Blackfin Icefish

(*Chaenocephalus aceratus*)

Size:	Length up to 70–72cm, weight up to 3.7kg
Distribution:	Northern part of Antarctic peninsula, islands of the Scotia Arc, Bouvet Island. Down to 750m but most abundant 90–345m deep
Identification:	Ghostly, pallid appearance with faint dark vertical banding on upper side. Very large head with body tapering sharply to tail. Wide, flat, toothy mouth and protuberant eyes, like a small crocodile

Icefish are found only in Antarctic waters. To survive near the freezing point of seawater – 1.8 °C (28 °F) these fish produce natural antifreeze proteins – glycopeptides – which prevent ice crystals forming in their blood. These proteins are 300 times more effective than conventional chemical antifreezes and their potential is of great interest to scientists involved in genetic engineering.

Lumpfish (Lumpsucker)

(*Cyclopterus lumpus*)

Size:	Length up to 60cm but usually 34–50cm. Weight up to 9kg but usually 2–2.7kg
Distribution:	Shallow coastal waters of Antarctic and north Atlantic
Identification:	Distinctive knobbly, scaleless body with bumpy ridge down back and tubercles down each side. Sucker on underside to hold on to rocks. Colours vary. Breeding males have brilliant reddish-orange underside and blue upper parts

This is an ugly fish for which only the Icelanders seem to have regard. For the rest of us the lumpfish is known solely for its roe, which is dyed red or black and sold as caviar. The lumpfish is extraordinary for the big variation between male and female. Indeed, they are named and cooked differently in Iceland. Apart from its roe, the female is generally considered less good to eat than the male.

LINED SEAHORSE (*Hippocampus erectus*)

SIZE:	Length up to 127mm
DISTRIBUTION:	Atlantic Ocean from Canada to Argentina
IDENTIFICATION:	Upright body, horse-like head, jointed armour. Prehensile tail. Dark lines on lighter background with 18–21 dorsal fin rays

The seahorse has to be patient when looking for food. It hooks on to a piece of sea grass or similar vegetation and waits for tiny crustaceans to drift by. With pinpoint accuracy it sucks each minuscule creature into its long snout, feeding for up to 10 hours and eating as many as 3,600 baby brine shrimps in a day. The female seahorse deposits her eggs in a brood pouch on the male. He incubates them until they hatch: around 500 popping out of the pouch, one at a time, and swimming free.

The world's smallest seahorse is *H. denise*, discovered in the Flores Sea, Indonesia, in 2003. It is 16mm long and lives up to 90m deep. Seahorse species around the world are threatened by trawling and irresponsible diving as well as over-harvesting for souvenirs and traditional eastern medicines.

GHOST CRAB *(Ocypode quadrata)*

SIZE:	Width 51mm. Length 44mm
DISTRIBUTION:	Southeastern USA, West Indies, Central and South America
IDENTIFICATION:	Square-bodied crab with pale-grey or yellowish shell. Large eyestalks and strong hairy legs

It is not surprising that this crustacean was named ghost crab. It remains hidden in its sandy burrow during the day and emerges at dusk to hunt for food. The ghostly pale colouring and the huge, spooky eye stalks certainly give it an eerie appearance, but equally spectral is its seeming ability to appear and disappear in the blink of an eye. This is partly because of its speed – it can run at up to 16kph – and partly because it is so well camouflaged against the sand, particularly at night.

Crabs do a good job in helping to clear up the tide line as they scavenge for food but the ghost crab does not endear itself to animal lovers as it preys on shore birds' eggs and chicks. On Prichard's Island, South Carolina, ghost crabs have even been seen dragging turtle hatchlings back to their burrows.

HORSESHOE CRAB
(Limulus polyphemus)

SIZE:	Length up to 6cm including tail
DISTRIBUTION:	Eastern coast of North and Central America
IDENTIFICATION:	Brownish-green shell shaped like a horse's foo long thin tail. Four pairs of walking and one pair of pushing legs

The sight of horseshoe crabs spawning is one of nature's greatest spectacles as thousands gather together on their chosen beaches in late spring. They arrive on shore on the high spring tides and the males (which are smaller) clasp the females, which tow them up the beach to fertilize the eggs immediately after laying. Up to 20,000 small, gree eggs are deposited in batches by each female and the waves wash a covering of sand over them. It is as well that they are so prolific as migratory shore birds feast on the eggs, fish eat the juvenile crabs and fishermen take adults for bait.

The horseshoe crab is also valued by the pharmaceutical industry. An extract of its blood is used in tests for bacterial contamination. This poses no threat to the species as scientists have devised a method of extracting blood and retuni the crab to the water relatively unharmed.

LOBSTER (*Homarus gammarus*)

SIZE:	Length up to 50cm. Weight 5kg
DISTRIBUTION:	Rocky coasts of northern Europe as far south as the Mediterranean
IDENTIFICATION:	Dark-blue segmented body with two large pincers

This handsome, aggressive crustacean is highly prized as gourmet seafood and more often seen on restaurant menus or fishmongers' slabs than in the wild. Consequently numbers are declining and prices rising, making this an even more attractive catch for the fishermen's creels. Lobster fishing is controlled by licence and those under 9cm long must be returned to the sea. Sometimes it's possible to find a small lobster in a rock pool and, if disturbed, it will scoot backwards at an astonishing speed and hide in a rocky crevice. Apart from man, the lobster has few enemies: its exoskeleton or shell makes effective armour and the huge claws are formidable weapons.

The American lobster (*Homarus americanus*) is larger. The biggest specimen caught weighed over 20kg. In 1996, some American lobsters were caught off the English coast but had probably crossed the Atlantic in the galley of a cruise ship.

HARLEQUIN SHRIMP (*Hymenocera picta*)

SIZE:	Length up to 50mm
DISTRIBUTION:	Tropical Pacific and Indian Oceans
IDENTIFICATION:	Stocky body. White or pinkish, splashed with brown, purple, pink or red spots. Pink spots often edged in purple. Flat petal-like antennae. Eyes on stalks

For such a beautiful creature, the harlequin shrimp is fairly brutish when it comes to eating. It feeds on live sea stars, digging into its prey's tube feet and tugging out the inner tissues over several weeks, until the victim dies. It favours *Linckia* sea stars which it finds by scent using its delicate sensory antennae. It grasps one of the star's legs with its own walking legs and does a handstand on its two main claws, lifting the star's leg and allowing it to crawl under. Once there it flips the star onto its back where it is powerless to resist the ensuing ravages.

The harlequin shrimp is highly prized by aquarium keepers but its need for live sea stars makes it difficult for beginners to keep. Consequently it is relatively rare in captivity and is not threatened by over-harvesting. Instead, it is a main attraction for divers and marine photographers.

Crown of Thorns Starfish

(Acanthaster planci)

Size:	Diameter 25–40cm (occasionally up to 80cm). Spines 4–5cm
Distribution:	Pacific and Indian Oceans
Identification:	Usually reddish but colour varies with location. Very sharp, poisonous spines and 12–19 arms

The crown of thorns starfish is eating Australia's Great Barrier Reef. Conservationists are so concerned about the booming numbers of this attractive but venomous echinoderm and about the damage it is doing to the famous coral reef that they have carried out culls. One theory is that over-collection of the starfish's main predator, the Pacific triton, might be allowing it free rein but other research shows that such population explosions have occurred before and are part of a natural cycle. Whatever the reason, coral is being consumed in huge amounts and the reef is gradually disappearing. The starfish eats by distending its stomach through its mouth, soaking the coral with digestive juices and sucking up the resultant 'soup'. Each animal eats up to 6 square metres per year, leaving behind the white coral skeleton. Its poison causes intense pain, nausea and vomiting in humans and turns the victim's skin blue.

Langoustine or Dublin Bay Prawn ▼ (*Nephrops norvegicus*)

Size:	Length up to 24cm, excluding claws
Distribution:	Eastern Atlantic from Iceland to the Mediterranean
Identification:	Small, pale-orange lobster. Long, slender claws have spiny ridges and white markings

This delicious shellfish has always been prized by the Italians who gave it the name scampi but it was not until the 1950s that the British began to appreciate them and fishermen stopped throwing them back. The Irish were a little quicker off the mark and, when finding them among their catch, they sold the tasty creatures to street vendors when the fishing boats came into Dublin Bay. Although sometimes called Norway lobster the langoustine is so small that fishermen referred to them as prawns and the name has stuck to this day.

The langoustine lives on muddy bottoms at depths of 200–800m, burrowing into the seabed to escape predators. Unfortunately, this is no defence against creel lobster traps that lie on the seabed, or trawler nets.

Common Shrimp

(*Crangon crangon*)

Size:	Length up to 90mm
Distribution:	Coastal waters from Norway to the Mediterranean
Identification:	Semi-transparent brown body, fan-like tail and long antennae

In the days before foreign holidays were the norm, British children's seaside holidays involved bucket, spade and shrimping net. These D-shaped nets were poked into rock pools or pushed into the sea by paddling infants hoping for something for their bucket, or their tea. In the northeast of England, shrimp fishermen progressed from wading into the sea with a hand-net to using a larger, horse-drawn net. Horses were later superseded by tractors.

The common shrimp, or brown shrimp as it is sometimes known, lives in shallow burrows in the sand and can change its colour to match its surroundings. It emerges at night to feed on small molluscs and fish, swimming backwards by flexing the abdomen and tail at considerable speed.

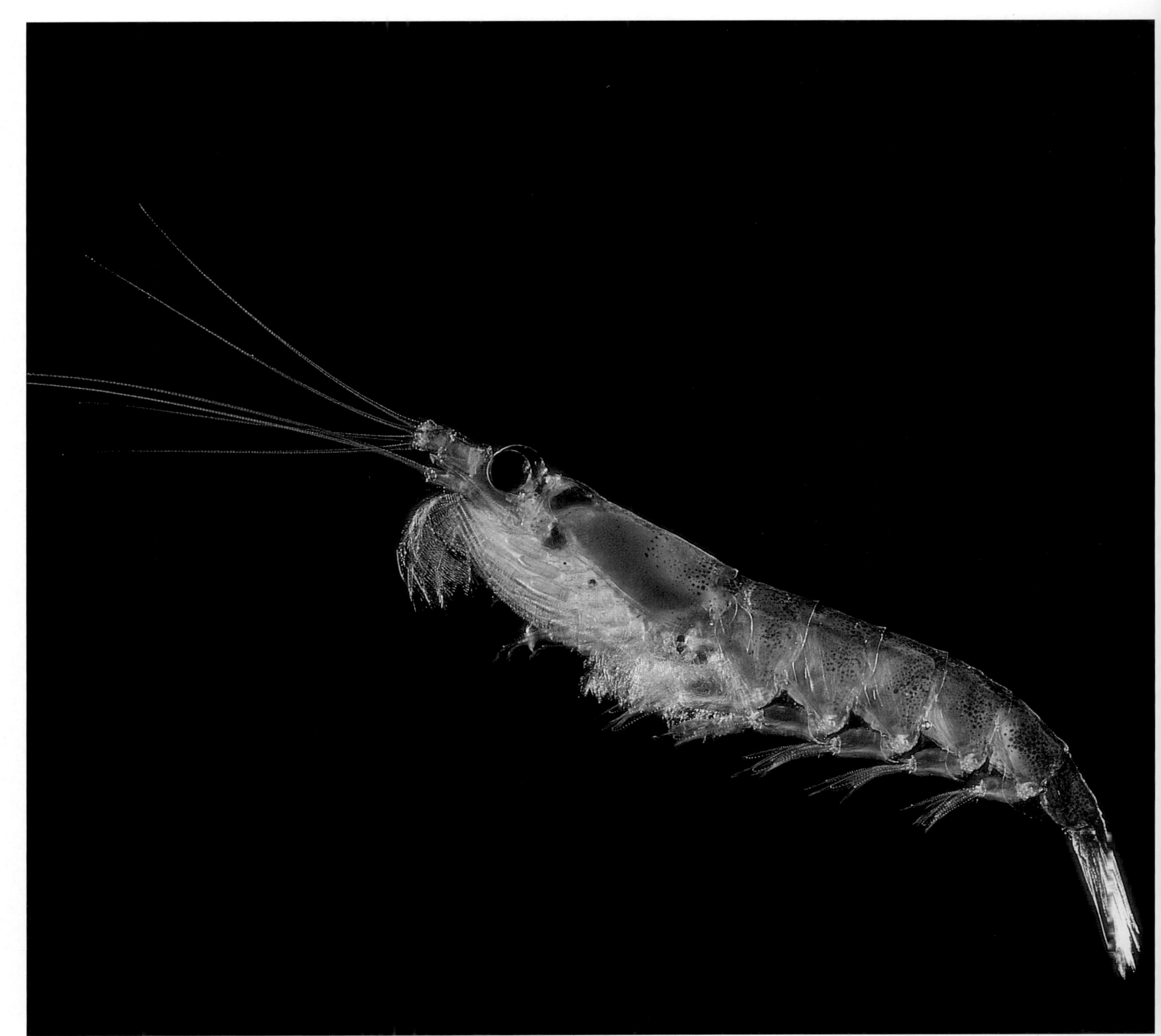

ANTARCTIC KRILL (*Euphausia superba*)

SIZE:	Length up to 4cm, weight 0.9g
DISTRIBUTION:	Throughout Antarctic waters. Descending to 90m during day, rising to surface at night to feed on phytoplankton. Often in dense swarms several kilometres wide
IDENTIFICATION:	Pink, translucent shrimp-like crustacean with hard exoskeleton, segmented body and many legs

Without a healthy krill population the whole food chain in the Southern Ocean, from seabirds to whales, would collapse. Krill is a general term used to describe about 85 species of open ocean crustaceans on which many animals depend, either directly or indirectly. *Euphasia superba* is the most abundant of them all. Scientists calculate that the biomass, the sheer collective weight and volume of krill, is the largest of any multicellular creature on the planet.

Fewer than 100,000 tonnes per year of all fish and crustaceans are harvested worldwide, yet in the 1960s it was suggested that a sustainable krill harvest alone could be around 150,000 tonnes per year. On this evidence commercial harvesting began in the early 1970s and the catch in 2003 was 120,000 tonnes, mostly used for human consumption, fish farm feed and sport fishing bait.

Sand Fiddler Crab ▲

(*Uca pugilator*)

Size:	Length 25mm, width 38mm
Distribution:	USA (Massachusetts to Mississippi, scattered in Texas), Bahamas
Identification:	Blue-grey irregularly-marked shell. One of the male's pincers is large and brightly-coloured

Several hundred fiddler crabs live in close proximity in colonies on sandbanks around salt marshes, with each crab fiercely defending its own burrow. The male attracts a passing female by waving his large cheliped or pincer and running towards her and back to his burrow entrance several times, to show her which is his. The large pincer is then drummed on the side of the burrow to entice her in. This is the point of no return: once she is inside, the male seals the entrance with mud.

To feed, the male uses his smaller pincer to scrape up a ball of mud and pop it into his mouth. Here edible matter is filtered out and the sediment deposited on the ground in pellets.

Red Swamp Crayfish

(*Procambarus clarkii*)

Size:	Length 5.5–12cm
Distribution:	North America. Introduced to Hawaii, Japan, North Africa and elsewhere
Identification:	Dark-red; wedge-shaped black stripe on abdomen. Sharp snout with mobile eyes and long antennae. Thin, tough exoskeleton. Five pairs of legs; long, narrow pincers

The red swamp crayfish is another example of a well-meaning intervention in nature which back-fired badly. This meaty little crustacean was taken to Asia and Africa as a food source and because it eats the snails which pass on bilharzia, or schistosomiasis disease, to humans. Unfortunately it is a master burrower and has destroyed riverbanks, dams, levees and water control structures in its new homes. It is also a host for many parasitic worms and flukes which affect vertebrates, including humans. Now many areas which brought in the red swamp crayfish are trying to get rid of it. In their native home, particularly the Mississippi basin, crayfish are controlled by predators – among them humans who enjoy their sweet, succulent meat.

Water Spider ▼

(*Argyroneta aquatica*)

Size:	8–15mm
Distribution:	Central and northern Europe
Identification:	Dull velvety-black when out of water

In still ponds and lakes, a silvery spider swimming among aquatic plants will be the water spider: the only spider in the world to live almost entirely under water. Its silvery appearance is caused by bubbles of air, trapped on its furry abdomen. After spinning a platform of silk and attaching it to submerged plants, the spider makes several journeys to the surface collecting air bubbles which it takes down to its underwater home. The bubbles rise and collect under the silk platform, pushing it up into a dome shape and providing the spider with its own private breathing space.

The water spider waits in the dome with its legs in the water ready to sense the vibrations of suitable passing prey. The unsuspecting insect receives a venomous bite and is dragged back to the dome to be consumed.

Waterhyacinth Grasshopper

(*Cornops aquaticum*)

Size:	Length 25–30mm. Weight 0.3g
Distribution:	South America. Introduced in South and East Africa
Identification:	Generally pale-green with dark stripe running length of body from bulbous eye to tail

The waterhyacinth doubles in size every 7–12 days, grows up to 1.8m tall and chokes every waterway it gets into. Having failed to rid lakes, rivers and dams using expensive machines and dangerous poisons, researchers in South and East Africa turned to a biological alternative: the waterhyacinth grasshopper. A colony of these little insects eats tons of hyacinths in a year and can clear large lakes which have become too clogged to be navigated. The female lays eggs near the crown of the hyacinth and newly emerged nymphs begin to feed immediately. This treatment is not available to hyacinth-throttled areas of North America, however, as the grasshopper also eats indigenous pickerel weed and would cause more problems than it cured.

Portuguese Man-of-war

(*Physalia physalis*)

Size:	Length (body) up to 30cm. Tentacles up to 20m long
Distribution:	Atlantic, Pacific and Indian Oceans, Caribbean and Sargasso Seas
Identification:	Translucent pink, blue or violet body. Long, blue or purple tentacles

This spectacular jellyfish is best admired from a distance or at least from the safety of a boat. Its long tentacles can inflict a painful sting to swimmers and even when dead and washed up on the beach the man-of-war's stinging cells retain their potency.

The Portuguese man-of-war is not a single organism but a colony of several hundred polyps. Beneath the floating body are clusters of reproductive and digestive polyps below which trail bright purple tentacles. This jellyfish does not swim but a ridge on the top of the float acts like a sail so the colony moves where the wind and tide take it. Small fish which drift among the tentacles are paralysed by the venom then drawn up to the digestive polyps and consumed. Some fish, such as the clown fish, produce a protective mucus, allowing them to feed on the tentacles which are constantly regenerated.

Invertebrates

BUTTERFLIES

Papua New Guinea was still a relatively wild and unexplored place when the British naturalist Alfred S. Meek was there in 1906 on a collecting trip. While there, he made a spectacular catch – the largest butterfly ever seen. Since then the world's rainforests have been hacked back for cocoa, rubber and oil palm plantations, agriculture and logging, and hardwood for the timber industry. However, there are some wonderful species remaining which vie for the title of most beautiful creature in the forest.

The specimen netted by Meek was a female **Queen Alexandra's birdwing** (*Troides alexandrae*), the largest butterfly in the world, with a wingspan up to 28cm. Nature has been no kinder than man: in 1951 the eruption of Mt Lamington destroyed 250 square km of prime habitat and today this species is only known in a small area of the Popondetta Plain. The males, which have iridescent yellow, pale blue and green markings on a black background, swarm around flowering kwila trees during the breeding season. Females, which are larger but more drab with cream markings on a dark, chocolate brown background, will not accept any male which has not visited the flowers. The female lays huge eggs, 4mm in diameter, on the leaves of the pipe vine (*Aristolochia schlecteri*) high in the forest canopy.

A strong contender for the world's most striking butterfly, the **blue morpho** (*Morpho menelaus*) is found in the rainforests of South and Central America where it can be seen flitting about in the canopy as it goes in search of flower nectar, tree sap and rotting fruit juice which it drinks with its long proboscis. The blue and mother-of-pearl upperwings are countered by brown, grey-black and reddish underwings which, when closed, look just like autumn leaves. Wingspan can be up to 18cm. The caterpillars have hairs which irritate humans. They feed on rotting fruit and fermenting fungi and, if threatened, produce a strong rancid butter smell.

Anyone visiting the rainforests of Queensland, Australia can enjoy the sight of the protected **ulysses** or **blue mountain swallowtail butterfly** (*Papilio ulysses*) by leaving a blue object up to 30m away from the forest edge. The spectacular bright blue and black male of this species will come to investigate, thinking that it has found a female. The female is more subdued in colour but shares the impressive swallowtail extensions on the rear wings. Wingspan is up to 14cm. The ulysses (of which there are 16 known sub-species in Australia and Indonesia) flies quickly and strongly through woodland and open country and eats citrus fruit. Its caterpillar is also impressive: green with a white underside, white strip across its front, rows of large white spots on top and a large white spike at the rear.

Blue morpho butterfly

Ulysses butterfly

MONARCH BUTTERFLY

(*Danaus plexippus*)

SIZE:	Wingspan 8.8–10cm
DISTRIBUTION:	North America
IDENTIFICATION:	Distinctive black-veined, orange wings with white spots on the dark margins. The males have one dark spot on each hind wing

One of the most impressive sights of the insect world must be the mass migration of monarch butterflies each autumn. In flight they appear as a flickering orange cloud and when they land on a tree they can completely obliterate its shape. Hundreds of millions of monarchs make an incredible journey of up to 4,800km from eastern United States and Canada to the mountain fir forests of Mexico. How they find the overwintering site is one of nature's unsolved mysteries. The great-grandchildren of butterflies which flew north the previous year return to the same site and sometimes to the same tree as their great-grandparents.

LONG-TAILED SKIPPER *(Urbanus proteus)* ▼

SIZE:	Wingspan 4.5–6cm
DISTRIBUTION:	Argentina to southern United States
IDENTIFICATION:	Long tail hind wings, bright blue-green on upper wing surface, brown or grey on underside

In late summer or early autumn, this beautiful butterfly is a common sight on fallow agricultural land. The males patrol their territory, constantly on the lookout for a receptive female. Various beans, peas or hog peanut plants are chosen by the female to lay her eggs, which she deposits singly on the underside of the leaves. When the larvae hatch, their main concern is to avoid becoming a tasty morsel for a passing bird so they concentrate on building a shelter. A leaf is folded like a tent and secured with silk, forming a safe haven for the caterpillar during the day. As the caterpillar grows it might need to use more than one leaf but it folds and secures each one in the same way, hence the common name 'bean leaf roller'.

OLD WORLD SWALLOWTAIL BUTTERFLY *(Papilio machaon)*

SIZE:	Wingspan 5–7cm
DISTRIBUTION:	Non-tropical Eurasia, North America and North Africa
IDENTIFICATION:	Yellow wings with black veins, lower wings have a curved band of blue ending in a reddish-orange eye spot

Swallowtail butterflies are some of the most beautiful butterflies in the world, named for the striking tails on their hind wings which resemble the streaming tail feathers of a swallow. On mainland Europe and North America the old world swallowtail is fairly widespread, inhabiting meadows, open hilltops and even some tundra areas. Two or three broods of eggs are laid singly between April and September. At first the caterpillars are black and white, resembling bird droppings to deter predators. As they mature, they turn green with black and orange rings. Now they are more visible to birds seeking a tasty meal, their first line of defence is to produce a foul smell from 'horns' on their head.

Southern Hawker Dragonfly (*Aeshna cyanea*)

Size:	Length 4.5–5cm
Distribution:	Europe from the Iberian peninsular and western Mediterranean areas, north as far as southern Scandinavia and east to the Caucasus
Identification:	Long, thin body with four large wings. Two large compound eyes and short antennae. The black bodies have two broad bands on the abdominal segments, which are blue in males and apple green in females

On warm still days in late summer dragonflies add another splash of colour as they chase flying insects, catching them with their legs and eating on the wing. Dragonflies are the subject of much folklore and fable, strangely associated with the devil. In Britain, one of its common names is 'devil's darning needle'. Although they are strikingly beautiful insects, they belong to the genus *Aeshna*, which means ugly or misshapen.

The southern hawker dragonfly is usually found near water, breeding in ponds, lakes, and ditches. They are territorial insects, and males will attack other males who enter their patch on sight. Dead wood or vegetation at the water's edge make ideal sites for the female to make holes and lay her eggs. The larvae hatch the following spring and spend two or three years underwater ambushing tadpoles and other aquatic insects before emerging one night in late summer to begin metamorphosis. Newly emerged dragonflies can sometimes be seen hanging from the stalks of aquatic plants waiting for their legs and wings to harden.

Dung Beetle (*Kheper aegyptiorum*) ▲

Size:	Length 3cm
Distribution:	Worldwide except Antarctica
Identification:	Grooved shield in metallic-green, pink or black. Flying wings are folded under hard covers

Observing a dung or scarab beetle rolling a ball of dung many times its own weight, the ancient Egyptians believed it was huge scarabs that kept the Earth revolving and the dung beetle became an important religious symbol.

To find their essential pat of dung the beetles fly after mammals using their acute sense of smell. The male makes the first ball and presents it to a female and if she accepts his offering they roll it away together, fighting off other beetles attempting to steal their prize. Together the pair will bury the ball before mating. As the male returns to the dung patch the female reshapes the ball and lays her eggs in the thin end.

Banjo or Violin Beetle

(*Mormolyce phyllodes*)

Size:	Length 75mm
Distribution:	Southern Thailand and Indonesia
Identification:	Flat brown banjo shaped beetle

This beetle bears a remarkable resemblance to the instruments after which it is named. Its flat front wings allow it to squeeze into crevices in the bark of fallen trees or under bracket fungi where it feeds on insect larvae or the fungus itself. Also known as a fiddle beetle or ghost walker, its distinctive shape has made it a collector's item and specimens are sold for about $25 despite the fact that they have been protected since 1992. In 2000, forestry officials in and around Bangkok handed out pictures of the violin beetle and 14 other rare, protected insects in an attempt to crack down on the trade. Its image lives on though, depicted on postage stamps in 2001 and 2003, and used as a model for jewellery.

Darkling Beetle (*Eleodes spp*)

Size:	Length 10–35mm
Distribution:	Worldwide
Identification:	Jet-black oval or oblong beetle with prominent head, and thick leathery wing covers

The darkling beetle has two very good reasons for standing on its head. In deserts with rainfall of less than 15mm a year, a light fog at dawn is the only other source of water, so the beetle tilts its weight forward allowing dew to condense and run down its back to its mouth.

The position is also used as a defence against predators and if this odd sight does not frighten them, the beetle can squirt a foul-smelling, foul-tasting secretion, thus earning its common name of 'stinkbug'. This deters most predators, but the grasshopper mouse has learnt to wedge the beetle's rear end into the soil and eat it head first, leaving the unappetising part to rot in the ground.

Leafcutter Ant ▼

(*Atta rodona*)

Size:	Length (workers)1.5–12.5mm, a queen is 19mm long
Distribution:	Costa Rica to Argentina. Similar species in southern USA
Identification:	Rust or dark-brown ant. Workers have three pairs of spines on the thorax and one on the back of the head

Beneath the floor of the tropical rainforest a complex colony of leafcutter ants runs a fungus farm with an efficiency many estate managers would envy. Five to eight million ants follow one of six trades according to their size, getting through as much forage per day as a fully grown cow. But the foliage is not eaten by the ants: it is fed to their cultivated fungus which in turn grows at a far from natural rate producing food for the whole colony. A medium sized tree can be stripped in one night as the cutting ants bite the leaves into tiny pieces and pass them to smaller, foraging ants who carry them home in a long line, holding the piece of leaf above their head.

Soldiers, gardeners and janitors complete the work force with only the drones mating with the queen.

Goliathus Beetle (*Goliathus cacicus*)

Size:	Length up to 10cm
Distribution:	Western equatorial Africa
Identification:	Bluish-white wing cases with dark markings. Male has tawny shield behind the head with black vertical stripes

Goliathus beetles are among the heaviest in the world with some reports of weights up to 100g. Of the five species, *Goliathus regius Klug* is the largest, measuring up to 150mm. When flying, the noise of their wings has been likened to the sound of tiny helicopters. They are also exceptionally strong and grip tree trunks tightly with their claws or tarsi.

When fallen trees in the tropical rain forests start to decompose, the soft, moist wood makes an ideal site for the female goliath beetle to lay her eggs. The larvae take several months to mature and during this time perform a valuable ecological service by tunnelling through the logs, thus hastening decomposition. Unlike the young of other scarabs, goliathus larvae prey on grubs and small insects rather than eating the wood itself.

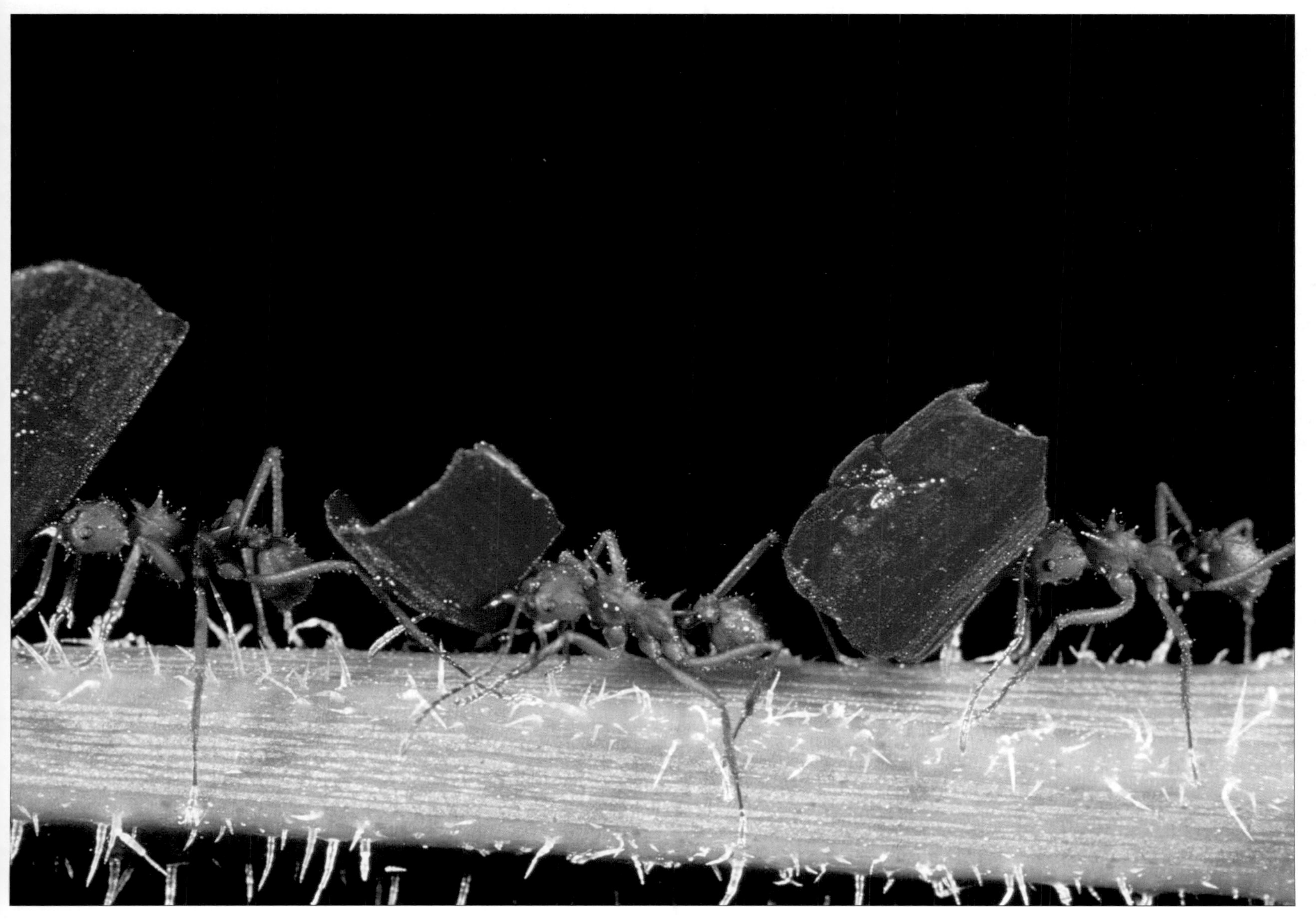

Termites

Without termites the world would be covered in vast compost heaps and there would be fewer animals. The 2,753 termite species eat dead wood, roots and grass, leaf litter, dung and humus, all of which makes up the most abundant organic matter in the biosphere. This cellulose plant wall material is converted into termites, which in their turn feed thousands of insectivorous reptiles, birds, amphibians and mammals, many of which are essential for other creatures further up the food chain.

In some tropical areas there are 10,000 termites per square metre of soil and one of the most important species in Africa is *Macrotermes bellicosus.* These termites build huge mounds, common throughout the sub-Sahara, out of saliva and soil. Each mound houses a single family, known as a colony, which is centred on a king and queen insect. The colony is made up of three types of termite, all of which begin life as identical larvae but develop differently according to diet, time of year and pheromones. Workers are most numerous and do all the building, feeding, cleaning and tending; soldiers protect the colony from predators such as ants and centipedes; reproductives are able to mate and create new colonies and include those that become king and queen.

The king's role is to provide sperm for the queen and she produces all the eggs for the colony, sometimes laying thousands a day. When she is full of eggs her body becomes so large (about 6cm long) that she cannot move and has to be constantly licked clean and fed by workers which, like the other termites, are about 10mm long.

All the soldiers are females and they spit corrosive glue at their adversaries. However, they cannot deal with large predators like the aardvark, which can wipe out a colony in one visit. When a mound is overwhelmed by driver ants, workers rush to the royal chamber and seal themselves in. If they survive the attack they form the basis of a new colony.

The tall porous spires on top of a termite mound act as lungs, dispersing heat and carbon dioxide and taking in fresh air, which sinks to air cellars beneath the main living chambers, most of which are below ground level.

Macrotermes eat dead plant material softened by fungus but this is in short supply in the dry season so they create special fungus chambers in the mound. Here they use saliva and animal droppings to make combs on which fungus grows, breaking down the faecal matter and making it digestible.

Termites are said, by those brave enough to eat them, to taste of lettuce.

Termite queen and attendants

Seventeen-year Cicada

(Magicicada septendecim)

Size:	Length up to 3cm
Distribution:	Northern, midwestern and eastern United States
Identification:	Black body with broad orange stripes on the underside and an orange spot on the thorax. Legs and eyes are reddish-orange. Two pairs of clear wings with orange veins

After living for seventeen years in darkness underground, the nymph of this cicada emerges to enjoy the sunshine for just five weeks before dying. The eggs might have been laid over several weeks but the nymphs not only know which year to emerge, they also know which night – and almost all of them emerge at the same time, crawling through the exit tunnel they started to build a few weeks earlier. During their short life above ground, the male cicadas congregate in large choruses, 'singing' to attract their mates and deafening those in the vicinity in the process. After mating the female cuts slits in twigs and lays her batch of 400–500 eggs. After nine weeks, the eggs hatch and the larvae drop to the ground then burrow into cracks in the soil.

Many myths and much folklore surround the periodical cicada, particularly among Native Americans, who were awed by its regular appearance at such long intervals. They are sometimes mistakenly called locusts, probably because their large gatherings remind people of the swarms of migratory locusts recorded in Biblical times.

Grasshopper (*Acanthacris ruficornis*)

Size:	Length 3.5–5.5cm
Distribution:	Throughout Africa south of the Sahara
Identification:	Yellow-brown, green or pinkish body (depending on terrain) with dark wings and dark stripe behind eye

These grasshoppers appear suddenly in gardens and open ground following the first summer rains and after seven moulting stages become adults by February or March. They are then ready to eat. People in northern South Africa, Zaire and the Sahel (the band of savannah south of the Sahara) are partial to fried grasshopper. They pull off the legs and wings before frying the live creature in a pan or roasting it in the embers of a fire. Most South Africans call this grasshopper a locust, but wrongly so, as it does not swarm. It eats the leaves of various small trees. The female lays about 120 eggs in a long egg pod which lies partly buried in soft soil. When the larvae emerge from this froth-filled pod in October they are green. They might remain that colour or change colour to match their surroundings.

Desert Locust ▲

(*Schistocerca gregaria*)

Size:	Length up to 65mm
Distribution:	North Africa
Identification:	Immature adults pink, sexually mature adults bright yellow when ready to breed. Non-flying 'hoppers' solid yellow with heavy black spots

The desert locust is one of the most destructive insects on earth. Each locust can eat its own weight of food in one day but it is the vast collective numbers that makes the swarm so ruinous to crops and pastureland. The largest swarm ever recorded contained an estimated 12.5 trillion locusts. It covered several hundred square km. Such swarms are so big that they are easily tracked by radar. Fortunately, only a few of the 300 species of locust and grasshopper found in Africa are this highly mobile – the majority lead a more sedentary lifestyle.

Dead Leaf Mantis

(*Acanthops falcata*)

Size:	Length 5cm
Distribution:	South America
Identification:	Varying colours from yellow to peachy pink and black. Forelegs more powerful than middle and hind legs, with rows of hooked spines along inner edges

There are almost 2,000 species of mantis in different habitats across the world and they are all shapes, sizes and colours. What they share is a gruesomely efficient hunting technique and a penchant for cannibalism. It is well-known that the female eats her partner, head first, after mating but this tends to happen more in captivity than in the wild. The dead leaf mantis, like the others, relies on camouflage as a first line of defence against predators like birds, lizards or frogs, but other larger species – and some are 30cm long – will actually fend off attackers with those fearsome front legs. The mantis hunts by waiting stock still – its legs gathered up as if praying – until an insect or spider comes by. Then it lashes out and snares the victim in the spined crooks of its legs, bites off the head and munches away at leisure.

Oriental Cockroach ▶

(*Blatta orientalis*)

Size:	Length 2.5–3cm. Weight, male 0.3g, female 0.8g
Distribution:	Worldwide
Identification:	Deep-brown flat body. The male's wings reach almost to the abdomen, the female only has wing pads

The Oriental cockroach is found in houses and buildings everywhere and around rubbish or sewers outside in warm weather. It likes warm, damp areas and often inhabits cellars, or seeks out higher levels for warmth. It will eat whatever it finds, often contaminating food after its foray into decaying rubbish, and is considered to be one of the worst pests in the world. Very active, and capable of running and flying very fast, cockroaches are notoriously difficult to catch and exterminate.

The larger American and Australian cockroaches can also be found in Europe but are less common than the Oriental species.

Glow Worm

(*Lampyris noctiluca*)

Size:	Length, female, 1–1.5cm, males smaller
Distribution:	Throughout Europe
Identification:	A dark-brown or blackish body, the male has two pairs of wings, the female has none, but has a segmented body and threadlike antennae

The glow worm is not a worm, it is actually a beetle. Although the male and the larvae glow slightly, the female produces the most noticeable light. She bends her abdomen to display her glowing organs in a bold attempt to attract a flying male. It might be thought that this would also attract predators, but studies have proved that they associate the luminescence with the glow worm's bitter taste and are repelled.

Female cockroach with egg pouch

▲ Common Warble Fly *(Hypoderma lineatum)*

Size:	Length 2cm
Distribution:	Sub-Arctic region
Identification:	Small, tawny-yellow and black fly

The female warble fly, a harmless-looking insect, can detect caribou from a great distance and can fly non-stop for 400km to find them. She lays her eggs on the caribou's legs. When the larvae hatch they burrow through the skin and work their way up to the animal's back. Here they form a cyst or warble, making a breathing hole in the hide. In spring, the larva emerges through the breathing hole before developing into an adult fly. Though it is a pest and parasite to the unfortunate caribou, the warble fly larva is considered a delicacy by some of the Inuit.

Ichneumon Fly *(Amblyteles armatorius)* ▶

Size:	Length 2–5cm, plus 3cm ovipositor
Distribution:	Europe, North America and Asia
Identification:	Slim, black body with wasp waist, pale-yellow or white marks on the abdomen, orange legs and long flexible antennae

The female ichneumon fly with her long ovipositor is often mistaken for a wasp with a huge sting. She is completely harmless but her larvae can be deadly. The larvae of insects such as wood wasps lie deep in fallen timber, where the ichneumon fly can sense their presence. She uses her ovipositor to pierce the wood and lay her egg on or next to the host, taking 20–40 minutes to complete the operation. When the egg hatches, the ichneumon larva feeds on the body of its host. Gruesome as this sounds, it is one of nature's ways of keeping insect pests under control.

MOSQUITO (*Aedes hexodontus*)

SIZE:	Length 7–8mm
DISTRIBUTION:	All circumpolar north regions
IDENTIFICATION:	Long slender body, long proboscis, scales on the veins of the wings, feather-like antennae

The disease-carrying mosquito is indirectly blamed for approximately one million human deaths each year. The majority of species are found in the tropics but the greatest concentration is in the Arctic tundra where clouds of newly hatched insects can block out the sunlight. As the spring snow melts thousands of square km are flooded, providing perfect mosquito breeding ground.

Only the female mosquito bites. She needs protein to develop her eggs and makes life a misery for man and beast in her hunt for protein-rich blood. Inserting her proboscis and injecting an anticoagulant, she will suck out three or four times her original weight in blood. She is not immune from biting herself. Midges lie in wait and sometimes rob the engorged mosquito of her bounty. Rafts of eggs are laid on still water and usually lie dormant until temperatures rise in the spring. Both the eggs and larvae can survive the winter frozen in ice.

Tarantula Hawk Wasp

(*Pepsis formosa*)

Size:	Length 20–38mm
Distribution:	California and Mexico
Identification:	Metallic blue-black body, reddish antennae and red wings

For the squeamish, there are many details of the everyday behaviour of parasites that do not bear close scrutiny. Of these, the way the female tarantula hawk wasp ensures a well-fed infancy for her young must be one of the most gruesome. She locates a tarantula by smell and injects her venom. The spider is paralysed almost immediately but not killed. Despite the spider's being several times her own weight, the wasp drags it back to her own burrow. A single egg is laid on the spider's abdomen before the live-burial chamber is sealed. When the larva hatches it has fresh spider meat from the still living tarantula and eats its way in, saving the vital organs until last, so ensuring the meat stays fresh for as long as possible.

The bright colours of the tarantula hawk wasp serve as a warning: its sting is said to be extraordinarily painful.

Fat-tailed Scorpion

(*Androctonus australis*)

Size:	Length up to 10cm
Distribution:	In Africa: Algeria, Chad, Egypt, Libya, Mauritania, Somalia, Sudan and Tunisia. Elsewhere: Israel, India, Pakistan, Saudi Arabia and Yemen in Asia
Identification:	Long, segmented yellowish body, the last five abdominal segments appear tail-like and end with the venom glands

This is one of the world's most dangerous scorpions, causing several deaths each year. The sting can cause temporary paralysis, convulsions, cardiac arrest or respiratory failure. It inhabits dry stony, desert areas living in natural crevices during the heat of the day and is not averse to using cracks in houses for its home.

A rather more endearing habit of the scorpion is its mating ritual. The male holds out his pincers when approaching a female and leads her into a courtship dance. After mating, the female gives birth to 25–35 young that she catches in her folded legs as they are born. She then helps them up onto her back where they remain for a week or two.

Black Widow Spider

(*Latrodectus mactans*)

Size:	Length 8–10mm (female), male roughly half this size
Distribution:	Southern states of USA, Canada, Mexico, West Indies and South America
Identification:	Shiny black long-legged spider. Female has red hourglass-shaped mark on abdomen and one or two red spots on back

The black widow spider is so named because she occasionally attacks her partner after mating and eats him. However, this is the exception rather than the rule as she is not normally aggressive, even to humans. But when cornered the black widow will bite, injecting highly toxic venom and leaving a characteristic double puncture wound. The venom is 15 times more potent than that of a rattlesnake but the amount injected is usually too small to be fatal. Interestingly, one of the symptoms following the bite is painful rigidity of the abdominal wall leading to a misdiagnosis of appendicitis, which has been known to result in death from unnecessary surgery rather than from the bite itself.

Mexican Red-kneed Tarantula (*Brachypelma smithi*)

Size:	Leg span 15–18cm
Distribution:	Mexico, southwestern United States and Panama
Identification:	Large black or dark-brown spider with red or orange joints on each leg

This spider, despite its starring role in many a horror film, has a fairly docile temperament and is becoming increasingly popular as a pet. The American Tarantula Society encourages breeding in captivity as this species is protected and cannot be exported from Mexico.

In the wild, the Mexican red-kneed tarantula acts more as we would expect. It hunts at night, lying in wait for an unwary frog or lizard then pouncing on its quarry. Holding its prey with all eight legs, the tarantula injects venom through two hollow fangs, paralysing its victim and liquefying its internal organs. The pre-digested fats and proteins are sucked out leaving behind the hollow carcass.

Acknowledgements

The publisher would like to thank Oxford Scientific Films for kindly providing the photographs for this book. We would also like to thank the following for their kind permission to reproduce their photographs:

MAMMALS
Burchell's or Plains Zebras Mike Hill (10-11 and 84-85); Polar bears Daniel Cox; Killer whales Kim Westerskov; Beluga whale Doug Allan; Walrus Daniel Cox; Harp seal Daniel and Julie Cox; Weddell seal Ben Osborne; Arctic fox Owen Newman; Arctic wolf Daniel Cox; Arctic hare Ted Levin/AA; Ermine; Brown Bear (Grizzly Bear) Daniel Cox; Moose W. Shattil and B Rozinski; Reindeer Johnny Johnson/AA; Beaver Daniel Cox Musk ox Lon E Lauber; Wolverine Daniel Cox; Lynx Daniel Cox; Fallow Deer Tipling; Muntjac Chris Knights/SAL; Wild boar K G Vock/OKAPIA; Badger Mark Hamblin; Red fox Mike Powles; Giant Panda (and on page 316) Daniel Cox; Tasmanian devil Steve Turner; Koala (and on back jacket) Steve Turner; Common wombat Daniel Cox; European Wildcat Norbert Rosing; Small Spotted Genet Jorge Sierra Antinolo; Raccoon Tom Ulrich; Pine Martin Michael Leach; Polecat Mark Hamblin; Groundhog (Woodchuck) Numbat Bert and Babs Wells; Peter's epauletted fruit bat Partridge Films; Wahlberg's fruit bat osf; Weasel Mark Hamblin; Common Rabbit O.S.F.; Eurasian red squirrel Niall Benie; Grey squirrel Richard Packwood; Black Rat Robin Redfern; Brown rat Keith Ringland; Chipmunk Niall Benvie; Hamster osf; Eurasian common shrew Barrie Watts; Edible dormouse Alastair McEwen; Harvest mouse Osf.; Grey wolf Charles Palek/AA; Vicuna Tui de Roy; Chamois Richard Packwood; Moufflon Jorge Sierra Antinolo; Llama Rick Price/SAL; Alpine ibex Ben Osborne; Yak; Bighorn sheep Stan Osolinski; Asian Black bear Judd Cooney; Bobcat Tom Ulrich; cougar Steve Turner; Snow Leopard Daniel Cox; Mountain Tapir John Chellman/AA; Hyrax Stan Osolinski; Hoary Marmot Tom Ulrich; Chinchilla Michael Leach; Michael Fogden; Orynx Mike Hill; Addax Berndt Fischer; Dromedary camel Mickey Gibson; Bactrian camels Colin Monteath; Spotted skunk Tom Ulrich; Coyote Bob Bennett; Dingo Roger Brown; Meerkats David MacDonald; Hamadryas baboon Mike Hill; Fennec fox Eyal Bartov; Sandcat Alain Dragesco-Joffe; porcupine; Red Kangaroo K. Gowlett-Holmes; Grey kangaroo Steve Turner; Rabbit-eared bandicoot Bert & Babs Wells; Gerbil, Elephants walking front endpaper) Martyn Colbeck; African elephant Martyn Colbeck; African elephants (mother and calf) Martyn Colbeck; Black Rhinoceros David Cayless; White Rhinoceros Tim Jackson; Wildebeest Richard Packwood; Bison Impala Stan Osolinski;Giraffe Martin Colbeck; Giraffe (head) Martin Colbeck Burchell's or Plains Zebras Mike Hill;Greater Kudu; Sable Ariadne Van Zandbergen; Indian Black Buck Antelope Stanley Breeden;Pronghorn; Springbok Stan Osolinski; African Lion Adam Jones; lioness and cubs drinking (and on page one) Peter Lillie; Spotted hyena Alan J. Hartley; Cheetah Stan Osolinksi; Przewalski's Horse Bill Paton/SAL Warthog John Downer; Olive Baboon Steve Turner; Caracal William Grey; Black-tailed prairie dog Marty Cordano; Ratel or Honey badger Mary Plage; Aadvark Brian Kenney; Quokka Eric Woods; Spectacled Hare Wallaby Bert and Babs Wells; Grasshopper Mouse; West Indian Manatee (and on jacket flap) Herb Segars/AA; Water Buffalo Stan Osolinski; Hippopotamus Lee Lyon/SAL; Otter Bridget Wheeler/SAL; North American river otter Alan and Sandy Carey; Water Mongoose ; Duck-billed platypus Daniel and Julie Cox; muskrat Tom Ulrich; Northern Water vole Tony Tilford; mink Marianne Wilding/SAL; Blue WhaleR. Ellis /OKAPIA; Humpback Whale David Fleetham; Sperm Whale Thoma Haider; Black Right Whale Des and Jen Bartlett/SAL; Sei Whale Gerard Soury; Common dolphin Gerard Soury; Bottlenose Dolphin Howard Hall; Dugong David Fleetham; Sea Otter Daniel Cox; Orang utan Konrad Wothe; Bonobo/ Pygmy chimp Martyn Colbeck; Chimpanzee Mike Birkhead; Golden lion tamarin Chris Sharp; Common Gibbon; Common Marmoset Michael Dick/AA; Mandrill Zig Leszczynski/AA; Probiscis monkey Michael Dick/AA; Long-tailed Macaque David C. Fritts/AA; Red howler monkey Raymond Menzies; Aye-aye David Haring; Slender Loris David Haring; Common Cuscus Konrad Wothe; Striped Possum; Tree porcupine Alan Root/SAL; Three-toed sloth Norbert Wu; Binturong Mickey Gibson/AA; Common Long-nosed Armadillo Paul Franklin; Giant PangolinBruce Watkins/AA; Tiger Dinodia picture agency; Clouded Leopard Alan & Sandy Carey; ocelot Brian Kenney; Jaguar Nick Gordon; Asian elephant (also on page two) Stan Osolinski; Bongo Stan Osolinski; Okapi John Boyd; Brazilian Tapir Michale Fogden; Short-tailed Leaf-nosed Fruit Bat Joe McDonald/ AA; Front cover tiger: Bob Bennett, Back endpaper: Masai Giraffe Robert Nosing; Wildebeest in the sunset (8-9) Mike Powles, Mountain lion with cub(320) Michael Sewell

BIRDS
Lesser flamingo (148-9) Mark Deeble and Victoria Stone; Emperor penguins Doug Allan; Macaroni penguins Mike Hill; Adelie penguins Steve Turner; Wandering Albatross; Southern Giant petrel Doug Allan; Greater Snow goose Owen Newman; Willow ptarmigan Daniel Cox; Atlantic puffin Richard Packwood; Snowy sheathbill DanielCox; Ivory gull Chris Knights/SAL; Arctic tern Richard Packwood; White-tailed eagle Berndt Fischer; Siberian crane Tom Ulrich; Buff-breasted Sandpiper Richard Kittlewell/ AA; Gyrfalcon Tom Ulrich; Tundra swan Edward Robinson Bewick Swan Ronald Toms; Snowy owl E.R. Digginger/AA; Great grey owl Philippe Henry; Snow bunting Niall Benvie; Goldcrest Chris Knights/SAL; Tawny owl Tony Tilford; Barn owl Berndt Fischer; Wild turkey Gary Griffen /AA; Common pheasant Roland Mayr; Acorn woodpecker Partridge Films Ltd; Baltimore Oriole Ken Cole/AA; Common Nightingale Tony Tilford; Blue jay Daybreak Imagery; Eurasian cuckoo Mark Hamblin; Common Swift; Robin Mark Hamblin; Wren Conrad Wothe; Golden Eagle Konrad Wothe; Bald eagle in flight Daniel Cox; condor Mark Jones; Clark's Nutcracker Tom Ulrich; Blue Grouse Matthias Breiter; sunbird Tim Jackson; Water Pipit Mike Brown; Red Crossbill Chris Knights; Steller's jay Leonard Lee Rue III/AA; Lappet-faced vulture Steve Turner; Emu Michael Fogden; Ostrich Christopher Grizmek/OPAKIA; Swainson's hawk Tom Ulrich; Sociable weaver Tim Jackson; Road runner James H. Robinson; Burrowing owl James H. Robinson; Cape Griffon vulture Tim Jackson; Secretary bird Martyn Colbeck; Red-billed Hornbill Partridge Films; Greater prairie chicken Daybreak imagery; Hammerkop Tim Jackson; Yellow-billed oxpecker Steve Turner; Scarlet Ibis Frank Schneidermeyer; Grey heron Peter Clark/SAL; Marabou stork Richard Packwood; Osprey Michael Leach; American bittern Berndt Fischer; Shoebill Adam Jones; Canada goose Stan Osolinksi; Lesser flamingo Stan Osolinski; Takahe John McCammon; Common Kingfisher D.J. Saunders; Mandarin duck Ian West; Mallard Mark Hamblin; American White Pelican Marty Cordano; Eider Niall Benvie; Common Cormorant Alain Christof; Northern Gannet Eric Woods; Booby Mike Hill Sooty Tern Richard Herrman Turnstone George Reszeter Knot Mark Hamblin; Great Frigate Bird Mary Plage; Common peafowl Michael Richards; Resplendent Quetzal Michael Fogden; Harpy eagle Tui de Roy; Toco Toucan Konrad Wothe; Hoatzin Michael Sewell; Australian Cassowary Steve Turner; Electus parrot Tony Tilford; Scarlet Macaw Brian Kenney; Rufuous-breasted hermit hummingbird Robert Tyrell; Bird of Paradise Tony Tilford; Vogelkop bowerbird Richard Kirby;

FISH, CRUSTACEANS AND OTHER AQUATIC CREATURES
Clown anemonefish David Fleetham (268-9 and 280); Arctic Cod Doug Allan; Blackfin icefish Doug Allan; Lumpfish (lumpsucker) Mark Webster Antarctic krill Chris J. Gilbert; Red sock-eye salmon Richard Hermann; Archer fish osf; piranha Tony Allen; Water spider Harry Fox; Fiddler crab David Fleetham; Great white shark David Fleetham; White-tipped reef shark David Fleetham; Manta ray David Fleetham; Northern bluefin tuna Richard Herrman; Mackerel David Fleetham; Atlantic herring Zig Leszczynski/AA; Lion fish Zig Leszczynski/AA; striped Marlin Richard Herrman; Tiger grouper Joe Dorsey; Striped Cleaner Wrasse osf; Leatherback Turtle Green Sea Turtle David Fleetham; Loggerhead turtle Gerard Soury; Salt water crocodile Tobias Bernhard; Banded Sea Snake Michael Fogden; Lined Sea horse Laurence Gould; Ghost crab Prof Jack Dermid; Horseshoe crab David Cayless; Lobster Mark Webster; Harelquin shrimp David Fleetham Portuguese man-of-war osf; Crown of thorns starfish Mark Webster; Langoustine or Dublin Bay Prawn & Common Shrimp Paul Kay

INVERTEBRATES
Monarch butterflies Mantis Wildlife Films (292-293) Mosquito osf; Common warblefly London scientific films; Ichneumon fly Jame H. Robinson; Seventeen-year Cicada Breck P. Kent: Cockroach Paulo de Oliveira; Old World swallow tail butterfly Michael Leach; Southern Hawker (Dragon fly) Alastair Shay; Dung beetle Stan Osolinski; Monarch butterfly; Darkling beetle Michael Fogden; Fat-tailed scorpion London Scientific Films; Red-kneed tarantula Martyn Chillmaid; Black widow spider Scott Camazine; Long-tailed Skipper Stan Osolinski; Termite queen and attendants Kjell Sandved; Goliathus Beetle; Blue morpho butterfly Kjell Sandved; Ulysses butterfly Mantis Wildlife Films; Leafcutter ant Richard K la Val/AA; Dead Leaf Mantis osf

REPTILES AND AMPHIBIANS
Sidewinder (232-3); Boreal Chorus Frog Allen Blake Sheldon/AA; Western Painted Turtle Zig Leszczynski/AA; Common toad Paulo de Oliveira; Adder or Viper Mark Hamblin; Fire Salamander Michael Fogden; Common frog Paul Franklin; Great crested newt Paul Franklin; Pit Viper Michael Fogden; Western diamondback rattlesnake Tom Ulrich; Coral snake Mike Linley/SAL; Black mamba Brian Kenney; Asian or Indian Cobra John Mitchell; Frilled lizard Steve Turner; Starred Tortoise Zig Leszczynski/AA; Mangrove snake (sp) (borneo) or Mangrove Snake Norbert Wu /BrianKenney; Grass Snake Chris Knights/SA; Common Sanpping turtle Breck P. Kent/AA; American alligator Philippe Henry; Cuvier's Dwarf Caiman Joe McDonald/AA; Nile Crocodile Hilary Pooley; Nile Crocodile walking Mark Dreeble & Victoria Stone; Green Iguana P.J De Vries

Bibliography

Alderton, David: Turtles and Tortoises of the World (Blandford Press, London) 1988

Arnold, Nicholas E: A Field Guide to the Reptiles and Amphibians of Britain and Europe (Collins, London) 2002

Attenborough, David: The Life of Birds (BBC Books, London) 1998

Attenborough, David: The Living Planet (Collins/BBC, London) 1984

Aulagnier S, Thévenot M: Catalogue des Mammifères Sauvages du Maroc (Travaux de l'Institut Scientifique, Série Zoologie: 41, 1–164) 1986

Behler, John L & Deborah A: Alligators and Crocodiles (Colin Baxter Photography Ltd, Grantown-on-Spey) 1998

Briggs, Mike & Peggy: The Natural History of the British Isles (Parragon, Bath) 2003

Burton, John A: Wild Animals (Collins, London) 1998

Byatt, Andrew, Fothergill, Alistair, Holmes, Martha: The Blue Planet (BBC Worldwide Ltd, London) 2001

Davidson, Alan: North Atlantic Seafood (Penguin Books, London) 1980

Dudley, Nigel: Forests and Climate Change – a report for WWF International (WWF) 1998

Gould, Edwin, McKay, Dr George: Encyclopedia of Mammals (Academic Press, San Diego) 1998

Greenaway, Theresa: Swamp Life (Dorling Kindersley, London) 1993

Hoyt, Erich: Creatures of the Deep (Firefly Books, Ontario) 2001

Kingdon, J: The Kingdon Field Guide to African Mammals (Academic Press, London and New York: Natural World) 1997

Manning, Aubrey & Stamp Dawkins, Marian: An Introduction to Animal Behaviour (Cambridge University Press, Cambridge) 1998

Marven, Nigel: Incredible Journeys (BBC Books, London) 1997

Matthiessen, Peter: Tigers in the Snow (North Point Press) 2000

Mattison, Chris: Frogs and Toads of the World (Blandford Press, Poole) 1987

Mattison, Chris: Snakes of the World (Blandford Press, Poole) 1986

Morris, Desmond: Animal Watching (Arrow Books, London) 1991

Mound, Laurence: Eyewitness Guide – Insect (Dorling Kindersley Ltd, London) 1990

National Geographic Magazine

Philip's Nature Encyclopedia (George Philip Ltd, London) 1998

Poole, Joyce: Elephants (Colin Baxter, Grantown-on-Spey) 1997

Preston-Mafham, Rod & Ken: Spiders of the World (Blandford Press, Poole) 1984

Rehsteiner, Ueli, Geisser, Hannes, Reyer, Heinz-Ulrich: Singing and Mating Success in Water Pipits: One Specific Song Element Makes all the Difference (Zoological Institute, University of Zürich) 1997

Stewart, Robyn: Nomads of the Serengeti (Struik Publishers, Cape Town) 2002

Various contributors: Crocodiles and Alligators (Blitz Editions, Leicester) 1992

Various contributors: Marvels and Mysteries of Our Animal World (Reader's Digest Association, New York) 1964

Index

R

S

T

V

W

Y

Z